MISSION 115: SCHWEINFURT

THE MOST DEADLY MISSION OF THEM ALL...

BLACK THURSDAY

"SUPERB!
The 'longest day' for the B-17s
in World War II."
—*The New York Times*

"A PROUD AND HONEST BOOK.
It's all here . . . the raw, vital courage of the men,
the beauty and malleable endurance of the B-17s, the
dark, deadly blossoms of flak, the incredible frenzy
of the attacks by more than 1,000 German aircraft."
—*The Chicago Tribune*

THE BANTAM WAR BOOK SERIES

This is a series of books about a world on fire.

These carefully chosen volumes cover the full dramatic sweep of World War II. Many are eyewitness accounts by the men who fought in this global conflict in which the future of the civilized world hung in balance. Fighter pilots, tank commanders and infantry commanders, among others, recount exploits of individual courage in the midst of the large-scale terrors of war. They present portraits of brave men and true stories of gallantry and cowardice in action, moving sagas of survival and tragedies of untimely death. Some of the stories are told from the enemy viewpoint to give the reader an immediate sense of the incredible life and death struggle of both sides of the battle.

Through these books we begin to discover what it was like to be there, a participant in an epic war for freedom.

Each of the books in the Bantam War Book series contains a dramatic color painting and illustrations specially commissioned for each title to give the reader a deeper understanding of the roles played by the men and machines of World War II.

BLACK THURSDAY

MARTIN CAIDIN

BANTAM BOOKS · TORONTO · NEW YORK · LONDON

BLACK THURSDAY

*A Bantam Book / published by arrangement with
Elsevier-Dutton Publishing Co., Inc.*

PRINTING HISTORY
*E. P. Dutton edition published October 1960
Bantam edition / February 1981*

*Drawings by Fred L. Wolff.
Map by Ben Klaessig.*

ISBN 0–553–13582–1

Published simultaneously in the United States and Canada

PRINTED IN THE UNITED STATES OF AMERICA

0 9 8 7 6 5 4 3 2 1

CONTENTS

PART I
BACKGROUND TO THE MISSION

PART II
THE MISSION BEGINS

CONTENTS

PART III

ATTACK

PART IV

THE SUMMING UP

ACKNOWLEDGMENTS

I am deeply grateful to Colonel Budd J. Peaslee, United States Air Force, Retired, who spared no effort to assist me in the task of bringing this epochal air battle back to life. As the air commander of Mission 115, the daylight bombing attack on Schweinfurt, Germany, on October 14, 1943, Colonel Peaslee's contribution is unique. Both as a fighting man and as an observer, he is rich in emotion, courage, and understanding. Without his unselfish assistance and suggestions and kind permission to study and quote from the manuscript of his recollections of the attack, this book would not have been possible. As with any such project, of course, many other people have also contributed greatly to it. My sincere thanks to Beirne Lay, Jr., formerly Lieutenant Colonel, U.S.A.A.F., a great combat pilot and a gifted writer of the air. The staff of the Research Studies Institute, Air University, United States Air Force, have also spared no pains in their close cooperation; among them I wish to extend my thanks particularly to Margaret Kennedy and to Colonel Laurence Macauley, U.S.A.F. I am no less grateful for the aid of Dr. Albert F. Simpson, chief, U.S.A.F. Historical Division, who has brought to the documentation of the history of air warfare remarkable skill and knowledge of the subject.

For many hours spent in the air with him, in airplanes small and large, and for his patience and skill as a teacher my thanks to the late Lieutenant Colonel Keith M. Garrison, U.S.A.F. Keith Garrison was in a B-17 on Mission 115; the machine in which he flew his last mission, seventeen years later, was the mighty B-52 of the Strategic Air Command. I am grateful for the ready assistance and suggestions of Carl B. McCamish and of H. M. Mason, Jr., who have always supported and aided my projects. Major Raymond Houseman over the last several years has kept up his own private project to accumulate material for this book, and I owe much to him for his efforts. These acknowledgements would be far from complete if they did not express, finally, my gratitude to Major James F. Sunderman, U.S.A.F., who has worked for many years with me on airpower projects, and whose ready and willing support of these efforts has contributed to them greatly.

M.C.

FOREWORD

The battle fought on Black Thursday stands high in the history of American fighting men. It will be long remembered, like the immortal struggles of Gettysburg, St. Mihiel and the Argonne, of Midway and the Bulge and Pork Chop Hill.

Tens of thousands of our airmen fought in desperate battles in the sky during World War II. From China to the Aleutians, from Australia through the Philippines and across the Southwest Pacific, through the Central Pacific, in Africa and the Mediterranean, and across the length and breadth of Europe, American fliers engaged in combat with the Germans, the Japanese, the Italians.

In all these battles one stands out among all the others for unprecedented fury, for losses suffered, for courage. This was the battle on Black Thursday, Mission 115 of the VIII Bomber Command from bases in England to the savagely defended German city of Schweinfurt. It was a battle in which we suffered unprecedented losses, and a battle that we cannot in honesty remember as having produced the results we had hoped for, or that hurt the enemy's war effort as much as we had believed.

Yet it is an aerial struggle remembered with great pride, for it demanded the utmost in courage, in skill, in carrying on the fight in the face of bloody slaughter. All these things, and more, make up the story of Black Thursday, of this book.

Re-creating the events of the Schweinfurt attack presented complex problems in assembling and coordinating the experiences of a great many men and units and arranging them in relation to time and movement. The air is a fluid medium, and the fight raged across many hundreds of miles thousands of feet above the earth. There were thousands of participants,

friendly and enemy, and a vast expanse of the European sky
was their battleground.

You cannot revisit the scene of conflict, for there is only
the sky, washed clean and unscarred. You cannot walk the
battleground, pointing out a hill or a road, a valley or a pass,
a stretch of level or rocky ground, and say: "This is where it
happened."

You cannot query bystanders or noncombatant witnesses to
the fight, for they were far below, on the ground, and saw
only the war-tossed debris of that struggle in the form of
flaming craft, drifting parachutes, trails of smoke, charred
bodies, and terrible explosions.

To write *Black Thursday* I have talked at length with many
survivors of the mission. The recollections and written notes
of Colonel Budd J. Peaslee, Air Commander of the bomber
force that invaded Germany on October 14, 1943, to whom I
am indeed grateful for having kept so disciplined a record of
his participation in that fight, have been especially valuable.
But dozens of other men have also told me of that memorable
day in the air. I have compared their recollections with the
official histories of Mission 115. At the Research Studies
Institute of the Air University of the United States Air Force
I have pored over thousands of sheets of paper, the official
records of the mission. The handwritten notes of returning
crews, the official reports of pilots and bombardiers and
gunners and radiomen and navigators, have also been exam-
ined. The interrogation reports of intelligence and debriefing
officers have been studied. I have read the detailed reports of
men who fought that day and returned to their bases, of men
who were shot down, later escaped from the German *Stalags,*
evaded pursuit, and eventually returned to England.

I have gone through the final reports of the headquarters of
the Eighth Air Force and of its combat arms, the VIII
Bomber Command and the VIII Fighter Command. There
were also the records of the United States Strategic Bomb
Survey, which afford a 20–20 hindsight of the attack and its
results, and include the papers of German industrialists who
were in the attacked ball-bearing plants during the raids and
afterward. I have also studied German fighter command
reports, and have talked with German pilots who flew that
October day against our bombers.

In addition to all these firsthand verbal reports and documentary records, accounts, and analyses, there were thou-

sands of feet of film to be studied: films taken by the Germans, taken by gun cameras in the Messerschmitts and Heinkels, Junkers and Focke-Wulfs and other fighters, and films taken by crewmen aboard the battered Flying Fortresses of VIII Bomber Command.

These are the sources that made up this story. When the manuscript was completed, it was read by the Historical Division and the Security Review Branch of the United States Air Force, by Colonel Peaslee, who led the mission; and by others who flew Mission 115 and in so doing contributed to a brilliant accomplishment in the history of our combat in the air. I am grateful for their valuable suggestions. Responsibility for any inadvertent errors, however, is mine.

What you read in *Black Thursday* is a compilation of all this material, and has been derived from the sources described above, except where other sources are specifically identified in the text.

This does not, of course, tell of all of the many contributors to this book, some of whom are named in the acknowledgments. Lieutenant Colonel Garrison, for example, as we cruised high above the earth in a bomber, would describe some of the things that happened that day seventeen years ago. I had hoped to be able to weave into this story of Mission 115, in detailed incidents, and with his name, more of the story of my good friend Keith Garrison. Much of the combat material in *Black Thursday* comes from men such as Keith.

When I was preparing my notes for this book, I received a letter from Keith Garrison, telling me of the material he was preparing for my use. "I hope," he wrote, "to have the material assembled before too long and I will quickly send it along for your evaluation. It won't be a finished or a polished job; SAC doesn't afford us the luxury of secretaries, and I'm getting this out late at night, after flying all day. It will come—all of it—straight from the old ticker, as I can remember most of the details as if it happened only yesterday, and not seventeen years ago.

"My story will be different, as it will be from the other side of the ledger. We were anything but in the policy-making end of the game at that time—as a matter of fact, you couldn't get much farther down on the totem pole as far as chain of command was concerned. We were nothing but a line combat crew hanging on by our toes and trying just to stay alive. By virtue of surviving this mission, my third, and several following in which we suffered heavy loses, I inherited the job of squadron navigator and then started flying group, wing, and division lead missions, even though I was only nineteen years old and less than six months out of flying school. At the October 14 stage of the game, however, we were flying in the low squadron of the low group over the target, near the end of the bomber stream in the order of battle, and you can't get much more vulnerable than that.

"I'm sorry for the delay in getting all this stuff to you. I have been so busy learning my new job and getting a recheck in the B-52 that I haven't had a moment of spare time. But this is something that I really want to do—and I will make the time."

It is painful to write that Keith never found the time that he needed. Three days after he wrote this letter to me Keith Garrison was killed in the flaming crash of his B-52 bomber.

In a way, I hope that this book will stand as a strong and living memory to Keith and the men with whom he flew then, and through all the years since Mission 115. You will not find Keith Garrison's name throughout this book, as you will find the name of his former commander, Budd Peaslee, but he is there, for this, too, was Keith's battle.

I have flown also with Budd Peaslee, and he, too, recaptured some of the feelings, the emotions, the fears that occupied his mind on that terrible day in the air.

This is the story of these men and thousands of other American airmen—a story of which our nation can be most proud.

MARTIN CAIDIN

PROLOGUE

Over the English countryside a thick fog saturates the air. The pre-dawn darkness of October 14, 1943, is black, cold, and dismally wet. The morning fog squeezes its dank touch into the barracks room, one of many at a sprawling bomber airdrome in the Midlands. It pervades the nostrils and chests of sleeping men, hangs in a tenacious and clammy grip to the curving walls and ceilings of the Nissen hut, slicks the floor with a greasy film. The blankets feel wet, clothes are damp; one could almost reach out and squeeze the water from the air.

It is the bottom of a black ocean of dampness.

The room is dark, and from different directions, in this center of damp nowhere, comes the low sound of fortress gunners breathing deeply. Most of them breathe steadily. But not all. From one bunk there issue sounds of unease, of a body moving under the blankets. In the dark it cannot be seen, but the gunner's face is contorted, he cries out soundlessly, his fingers twitch and curl back on unseen tiggers.

Perhaps, if these men could foretell that October 14 would be seared into the history of the United States Army Air Forces as the fateful Black Thursday, their sleep would not be so deep, there would be more figures moving in nightmare, more fingers closing around imagined gun handles, twitching toward unreal firing buttons. But no man ever knows, the night before, and most of these men, already veterans of the growing, flame-lashed air battles over the continent of Europe, have found little solace in idle or fearful speculation about the morrow. There is no pattern by which they may ever know which one of the hundreds of targets, near or far, is to be their next.

Not all the men sleep. Some are awake, but their consciousness is a heavy thing. They stare sightlessly into the dark, feel the discomfort of the cold and the dismal humidity. Others are shapeless mounds, invisible faces beneath the tiny red glow, alternately brightening and dimming, as a man draws deeply on a cigarette, glimpsing briefly the swirl of smoke as it vanishes into the blackness. They are awake, and now sounds—sounds they have been expecting and waiting for—impinge on their troubled rest. There are the first subdued noises of the awakening of other men. A distant door slams faintly somewhere beyond the corrugated-steel wall. Then there comes the growing tread of approaching footsteps. A man can check off these steps; if he has been here long enough, survived enough battles, he knows exactly when they will pause at the door of his hut. In the darkness he sees in his mind a hand reaching for the knob, hears a shuffle of those feet, the barely perceptible sound of the door opening on damp hinges. The feet are inside; the door is closed once more and pushed tight. The feet move again, very close now, past the cot; then they stop and there is the sound of a hand brushing against clothing.

A single match flares yellow, stabbing through the blackness, lighting a grotesque figure, thick and bulky in his heavy sheepskin jacket and flying boots.

Then blinding light as the squadron operations officer hits the wall switch. The room is cold and wet and stinking, but if a man snuggles down deep enough into his blankets and wraps the ends around his feet and burrows his head into the pillow, he can elude the cold. The light is more than a disagreeable glare in unaccustomed eyes; it means a rude and unpleasant entry into the wet and the cold.

The men who are awake lift their heads wearily to stare at the officer. Eyes follow him silently, blankly, as he reaches the center of the hut in a measured stride, then stops. Because not all the men are flying today, and because sleep is a precious thing, he reads from the list in his hand in a low voice. As the names are spoken, those men who have been tagged by the operations roster groan wearily, or without sound push their blankets aside and slide their feet to the cold floor. Some sit there, unfeeling, unthinking, for long seconds; others light cigarettes or curse softly for the sheer sake of cursing. Almost all shiver slightly from the dampness and chill that swiftly replace the pleasurable warmth of the bunks.

When he has read the last name, the officer looks around for a moment, absently folding the little white piece of paper and shoving it into a pocket. The summons to fly into Germany has been given. "Briefing's at 0700," he says softly, and walks to the door. It opens and closes, and the officer, outside, treads once again through the wet and cold toward the next hut, where the same scene will be re-enacted. Another slip of paper, another list of names, another summons. To what? Death, wounds, terror? Death and wounds are imponderables; they are maybes. But terror is not, and many will feel its suffocating embrace before the day is out. They do not even think of it; they know, and accept its inevitability.

Some miles away, across the flat countryside of the Midlands, a light, cold, persistent rain falls from the sullen clouds hanging low over another heavy bomber base at Thurleigh, about fifty miles north of London, where the 40th Combat Wing has its headquarters.

On his cot, Colonel Budd J. Peaslee opens his eyes. Later, much later, when October 14, 1943, has entered into history, Colonel Peaslee will think of what has passed. Of this moment he will write in his personal notes: "I can see nothing but complete darkness. I hear water dripping from the eaves of my hut, spatting sharply against the sodden ground. In the distance I can hear the muted rumble of many engines—they have been rumbling all night. At times the rumble changes to a high, penetrating tone as some mechanic winds one up to full throttle, but there is always that dull, monotonous background of sound. Thousands of men have been working while I slept—they have worked throughout the black night in the rain and cold. They have worked on bombers and fighters, repairing previous battle damage, tuning engines, loading bombs, and readying thousands upon thousands of rounds of .50-caliber ammunition. The lights have burned all night behind the blackout curtains of our headquarters as navigators pored over their charts and intelligence officers studied flak maps and plans of enemy fighter fields."

Today Colonel Peaslee will be the air commander of the First Bomb Division. He will lead the Eighth Air Force over Germany.

"I went to bed but I did not go to sleep at once," he recalled as we talked. "It's more than difficult to go to sleep at will when you are planning a long trip over strange and hostile roads, along which there will be known hazards. Scenes from past missions meandered across my memory as brightly as they did on the nights immediately after those raids. . . .

"I did not know that before another night had come I should have witnessed a play—a drama of life and death—whose every action would never fade from my mind. It would be set on a vast stage, the sky over Germany, and the actors would be my flying friends, my brothers in arms, with the German Luftwaffe portraying a bloody and unrelenting villain. I did not know. Sometime during the night I drifted off to sleep."

And now it is almost morning. The darkness begins slowly to lighten toward the east, although almost imperceptibly through the fog and the drizzle. At these two American bomber bases and sixteen others, all across the Midlands, the men dress quietly, more than three thousand of them. They do not wish to disturb the oblivion of their sleeping comrades. They pull on boots, jackets, pick up helmets, gloves, oxygen masks, and other personal items. They file out-of-doors. The last man in each barracks switches off the light and eases the door shut quietly, envying the others in their slumber, huddled islands among the sea of empty beds.

An empty bed. Who could believe it holds such meaning? How many men have slept in one particular bed? Men never to return, never to come home from the terrible arena of the thin, high air over Germany, men who failed to run successfully the gauntlet of machine guns, cannon, anti-aircraft shells, rockets, aerial bombs and mines, broken wings and flaming tanks and shattered cockpits. . . .

Empty beds. Tonight, as October 14, 1943, passes into history, more than six hundred of those beds will remain empty.

BLACK THURSDAY

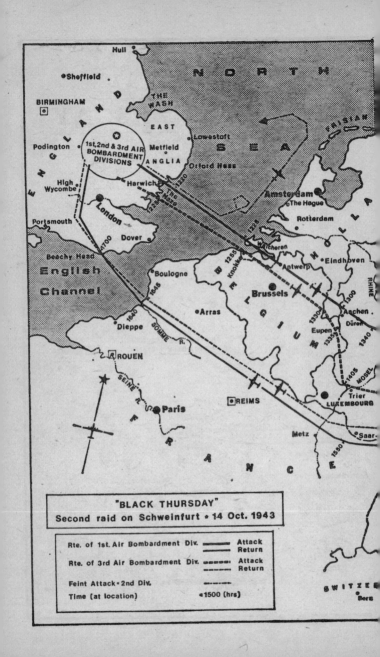

"BLACK THURSDAY"
Second raid on Schweinfurt • 14 Oct. 1943

PART I

BACKGROUND
TO THE MISSION

BOLERO, SICKLE, CBO

Even experienced veterans of strategic air warfare in the European Theater of Operations found it difficult to believe, in October, 1943, that only fourteen months had passed since the first American heavy bombers had ventured forth from British soil into the skies over German-dominated Europe.

At thirty-nine minutes past three o'clock in the afternoon of August 17, 1942, the last of 12 B-17E Flying Fortresses of Colonel Frank K. Armstrong's 97th Bomb Group, first American heavy bomber unit to arrive in England, lifted from the main runway of the American airdrome at Grafton Underwood. The names of these giant four-engine raiders spoke of crew enthusiasm—*Baby Doll, Peggy D., Big Stuff, Butcher Shop, Yankee Doodle, Berlin Sleeper, Johnny Reb, Birmingham Blitzkrieg, Alabama Exterminator.*

The bombers assembled in tight formation, and in a steady climb wheeled for the English Channel, pointing their noses toward the target in France—the city of Rouen. Four Royal Air Force squadrons of Spitfire IX fighter planes flew close escort to the target area. Five Spitfire squadrons picked up the bombers as they left the smoking target, and escorted them back to England.

In that first attack by American heavy bombers in the European Theater of Operations, the tiny force dropped a total of 36,900 pounds of bombs from an altitude of 23,000 feet. Approximately half the bombs fell in the target area.

Anti-aircraft fire inflicted slight damage on two bombers. Three Messerschmitt Me-109 fighters attacked the formation, but failed to damage any of the B-17's. The only casualties of the Flying Fortress debut over Europe occurred on the return flight from the target. A bombardier and navigator of one B-17 were slightly injured when a pigeon smashed itself against the plexiglas nose and showered the crewmen with flying particles.

The target—the Sotteville marshaling yard in Rouen, with its large locomotive depot and rolling-stock repair shops of the Buddicum concern—was not seriously damaged, and operations were affected only negligibly. The attack, however, was immeasurably more important in terms of policy decisions for the United States than it could possibly have been in respect to the bombed marshaling yard. For behind the 12 bombers as they droned over France lay a story of long debate and bitter controversy.

In this summer of 1942 the strategic and logistic plans of the Allies, most especially those concerning the proposed aerial bombardment by the army air forces of occupied Europe and Germany, floundered in a state of extreme uncertainty. That Germany must be subjected at the earliest opportunity to the greatest possible weight of heavy aerial attack was beyond dispute. The question around which revolved the uncertainty of decision was to what extent the United States would commit its heavy bombardment strength to Europe at the expense of offensive operations in the Pacific, where the Japanese still enjoyed the heights of their overwhelming victories.

As part of the preparation for the invasion of Nazi-occupied France under the code name of BOLERO, the United States during the spring of 1942 committed its operational planning to building up a major heavy bombardment striking force in the British Isles, with the goal of eventually crippling the German war machine. On January 28, 1942, the army air forces had activated the English Air Force; three months later, in April, the Eighth was committed to BOLERO. One month later, in May, the paper plans assumed initial substance, when advance units of the fledgling air command —which was to become the most powerful striking force in the world—crossed the Atlantic and arrived in England. It was a harrowing transfer of air power to an advanced base, for the Flying Fortresses and the Liberators had to fight wild Atlantic storms, and more than a few bombers and their crews disappeared in the reaches of the angry ocean expanse.

The early life of the new command was essentially a frenzied nightmare of jumbled logistics and shortage of men and planes. Under the leadership of Major General Carl A. Spaatz, the Eighth was organized into bomber, fighter, composite (training), and service commands. General Spaatz's headquarters for the Eighth Air Force was located in the suburbs of London, at Bushy Park, Teddington, and carried the coded designation of WIDEWING.

To Brigadier General Ira C. Eaker went all the headaches of the Eighth's initial bomber force, the VIII Bomber Command. On April 15 General Eaker established his headquarters for the Bomber Command in a girls' school (from which the students and other tenants had been hurriedly evacuated) at High Wycombe in Buckinghamshire, some thirty miles west of London. This headquarters became well known by its code name of PINETREE.

Easing the burden of Eaker's problems was the superb cooperation offered by the British. The Royal Air Force Bomber Command was a combat-proved organization, and its growing strength and skill in air operations were beginning to exert a telling effect upon Germany's industrial war machine. While the forces under Eaker were still embryonic and struggling to gain some semblance of aircraft strength, the British were hammering with massive blows at Germany.

Those were the days when the Bomber Command of the Royal Air Force was hurling massed waves of bombers at the industrial might of the Ruhr, and when the heavyweights of that command—the Stirlings, Halifaxes, and Lancasters—began to lift bomb tonnages well above a thousand to two thousand tons per raid. The Royal Air Force's campaign of aerial attack against Germany was accomplished fact, as were the increasing number and violence of the raids against the enemy.

Early in 1942 British authorities began their build-up of the airdromes and installations that would house and maintain the many elements of the Eighth Air Force. If there were differences of opinion and at moments some bitter arguments, these arose more from the vexing problems created by the Americans' constantly changing their plans than from any vacillation in operations on the part of the British.

To meet the requirements of its varied organizations, the Eighth Air Force received from the British a total of 127 airdromes and all other installations and facilities necessary to sustain the bombers, fighters, service, and maintenance units, and supporting organizations.

As for the growing pains of the VIII Bomber Command, they arose almost inevitably from the rapidly growing size and changing organization of the command. The British, however, managed the greater portion of the time to keep pace with the needs of the American units that flooded into England.

Originally the proposals set forth under mutual agreement stated that the VIII Bomber Command would take over from the Royal Air Force five areas in the region of East Anglia, northeast of London, with 15 airdromes contained within each area. In addition, the VIII would also assume tenancy of any satellite airfields that might be necessary to accommodate additional aircraft, personnel, and facilities for operations.

By May of 1942 the British and Americans were in agreement on the location of the bomber airdromes. Into the Huntingdon area and adjacent sections of East Anglia went the army air forces' heavy bombers, and the airdromes of Grafton Underwood, Thurleigh, Molesworth, Little Straughton, Kimbolton, Polebrook, Chelveston, and Podington became the "veterans" of VIII Bomber Command.

There is ample evidence of the outstanding cooperation afforded the American bombing organization by our British allies. In General Eaker's report of June 19, 1942, to General Spaatz, he wrote of the British that they had "cooperated 100 per cent in every regard. They have lent us personnel when we had none, and have furnished us clerical and administrative staffs; they have furnished us liaison officers for Intelligence, Operations, and Supply; they have furnished us transportation; they have housed and fed our people and they have answered promptly and willingly all our requisitions; in addition they have made available to us for study their most secret devices and documents. We are extremely proud of the relations we have been able to establish between our British allies and ourselves. . . ."

As the VIII Bomber Command gained experience, it was eventually able to reduce its requirements from the 75 major airdromes originally authorized to 62 fields. Originally the United States bombing arm included three wings in East Anglia, the 1st Bombardment Wing under the command of Colonel Newton Longfellow, with headquarters at Brampton Grange; the 2d Bombardment Wing under Colonel James P. Hodges, at Old Catton; and the 3d Bombardment Wing, under Colonel Charles T. Phillips, at Elveden Hall. For smooth functioning in combat, the internal organization of the command was adapted as quickly as possible to the communications system of the Royal Air Force and finally the American Bomber Arm was permanently organized into bombardment wings. B-17 heavy bomber groups went, in this reorganization, into the 1st and 4th Wings; B-24 heavy bomber groups into the 2d Wing; and the B-26 medium bombers into the 3d Wing.

No one in those days would have anticipated that Eaker's disorganized bomber force would within the next thirty months expand and grow in power until it constituted fully half the anticipated combat group strength of the entire army air forces.

The Rouen attack involved a total of 160 officers and enlisted men airborne. Two and a half years later a single mass bomber attack by the VIII would send—in heavy bombers alone—more than twenty-five thousand fighting men into the air over Germany.

As subsequent events proved with overwhelming impact, the original Allied planners who formulated the machinery to attack the German positions in Europe tended in the first place grossly to underestimate the fighting skill and capacity of the Germans, and, secondly, to overestimate in even more unrealistic fashion the fighting capacity of the Allied forces. It is difficult to accept the validity of the strategy established in April, 1942, under Operation ROUNDUP, which called for an Allied invasion across the English Channel in the spring of 1943. But even more bizarre was the conviction at that time that, if urgently required, the Allies could accelerate their invasion plans and—successfully—move up their proposed assault against the Continent to September, 1942. Despite its impressive code designation, this Project SLEDGEHAMMER would have been, we are aware today, doomed to murderous defeat at the hands of the more seasoned, better organized, and better equipped German defense forces.

By August, 1942, as a result of unremitted controversy at high levels as to the distribution of American bomber strength between the northern European, Pacific, and Mediterranean theaters, the plans for BOLERO were waxing uncertain. The invasion of North Africa in the autumn of 1942 had been decided upon in July, and this new venture, designated as TORCH, led to the further diversion of the air build-up that had been planned for BOLERO.

Thus the aspirations of the army air forces for an early

and growing assault against Germany, from their very inception, had to suffer from the more pressing demands of areas where sea and ground forces, as well as those of the air, were engaged or would be soon engaged with the enemy. Simultaneously with its series of disappointments, the Eighth Air Force watched its British contemporaries in the Royal Air Force Bomber Command accelerate their own powerful effort in the mass bombing of German cities. The Royal Air Force program was simplicity itself: hurl every possible ton of high explosives and incendiaries into Germany, and rip and burn the cities to the ground.

After the landings in Morocco and Algeria in November, 1942, the fighting in North Africa, which sorely taxed the already heavily strained American and British capabilities, forced the Allies to postpone indefinitely their plans for a strike across the Channel. As the North African campaigns progressed through the winter and into the spring of 1943, however, it seemed that the requirements of that theater would wane appreciably, to the benefit of BOLERO. The British in the Western Desert had at least swept the Germans from their main positions in that area, and the American and British forces moved slowly toward a meeting in Tunisia where the surviving German elements could be crushed and all of North Africa secured. By early spring, 1943, these objectives were in sight; BOLERO, however, suffered once again from demands of other theaters for air-power forces which the BOLERO planners had expected would be placed in their hands. Commanders in the Pacific Theater were up in full cry for air power. Fifteen bombardment groups that had originally been committed for assignment to BOLERO instead went the other way around the world, dispatched to the air forces fighting the Japanese.

As this internal struggle to obtain weapons and manpower was fought in the high command and within the army air forces, the master plan called CBO—Combined Bomber Offensive—went into higher gear. CBO was conceived early in the war, and received its official authorization at the Casablanca conference early in 1943, and as rapidly as possible it was implemented with the growing strength of the VIII Bomber Command into a functioning reality.

CBO is best defined as the combined effort on the part of the United States Army Air Forces and the Royal Air Force to prepare the way for the storming by invasion of Europe, with each air force operating on the basis of its own particular capabilities and concepts, the Royal Air Force with its operations at night in attacks against strategic areas, and the army air forces striking at particular targets in daylight.

As it was planned and defined in early 1943, CBO specified a mission in which the Luftwaffe was to be engaged and destroyed in aerial battle, and through bombing, as a prerequisite to OVERLORD, the invasion by ground forces of the European continent.

By the end of June, 1943, the strength of the Eighth Air Force passed the 100,000 mark. During this same period VIII Bomber Command reached a strength level of 40,000 men, or nearly half of the entire Eighth Air Force. Its new commander, who took over from General Eaker, was Brigadier General Frederick L. Anderson, who had served as Deputy Director of Bombardment at army air forces' headquarters since January, 1942. Thirty-eight years of age, General Anderson, a West Point and Kelly Field graduate, had served five years in the Philippines and had later directed bombardier instruction at the Air Corps Tactical School.

By mid-1943 the organization of the combat bases in England had stabilized around a set pattern. The combat group of each base comprised the core of the installation, and around this central unit revolved the remainder of the base organization. Each combat group of heavy bombers was made up of three or four squadrons, averaging 1,600 men to each bomber group. To service each of these bases there were usually an ordnance company; quartermaster, signal, chemical warfare, and military police detachments; a service squadron, a detachment of the service group headquarters, and a headquarters squadron. In addition, there were units for finance, weather, gas defense, and other specialized services, and attached infantry. The service units added approximately five hundred men to the combat group, bringing the total strength at each base to an average of 2,000 men.

In September, 1943, just before Mission 115 against Schweinfurt, the VIII Bomber Command underwent command reorganization. The 1st and 2d Bombardment Wings were redesignated as the 1st and 2d Bombardment Divisions (H[1]), and the 4th Bombardment Wing was redesignated as the 3d Bombardment Division (H). The old 3d Bombard-

---

[1]Heavy.

ment Wing—made up of B-26 Marauder medium bombers—had been transferred in June to the VIII Air Support Command.

Under the new system, several bomber groups flew in combat under command of a wing, and several wings made up an air division. Each wing organization was identified only by its command status, and the personnel maintained their headquarters at a group airdrome.

By the close of September, 1943, there were active in the VIII Bomber Command these groups: the 100th, 381st, 384th, 385th, 388th, 390th, 482d, 389th, and 392d.

Each new bomber group airdrome assumed an appearance familiar from the other fields spread through the command's area. Great pains were taken in construction to assure the maximum benefit of camouflage, and the fields with their many installations blended skillfully into the surrounding countryside. A rule in construction was the widest possible dispersion of all major installations and facilities in order to reduce vulnerability to German air attack.

Bordering the runways were the repair and supply services; from two thousand feet to a mile from this area would be found the headquarters site, and here were the offices of administration and operations. Close to the living quarters, as a general rule, were the mess halls, post exchanges, a large shower bathhouse, clubs for officers and enlisted men, and quartermaster supply warehouses.

From seven to eight housing sites, widely separated by a mile or more, contained the group and base personnel, and this dispersion, while promising greater protection from German bombs, was a curse on the men. The main form of transport was the bicycle, not because of a love for athletics; a bike was simply a necessity for getting around without long and wearying trudges, often in rain or fog, through the thick mud of the fields. Technical personnel had the choice of walking (or riding their bicycles) over a distance each day of up to nine or ten miles, simply to move between the areas where they worked, ate, and slept.

Each of these group airdromes was the scene of a constant influx of new strength, of more bombers; of construction work carried on at all hours; of steady toil by mechanics and ground crews modifying the bombers as fast as they arrived from the States; of endless training in the air and on the ground—a vast, churning activity heralding the build-up of strength to that point when an armada, in fact as well as description, could penetrate Germany's skies and inflict punishing blows on the Reich's war machine.

Behind this build-up of strength was a burning question of strategic import, the solution of which would decide beyond further readjustment of plans the logistics and strategy of BOLERO. Could the combined British and American heavy bomber forces strike the German industrial machine and the war economy so effectively that the planned cross-Channel invasion would be accomplished at appreciably less cost? The use of strategic air power to cripple the industrial strength of the enemy was in every respect, at that time, little more than a concept, and not a policy which had proven itself. Accordingly, it suffered sorely from continuing opposition from the more conventional planners, who held strongly to the role of air power subservient to the established needs of sea power and ground forces.

And, supposing that strategic air power *could* so weaken the German industrial and war machine as to make surface attack against the continent possible without the frightful losses it would otherwise cost, could it accomplish this objective without stripping other combat theaters in the world of their critical air-power requirements? To win the battle over Europe while losing half the rest of the contested planet would indeed be a worthless venture.

There existed one great final question, which still had to be answered, presuming even that the first two were satisfactorily resolved. Could this promised ravaging of the German industrial complex and its military defense structure be achieved within a percentage of acceptable losses in combat? This was the greatest of the many unknowns at the time: assuming all else lay within the potential of the heavy bombers as a striking force, there hung over the entire campaign the threat of disastrous losses at the hands of a fighter defense system acknowledged to be the equal of any in the world. The Flying Fortress was an aerial porcupine of sorely questioned ability; no less so was its sister craft, the B-24 Liberator.

The British made no attempt to conceal their feelings about these two bombers; bluntly they informed the American commanders that their daylight attacks were doomed to catastrophic losses and defeat at the hands of the powerful German defense system. The Germans had tried daylight bombing against England, and been shattered in the attempt;

later, the British had attacked European targets in daylight, and suffered appalling losses both from German fighters and from anti-aircraft. The same, they warned, would be the lot of the American heavy bombers.

It was difficult for the British to accept the defensive power that the B-17 promised. It featured extraordinary structural strength, and its ruggedness meant that the airplane would return from the combat missions even when slashed to ribbons by enemy fire. Its one great fault lay in its susceptibility to fire; throughout the war there was a continuing attempt to reduce the inflammability of the Flying Fortress in respect to its fuel tanks.

In firepower, nothing like this airplane had ever before been seen. As many as thirteen .50-caliber machine guns, firing from hand-held gun positions plus power turrets, gave the B-17 an unprecedented field of defensive fire. The B-17F models mounted two to four machine guns in the nose, two guns in a power turret atop the fuselage directly behind the pilots' compartment, a single machine gun farther aft that was operated from the radio room, two guns in a power-operated ball turret in the belly, a single gun firing from waist positions to the rear of the airplane, and two machine guns in the tail.

No matter what its position in the air, a fighter could be subjected to a withering blast of fire from the many guns of the bomber; often several gun positions could bring their weapons to bear on a single airplane. As the war progressed, improvements in the firepower arrangement were incorporated into the bombers; gun positions were modified for better field of fire, turrets were "cleaned up" and afforded the gunners better visibility, and a power-operated "chin turret," mounted directly beneath the nose, gave better protection against the deadly frontal attack of German fighters.

Like its B-17 sister ship, the B-24 Liberator was a big, heavily defended bomber. It lacked the total number of guns of the Fortress, but the B-24 nevertheless featured power turrets with two guns each in the nose, upper fuselage, belly, and tail, plus the two waist guns, for a total of ten .50-caliber weapons.

The Fortress was not only rugged and superb on the controls, but it was the steadiest flying platform ever built. This was of vital importance in maintaining tight defensive formations, where the crisscrossing field of defensive firepower, plus the controllability of the plane and its ability to absorb staggering punishment, often meant the difference between acceptable losses or an outfit's being cut to pieces and scattered.

In these characteristics the Liberator was less richly endowed. Faster than the B-17 and able to carry a heavier bomb load over a greater distance, it could not sustain the battle damage that the B-17 accepted and survived. Attempts to improve the defensive firepower and armor plating of the B-24 so overloaded the airplane that it assumed dangerous flying characteristics, and its stability was sorely compromised; the modifications were dropped. The B-24 was an excellent weapon, and because of its flight performance characteristics, it proved to be of outstanding success in the vast reaches of the Pacific Theater. Against the "big league" of German opposition, however, it was the B-17 Flying Fortress that ranked as the prime combatant.

Each airplane flew with a normal crew of 10 men; depending on the mission to be flown, this could vary from nine to 11 crew members. Both machines had four radial engines, each of 1,200 horsepower; the B-17, fully loaded—thirty tons—had a speed of approximately one hundred and seventy miles per hour. The B-24 was slightly faster.

They were both able to operate at altitudes up to 27,000 feet in formation; what was a valuable weapon in the Pacific —height—became meaningless against the superb German fighters, which with no effort flew to 38,000 and 40,000 feet and streaked down, the sun behind them, to rip into the bombers.

With all its armor, guns, self-sealing tanks, and special equipment, the B-17 had a normal radius of action from England of 600 to 700 miles, carrying 5,000 pounds of bombs. For shorter missions the bomb load could be increased by several tons; over a radius of 700 miles, the bomb load had to decreased. In this area the B-24 was a slightly better performer; it carried over the same range from 1,000 to 2,000 pounds more bombs than the B-17.

These are basically technical comparisons; it should be emphasized that despite any shortcomings, both the B-17 Flying Fortress and the B-24 Liberator were the weapons that, eventually, with long-range fighter protection, penetrated to all points of Europe and inflicted grievous blows against the Germans. They were not always employed wisely, but that is the fault of the planner, and not the machine. Perhaps the best proof of the quality of these machines, besides their superb combat records, was that the best German aeronautical science could not produce an aircraft to rank with these great American bombers.

This, then, was the background out of which eventually developed the massive bombardment of Germany from the air. At this time the Royal Air Force had amassed a vast body of experience; but unhappily for the VIII Bomber Command, not even the constantly growing might and mounting successes of the British could provide the insight desperately required for the solution of the weighty problems of the army air forces. The British technique for the use of long-range bombers was diametrically opposed to the American plan. Their selections of targets, their preference for lightly armed bombers, striking in nocturnal raids; the very bombs and methods of attack they employed, yielded little experience that the VIII Bomber Command could usefully apply to its own future role.

The British clearly preferred attack by the stars. They had whipped the German Air Force at its peak in daylight defense, and had demonstrated beyond all question the inability of the Luftwaffe to maintain daylight raids. The Germans had, however, proven themselves capable, even with a sorely weakened bomber force, of inflicting punishing damage and destruction upon England under the mantle of darkness. For these reasons, and because of their firm belief that daylight attacks were suicidal in the face of the vigorous and highly capable German fighter force, the British disdained the daylight bombing campaign.

The VIII's hopes could not have been more different. Essentially the army air forces' program called for a sustained daylight bombing campaign, carried out with high precision, which, rather than attempting to destroy entire cities in saturation raids, would wreck carefully chosen industrial objectives. The VIII's planners worried their hair gray trying to resolve the complex and interwoven factors of the excellent German anti-aircraft defense, the depth and efficiency of their own radar and fighter-control operations, and the known excellence of the Luftwaffe's. Still unresolved was the crucial question of the ability of the American heavy bomber to enter German air territory without escort and defend itself against the superb German pilot and his airplane. The curse of it all was that the best laid plans could be measured only through the sustained test of battle.

2

SCHWEINFURT

This message would be read to all crews at mission briefings the morning of October 14, 1943, prior to take-off for the attack against the city of Schweinfurt:

To all leaders and combat crews. This air operation today is the most important air operation yet conducted in this war. The target must be destroyed. It is of vital importance to the enemy. Your friends and comrades that have been lost and that will be lost today are depending on you. Their sacrifices must not be in vain. Good luck, good shooting, and good bombing.

(Sgd.) *F. L. Anderson,*
Brigadier General, U.S.A.A.F.
COMMANDING GENERAL
VIII BOMBER COMMAND

Anti-friction bearings, as essential components of virtually every mechanical device and weapon used in World War II, occupied a highly critical position in the war economy of Germany. Aircraft, tanks, armored and motor vehicles, a diversity of weapons, submarines and warships, electrical equipment, precision instruments, and plant machinery all depended on anti-friction bearings for speed and efficiency of performance. Bearings were literally the mechanical lubrication of the entire German war effort.

The consumption of bearings in German war industry was fantastic. In the month of December, 1943, the aircraft industry alone consumed 2,395,000 anti-friction bearings.

The modern designs of German fighters and bombers demanded many varieties of highly specialized bearings to overcome friction, since power units with low horsepower—weight ratios must carry heavy loads at high speeds. For engine medium bomber called for 1,056 anti-friction bearings. Its two motors and the instruments required hundreds more. Almost every aircraft had a specific bearings need for propellers, superchargers, pump drives, gear systems, reduction gears, as well as bomb sights, automatic pilot, and other control instruments. The aircraft industry without a continual supply of anti-friction bearings would literally be crippled to a state of impotence.

Tanks and motor vehicles that were capable of high speeds with heavy loads also demanded many anti-friction bearings throughout their construction. Similarly, weapons of all types depended on bearings for their accuracy and sustained use. The 88-mm. anti-aircraft gun, perhaps the most efficient such weapon of the war, used 47 anti-friction bearings, a single 200-cm. searchlight required 90.

The general-equipment industries, which produced military equipment as well as products that were essentially civilian in nature, required even more bearings than the industries that produced aircraft, tanks, motor vehicles, and a wide variety of weapons.

With an adequate supply of these bearings, the German industrial complex was a machine that functioned efficiently and adequately sustained the German armed forces. Without the bearings, that same machine would strangle itself to death.

It was obvious to Allied target analysts, once they had ascertained properly the role of the German ball-bearings industry, that the destruction of that industry was imperative. To make it the object of a systematic aerial campaign promised far-reaching results with minimum effort. In addition to the bearing industry's pivotal place in the German war economy, the industry was concentrated within several target areas rather than disseminated piecemeal throughout the nation, and once crippled its recovery would be a slow and costly process, during which the interrupted production would produce its disastrous results.

Importance of Bearings to the Economy

If a heavy bomber attack could cut the supplies of this one component so vital to the manufacture of diverse armaments, the strategic air campaign would create repercussions sweeping through all of Germany like a paralyzing shock. Should the planned attacks on Schweinfurt, the primary center of bearings production, prove successful, the many and varied users of bearings would begin to suffer the effects of shortened supplies within a month of the initial attack. "Nonmilitary users would suffer most" from an effective attack on the bearings industry, target analysts concluded, "with less critical military items such as trucks next in line. A nine months' loss of output, however, would be bound to reach even to producers with top priority. No countermeasurers would be able to avoid a 30 per cent drop in armament production as a consequence of successful attack."

Intelligence agencies reported to VIII Bomber Command that the delivery of bearings to customers was on a "hand-to-mouth basis," and that these customers carried "only small stocks of finished bearings." The industry stood in urgent need of depth and decentralization for its defense; and in the lack of these things it was unusually vulnerable to being crippled by only a few devastating attacks. Its disruption could at an early date seriously affect aircraft production—notably fighters, a primary objective at the VIII—and within three months exert its influence on the battle line itself.

Concentration of Industry

Because of the industry's concentration, target analysts felt strongly—and so they reported—that the "knockout blow" could easily be delivered. Plants in only six cities were believed responsible for 73 per cent of the entire output of bearings available to the German war economy, even including those supplies which could be obtained from neutral nations, or from German satellites. It was an extraordinarily "ripe" target, as shown in breakdown:

Schweinfurt	42 per cent
Stuttgart	15 per cent
Paris and Annecy	9 per cent
Leipzig and Berlin	7 per cent

The importance of these centers, intelligence reported to VIII Bomber Command, was increased enormously by their specialization in military anti-friction bearings.

Recovery Difficulties

"The most important factor determining recovery is the ability to reconstruct, but equally crucial is the possibility of the effect of the raids' being absorbed during the reconstruction and repair period."[1] Analyses of the German situation indicated strongly to the Allied planning groups that the "cushion"—the alternate means of absorbing the effects of bombing raids—could be effectively broken through.

One element of the cushion was the "lavish use of bearings in German designs, the result of the industry's long existence and excellent salesmanship."[1] German aircraft and armaments used more bearings than comparable American and British equipment, but the VIII's intelligence officers discounted the possibility that the Germans would be able effectively to reduce the number of bearings required in their planes and armaments. It would require at least six months and possibly one year to effect changes in design and to pass these changes on to the production line. Furthermore, technical difficulties would keep the savings in bearings consumption to a low point, and would localize the savings in industrial rather than military equipment. By its very nature, the heavy use of bearings dictated a continued use; it was, from the attacker's point of view, an excellent and vicious circle that held every promise of crippling the enemy war effort.

Intelligence estimated that the German stocks of semi-finished components in bearings plants would suffice for six months' production. Target analysts stated their belief that an effective attack on a bearings plant should result in the destruction of, or serious damage to, the bulk of these stocks, removing the possibility of their serving as the invaluable cushion during the post-raid period.

Target analysis personnel stated emphatically that the time required for pipeline delivery—the period of one month from the producer to the consumer—could not possibly be reduced. The Germans could strip nonmilitary industry of its supply of bearings, but this measure would provide only a very limited and brief assistance.

---

[1] United States Strategic Bombing Survey #2736–17; 7 November, 1945.

Could the enemy make up the loss of primary plants by turning to alternate sources of supply? What if they diverted more raw materials and machine tools to the bearings industry, and increased their imports from Sweden? The answers to these questions were most reassuring, for a complete breakdown of all outside sources showed that the bearings supply from them could not be increased by more than 5 per cent of the total requirement, and this was a "generous estimate." And to reconstruct the German factories and repair their bombed machines would involve a time period of at least six, and quite possibly twelve, months.

Of the VIII Bomber Command's summary of these factors, the United States Strategic Bombing Survey stated: "Such were the considerations that underlay the decision to attack. Attacks on production in just four cities—Schweinfurt, Berlin-Erkner, Stuttgart, and Leipzig—would, if successful, eliminate 64 per cent of Germany's sources of bearings supplies. Recovery would be slow, with reconstruction extending over the period of a year. The combined effects of destruction of installations and of semi-finished and assembled stocks would lead to an estimated loss of nine months' production, a loss which could be offset by compensating factors of cushion to only a small extent. Pipelines were already short, stocks in hands of consumers were small, and savings through redesign of military equipment would take too long to be realized. Better utilization of alternate sources of supply in the conquered or neutral countries would yield a paltry 5 per cent increase."

It became ever more obvious to the American bombing campaign strategists that all Germany would suffer a disastrous loss in the wake of a truly effective strike at the bearings plants. More and more machines, electrical equipment, and installations of all kinds requiring anti-friction bearings were needed desperately to sustain Germany's fight.

In July, 1943, a total of 33,560 supervisors, technicians, and skilled and semi-skilled workers constituted the labor force of the German bearings industry. In use within the Fatherland itself were 13,000 precision machine tools. The industry operated on a two-shift system of sixty hours per week per shift, although the actual hours worked varied in different plants. Male laborers of the Müller firm at Nürnberg, for example, worked twelve hours a day, seven days a week, while women worked twelve hours for six days on

machines and fifty-eight hours a week when on the inspection
bench.

In mid-1943 Schweinfurt was uncontestably the single most
important industrial center for bearings production. It was a
city of 60,000 population located on the Main River, in
northeastern Bavaria, seventy miles east of Frankfurt am
Main, and by virtue of its small size was even more suscepti-
ble to heavy air attack.

In July, 1943, Schweinfurt produced 45 per cent in quantity of all the bearings manufactured in Germany; in monetary
value it turned out 52.2 per cent of all bearings.

In Schweinfurt proper were the buildings of the Vereinigte
Kugellager Fabrik (VKF) and the factory of Kugelfischer
AG (FAG). VKF Works I and II employed in July, 1943,
7,844 workers; the FAG plant had 9,770 on its working staff.
In the sprawling industrial city of massive factories and
crowded areas of workers' housing were also two other plants
of lesser importance in the anti-friction bearings industry,
Deutsche Star Kugelhalter and Fichtel and Sachs.

Since 1942 the industry had been straining under a major
acceleration of its production program. Because of the critical concentration in Schweinfurt, in 1942 the major German
firms had mapped out a major dispersal program. The plan
was simple: no more than 39 per cent of the German
production of any type and size (for example, small ball
bearings, or medium tapered bearings) was to be located in
any one plant. But this dispersal still lay in the future.

Following a successful bearings industry attack, concluded
the target analysts, "nonmilitary users would suffer most, with
less critical military items such as trucks next in line. A nine
months' loss of output, however, would be bound to reach
even to producers with top priority. No countermeasures
would be able to avoid a 30 per cent drop in armament
production as a consequence of successful attack."

On the morning of August 17, 1943, the finger pointed for
the first time at Schweinfurt.

The date is significant for several reasons. Not only did it
initiate the first of 40 air attacks to come on the entire
bearings industry, the majority of which struck at Schweinfurt, but it marked the single greatest aerial assault so far in
the war against Germany. It was the greatest and also, in
terms of losses, the most disastrous.

The mission of August 17, 1943, on the first anniversary of

B-17 operations, was a double one. A total force of 376 Fortresses smashed at the bearings works in Schweinfurt and at the large Messerschmitt aircraft complex at Regensburg, one hundred ten miles to the southeast. In these attacks more bombers than ever before—315 B-17's—struck the targets in the deepest penetration to date into Germany, and they unleashed the unprecedented bomb load of 724 tons.

It was a day of savage air battles. In the attack against Regensburg, the Germans blasted 36 heavy bombers from the air. Twenty-four more Fortresses went down from the Schweinfurt force, making the losses for the day a staggering 60 airplanes and 600 men. In statistical terms, the Germans destroyed a prohibitive 19 per cent of the attacking force.

On this attack the 3d Bombardment Division was to send its Fortresses, equipped with long-range tanks, from England to Regensburg, and then to continue on directly, in a precedent-breaking shuttle-bombing flight, to advanced bases in North Africa. More limited in its range was the 1st Bombardment Division, which would strike Schweinfurt and then return on a reciprocal route, because of the range problem.

It was a day of perfect flying weather, and the Germans struck at the bombers with savage persistence and incredible courage. The attacks were constant; no sooner did one wave of fighters tear through the bomber formations, than a fresh force screamed in to fire. The fighter pilots went wild; they attacked in vertical dives and climbs, rolled through the formations, closed to point-blank range. On several occasions entire fighter squadrons struck in "javelin-up" formation, which made it difficult and often impossible for the Flying Fortresses to take evasive action. The Germans came in with fighters wing to wing, three and four and five at a time. They lobbed heavy cannon shells and rockets at the bombers, and even dropped parachute bombs to drift downward into the massed formations.

The Schweinfurt raiders bore the brunt of heavy attack not only all the way in to the target, but all the way back, with fresh pilots constantly hammering away at the formations. All types of fighters appeared—single-engine Messerschmitt Me-109's, Focke-Wulf FW-190's, and Heinkel He-113's, and twin-engine Me-110's, Me-210's, Junkers Ju-88's, Dornier Do-217's and FW-189's. In terms of air battle, it was the most intensive, violent, and without question the worst day in the memory of the American crews.

There was at least one bit of comfort for the mauled American crews in one of the final phrases picked up by radio interception. As the battle wore on and increased in its ferocity, the men in the B-17's heard the increasingly excited shouted cries of "Parachute!" and "Ho, down you go, you dog!" then a final gasp, *"Herr Gott Sakramant."*

The grim aerial struggle brought some astonishing moments. In a fortress named *X Virgin,* a waist gunner was killed by German fighters. In an unprecedented move, four men chose to bail out deliberately, so that the remaining crew would have enough oxygen to take the ship over the target and return. But this wasn't the end of a wild mission; over the target the bomb-release mechanism failed to work.

Quickly a wounded gunner left his station and worked his way to the bomb bays. With a screwdriver he loosened the shackles, and then jumped up and down on the bombs until they broke loose and fell free.

Or consider the B-17 known to her crew as *My Prayer.* Fire broke out in the airplane; out of control, she plummeted in a wild, helpless dive. The crew—except the pilot, copilot, and the top turret gunner, whose chute was damaged by flames—quickly abandoned the flaming, plunging Fortress.

The pilot, by superhuman strength, fought the B-17 out of its dive. Behind him the gunner, painfully wounded in the leg, succeeded with the copilot in smothering the blaze.

It wasn't over yet—they still had to get home with German fighters clawing in to finish off the cripple. The pilot flew the Fortress, the gunner worked the nose guns, and the copilot swung back and forth between the waist guns to hold off the enemy fighters as *My Prayer* whipped over Germany at treetop level.

"We came home at two hundred and ten miles an hour," said the pilot, "buzzing cities, factories, and airfields in Germany. It was the first legal buzzing I've ever done. We drew some fire, but I did evasive action and we escaped further damage. The people in Germany scattered and fell to the ground when they saw us coming, but in Belgium the people waved and saluted us. . . ."

Despite the cruel losses sustained, the bombers, reports the official history of the army air forces, "did an extremely good job. This was especially true at Regensburg, where they blanketed the entire area with high explosives and incendiary bombs, damaging every important building in the plant. . . ."

The results on August 17, at Schweinfurt, although not so impressive as those in the Messerschmitt complex, were encouraging. German records reveal that the two main bearing plants were struck by 80 large high-explosive bombs. Damage was especially severe at Kugelfischer, the main plant, where 663 machines were destroyed or so badly damaged as to be useless for many months. In this one plant the production of the vital ball bearings fell from 140 tons in July to 69 tons in August, and to but 50 tons in September. Not until November was there any increase in production.

In terms of the ability of the VIII Bomber Command to sustain losses in the air battle against Germany, the cost was prohibitive and almost disastrous. It was a grim prelude for Mission 115—Black Thursday. That was yet to come.

3

THE LUFTWAFFE

During the Battle of Britain in 1940, the German Air Force for the first time in World War II ran into a literal wall of opposition in the air. Convinced that the Luftwaffe was the qualitative superior of the Royal Air Force, the Germans suffered a terrible shock as well as appalling losses as the British Spitfires, Hurricanes, Beaufighters, all aided by the miracle of radar that permitted swift and accurate vectoring of climbing fighters to German formations, broke the back of the Luftwaffe's attempt to bomb England out of the war.

Defeated though they were over the British Isles, the Germans maintained an unquestioned air superiority over the continent. As the British improved their fighter planes, so did the Germans, and for many months there was no question but that the German pilot had the better of the odds in aerial combat over occupied Europe.

Beginning in the spring of 1942, however, the Royal Air Force not only improved in quality, but poured increasing numbers of fighters and bombers into the air, and stepped up the tempo of operations against the continent. This new offensive program dictated to the Luftwaffe the necessity for more effective defense against the accelerating British air activity; and while the British unquestionably were making headway, European skies continued in general to be the safe home grounds of the German Air Force.

Along the vast Soviet front the Luftwaffe, despite numerical inferiority, reigned supreme against an opponent suffering from inferior equipment, tactics, and pilots. Yet this vast aerial arena was beginning to exert its influence in the struggle for air supremacy by draining equipment and manpower from other fronts.

Upon this scene entered the specter of massed waves of

heavy bombers from England, flown by the Americans, and lesser numbers of these bombers from bases in Africa and, later, from Italy. For this much-heralded mass assault the German fighter pilot and his machine—to say nothing of the American bomber and its crew—were untested and unproven. To their credit, the Germans quickly, after initial B-17 operations, took heed of the threat that grew with alarming speed, and funneled extensive activities into the development of defenses to oppose the daylight raids against Germany which the B-17's and B-24's promised.

In their early attacks against the Fortresses bristling with heavy-caliber machine guns, the Germans proved poorly trained and ill-prepared for the new method of air warfare. In addition to the fact that the B-17 was a completely new type of opponent, the reports of its heavy defensive firepower proved a serious limiting psychological factor. The Germans apparently believed as strongly as we did in the ability of the Flying Fortress to live up to its name.

Early battles proved conclusively that existing German methods of attacking bombers would not avail against the B-17. Until the debut of the Fortress formations the firing attacks against bombers were made singly, or by the *Rotte,* a two-fighter formation. This failed to provide the attacker with firepower sufficient to destroy the B-17, with its outstanding structural strength, for the German pilots estimated that at least twenty to twenty-five hits with 20-mm. cannon shells were needed to bring down a Fortress.

In their first interceptions of the American heavy bombers, the Luftwaffe pilots followed their customary tactics of closing from the rear. Experience quickly taught them that this was begging for trouble. Against a formation of only 27 Fortresses, the fighters had to close with slow speed and must face the tremendous defensive array of no less than 200 heavy-caliber machine guns which would open fire at a distance of 1,000 yards.

By attacking from the front, the fighter pilots still had to accept the danger inherent in the defensive fire screen of the entire bomber formation, but they gained the vital advantage of enormously increasing the rate of closure, which reduced the effectiveness of the enemy guns; furthermore, they enhanced the possibility of scoring cannon-shell strikes in the critical areas of the cockpit, engines, and wing fuel tanks.

The success of the German fighter defense system—which

reached its bloody pinnacle in the defense of Schweinfurt on October 14, 1943—was owing in great part to the efficiency with which the Germans accepted the problem. In their attacks against the American formations, they drew heavily on night-fighter resources. They made this move despite the weariness of the night-fighter pilots and their preference for and experience in fighting as lone wolves. Yet these defects were more than compensated for by the extensive endurance of the twin-engine night fighters, their ability to follow with great precision the commands of ground vector controllers, and their heavy firepower. Later, after the disaster of Schweinfurt, American escort fighters rampaged through the heavy twin-engine German ships and exacted crushing losses; the big airplanes proved too cumbersome and vulnerable to the American fighters and were soon stricken from the mainstream of battle. Unhappily, however, this was not until after Schweinfurt.

Late in 1942 the concentrated mass saturation raids of the Royal Air Force Bomber Command, and the threat of United States Army Air Forces daylight precision bombing led to the institution of a major change in the anti-aircraft batteries and tactics of the Luftwaffe, to which 90 per cent of all the German flak batteries were assigned. Previously, the heavy A.A. guns had been spread out in batteries of four. To increase firepower and concentration in a given airspace, the guns were regrouped in batteries of six to eight heavy weapons. To defend particularly vital areas, the Germans formed their *Grossbatterien,* each made up of two or three of the larger groupings, with as many as 24 heavy guns firing under a single control.

This again went through another reorganization, as a result of which up to 40 guns were firing under single-command control. If the command site found the range properly, and accurately tracked the bombers in respect to height, lead, and position in space, the effect upon the bomber formations was catastrophic.

When the 12 B-17's of the Eighth Air Force made their first attack of the war against Rouen, Germany was expending little of her air power in daylight defense against bombers. Instead, her fighters and bombers were operating with brilliant effect along the Russian front and in the African desert, as well as creating a serious air defense against the nocturnal raids of the British. The total fighter force of the

Luftwaffe in Germany proper at that time included perhaps 130 machines. Daylight fighter strength in France amounted to another 300 airplanes, all well within German maintenance capabilities.

The year 1942 was a period of testing of daylight defenses on a minor scale, for the Americans as well as the Germans. By the beginning of 1943 the Luftwaffe recognized the full threat of American precision bombing, and made their first major moves to stem the attacks. Their avowed purpose went further than this; they planned, and believed they had the strength and the means, to break the back of the coming American heavy bomber offensive.

Unfortunately for the VIII Bomber Command, the first six months of 1943 were literally made to order for the German reorganization and marshaling of forces. The VIII's attacks were too infrequent, and they were insufficient in strength, to overwhelm the powerful and resilient German defense system. By their very nature the attacks enabled the Germans to perfect their daylight defensive system, to eliminate weaknesses, and to exploit their strength to the utmost. We could not have assisted the Luftwaffe in its defensive planning and preparations more than we did.

The VIIIth attacked—lightly and infrequently, for reasons explained in Chapter I—the cities of Hamm, Emden, Cologne, Bremen, Wilhelmshaven, and Kiel. This provided the perfect opportunity for the German fighter sector control headquarters to gain badly needed skills in *quickly* plotting the paths of the bomber groups and transmitting their height, course, speed, and formation to the fighter forces, which enabled the Germans to vector every available airplane to the scene of battle with great efficiency.

Moreover, this outsanding target plot system permitted the Germans again to use fighters which had carried out their attacks. Leaving the battle at high speed, the planes landed, and their pilots remained in the cockpit while skilled ground crews in minutes loaded new gun belts and refilled the fuel tanks. These fighters took off again quickly, to be vectored back into the combat scene. Thus they met the bombers as they returned from the attack. This greatly increased the effectiveness of the defense system; it enabled the Germans to use a hundred fighters, for example, with perhaps the impact of 150 airplanes.

The Germans also experimented with hundreds of other new devices which might increase their effectiveness in air defense. The 25th Experimental Commando, created personally by General Adolph Galland, chief of the German fighter forces, tested out the hundreds of suggestions that poured in from combat units, industry, or even the general populace. The 21-cm. mortar—an aircraft rocket that struck with terrifying effects against our bombers—was rushed into production. Aerial bombs were released against bomber formations, as well as aerial mines that drifted ahead of and into the groups. Cables with and without bombs were trailed in the air, to be dropped into the B-17 formations. Rocket batteries and cluster bombs with automatic photocell ignition, repeater-exploding rockets—all these and others saw combat trials.

These innovations were supplementary to the standard armament of the German fighters and of the bombers pressed into service as flying gun batteries. The weapons of the single-engine fighters included the 7.9-mm. (.30 caliber) and 12.7-mm. (.50 caliber) machine gun, and cannon of 15, 20, 23, 30, and 37 mm.

Perhaps the most effective of the German single-engine fighters was the Focke-Wulf FW-190, one of the greatest military planes of history. Powered with a 1,700-horsepower radial engine, the FW-190 flew faster than four hundred miles per hour, had amazing maneuverability, climbed rapidly, and carried the formidable armament of four 20-mm. cannon in the wings and two heavy machine guns mounted in the nose. Swift, agile, and heavily armored throughout its belly, it was an effective bomber destroyer.

Most famous of the Luftwaffe's fighters was the veteran of air battles in Spain, all across Europe and Africa, and in the Battle of Britain—the Messerschmitt Me-109. In its defense version the Me-109G was available in great numbers. With a top speed of more than four hundred miles per hour, extremely agile in the air, and able to fly to altitudes of 40,000 feet and above, the Me-109G was a superb fighting machine. As a bomber destroyer it carried two heavy cannon in underwing mounts, plus two heavy nose machine guns and a single cannon firing through the propeller hub. Both the FW-190 and the Me-109G could also accommodate rockets and/or aerial bombs.

The main twin-engine fighter was the Messerschmitt Me-110, a slow (350 mph) two-seated plane that had been slaughtered by the nimble Spitfires and Hurricanes of the Royal Air Force in the Battle of Britain. In speed, however, it was

Messerschmitt Me-110

greatly superior to the B-17, and with a combination of heavy cannon and machine guns in the nose—up to four cannon and two guns in some models—plus rocket batteries and/or bombs, the Me-110 was a deadly opponent. Its large size gave it great endurance; it could take off from bases far from the bomber stream and still attack the Fortresses.

The replacement for the Me-110, the Me-210 model, was available for the Schweinfurt raid, but in lesser numbers. Faster (390 to 410 mph), the Me-210 was also more heavily armored, and it stood a greater chance of absorbing and surviving the B-17's defensive firepower than its predecessor.

Many of the night fighters of the Luftwaffe were actually bombers, notably the Junkers Ju-88, one of the most versatile military machines ever produced by any nation. As a night fighter the Ju-88 was unusually well protected with armor plating, and would carry as many as six 20-mm. cannon, plus heavy machine guns, besides having the advantage of long endurance in the air.

The Fortresses that invaded Germany could expect to encounter not only these defending fighters, but variations of bombers and other fighters, like the swift, single-engine Heinkel He-113, in lesser numbers. The armament variations were many, and a single 37-mm. cannon shell might tear the wing right off a B-17. With rockets, aerial bombs, and other ordnance, Germany had created a virtual wall of fire in her skies.

The Rosarius Traveling Circus, which toured Germany in the summer of 1943, proved of invaluable aid. This was a flight made up of all flyable captured Allied aircraft, which visited German units to teach pilots the details and the techniques of our aircraft. It was a brilliant move. Unit leaders actually flew the captured airplanes—including the B-17—and were able thus to develop their attack techniques with what must be considered a unique advantage for a fighter force.

If we learned anything from the lessons of our air war in Europe, it was that it is impossible to label any aspect of that fantastic struggle in simple black and white. The German fighter defenses over their homeland became extraordinarily effective only because the Germans stripped other fronts of their air power. The Luftwaffe consumed a fantastic number of men, and expended in great quantities matériel, fuel, and airplanes. They threw into the defense of their industrial heartland nothing short of a superb and fantastic effort. Throughout the year 1943 virtually every new single-engine fighter airplane in the Luftwaffe went for the growing air-defense structure of Germany, at the expense of the other fighting fronts where planes were needed so desperately.

Further, many squadrons of Messerschmitt Me-109 single-engine fighters were actually *recalled* from the Russian front in the summer of 1943 to assist in the daylight defense of the Reich. The Germans singled out their best and most experienced fighter pilots from every front, and ordered them back to the homeland. The effects of this air-power drain were significant and critical, and they constituted a major contribution to the eventual defeat of Germany.

Messerschmitt Me-109G

Whatever the reasons, the most formidable aerial-defense system in history was at the peak of its strength and efficiency by the fall of 1943. By August—two months before the October 14 raid—the *permanent* daylight defenses of Germany included some six hundred Me-109 and FW-190 single-engine fighters, plus at least 180 twin-engine day fighters or "destroyers."

There existed as a defense against the mounting British raids (which in July–August, 1943, smashed Hamburg into a gutted, largely abandoned wasteland) a night-fighter force of nearly one thousand single-engine and twin-engine fighters. Those alone constituted nearly 20 per cent of the total operational strength of the Luftwaffe, and these heavily armed machines also were available for the defense of the Reich during daylight hours.

Because of the extended range of the October 14 attack by the B-17's—460 miles from their English bases—the Germans had available against them in operational condition some twelve hundred defending fighter aircraft. All these machines were able to fight in brilliantly coordinated attacks, and to coincide their efforts with the massed anti-aircraft fire from the ground.

And yet this incredible opposition was not all. Many of these airplanes would fly second sorties during the Schweinfurt raid, and thus in effect increase the aggregate number of fighters involved.

Because of the particular route of the bombers, the Germans were able to call upon many supporting fighter squadrons in France, Belgium, and Holland. It required no more than telephone calls on lines always open to transfer the fighters to German bases, and thus fit them perfectly into the system of ground vectoring.

The first assault against Schweinfurt, on August 17, contributed heavily to the masterful and bloody defense of that city two months later. The majority of the leaders of the German government reacted to the August raid with great shock. Albert Speer, Reichsminister of Armaments, warned that should the Americans continue to hammer in steady raids against the ball-bearings industry, then within sixty days the German armaments industry would suffer ill effects. Within four months, he emphasized with utmost gravity, reserves would be exhausted and the war economy would truly be crippled. The Germans heeded the warning all too well.

Thus the stage was set for the grimmest drama of the war in the skies. By the fall of 1943 the Luftwaffe had whetted its appetite and honed to the ultimate degree its skill against the unescorted daylight raids by the VIII's B-17's. The air-defense system of the Reich was at the very peak of its strength and its efficiency. Not simply in quantity of superb fighter planes and massed flak batteries, but in the skill and freshness of its pilots, in their courage, and in their unswerving belief that they would triumph.

PART II
THE MISSION BEGINS

4

FIRST MOTION

In the history of the army air forces in World War II, the second week of October, 1943, is listed as "most critical." The VIII Bomber Command made four major efforts during those seven days to destroy vital industrial targets within Germany.

On October 8, 399 heavy bombers left their bases to attack Bremen and Vegesack. A force of 357 of these aircraft struck their targets. Thirty bombers were shot down, 26 received major damage, and another 150 bombers were "slightly damaged."

The next day, October 9, 378 bombers went out, of which 352 struck their objectives at Gdynia, Danzig, Marienburg, and Anklam. German fighters and flak shot down 28 heavy bombers.

On October 10, the third attack in as many days, a force of 236 bombers attacked the city of Münster. Thirty bombers were lost to the enemy.

For the three-day period, the VIII Bomber Command had lost in battle a total of 88 heavy bombers and nearly nine hundred men. Several hundred bombers were damaged in varying degrees; a number of these never flew again. Within the aircraft that returned to England were dozens of dead and wounded.

Then came Schweinfurt, on October 14. . . .

Mission 115 begins in subdued fashion, invisible to the outside world. The scene is Pinetree, General F. L. Anderson's headquarters for the VIII Bomber Command at High Wycombe, and more specifically, in a square, large room with a high ceiling buried beneath thirty feet of reinforced concrete. Here five officers sit around a large table at what is known as the Daily Operations Conference. On the table there are thick sheafs of paper, charts and graphs, maps, photographs, messages, and scribbled notes.

These men may discuss the affairs of the day for perhaps forty-five minutes, or the conference may stretch out to four hours. When they have completed their meeting, they will have dissected in its most intimate detail an enemy city, its factories, labor force, products, shipments, its vulnerability. They will have discussed its anti-aircraft defenses, the German fighter forces along the route to the target and along the aerial pathway the bombers will follow to return to England. The route is carefully chosen; it is impossible to avoid the Messerschmitts and Junkers and Focke-Wulfs and Dorniers and Heinkels directly, but the route can skirt the bristling flak batteries of the Luftwaffe. These men who meet beneath the thick concrete walls leave nothing unsaid, nothing unanswered; they will weigh the vital nature of this city's industry against that of other cities, and they will fit this impending mission precisely into its place among those already past and those to come.

For this target, what size bombs? Incendiaries to high explosives in what proportion? All bombs internal, or thousand-pounders also to be slung beneath the wings? What about weather: at take-off, on the route, over the target, on the way home, and for landing? Escort? How far can the fighters provide cover? Thunderbolts or Spitfires, or both in a coordinated outward- and inward-bound escort mission?

On a large wall in front of the five officers is a giant map of Europe. The heartland of the enemy. It is a map laced with red lines—the "blood highways of the air," as they are aptly named—showing the aerial pathways to and from the targets of Germany proper and its occupied nations. The "Old Man" completes his discussions with his aides. For all intents and purposes, indeed, in full reality, the decision to attack, or to keep the bombers on the ground, for whatever reasons may exist, is his and his alone.

General Anderson stares into space for a long moment. He thinks now not simply in terms of statistics and tonnage and target analysis. These are human beings, flesh and blood, who make the statistics move, who change the lines on the graphs. For the moment the silence is oppressive, and it is gloomy. How many men will be killed *today?* How many were killed last week, and the week before? The general's hand slaps lightly on the thick wooden table.

He looks up. "All right. Schweinfurt it is, then."

"Schweinfurt it is, then. . . ."

The four words are the signal that opens a torrent of orders and movements. It begins as a trickle, a Warning Order that flashes from VIII Bomber Command headquarters to the air divisions scattered throughout England. The Warning Order is the command to grind into motion the vast and intricate machine of destruction that is the modern heavy-bombardment force. Behind the order are months of experience, bitter and bloody.

"Schweinfurt—that's the goddamned killer town," one officer mumbles as the order clatters from its teletype machine. Ahead are many hours of intense manipulation of men, machines, aviation gasoline, incendiary bombs, and high explosives. The coordination of the sprawling complex is truly a masterful effort, so that the VIII may spawn into the sky several hundred bombers, several thousand men, thousands of bombs, and hundreds of thousands of machine-gun bullets. Into the great formations that will wheel with throbbing majesty through the cloud-flecked skies must go fuel, oxygen, sandwiches, first-aid kits, bomb sights, maps, clothing, extra shoes, parachutes—all the many hundreds of small items that are essential to bring about that fateful moment when men in plexiglas wombs may peer through optical sights at cross hairs and toggle bomb switches that blink out rows of red lights.

The orders disseminate like electronic waves across miles of England. At 1815 hours on October 13 the 92d Bombardment Group at Alconbury receives its orders to load all B-17 aircraft with six 1,000-pound bombs each. At 2335 hours of the same day Field Order 220 arrives from the 1st Bomb Division. The group will brief the crews at 0700 hours on October 14, and commence take-off at 1012 hours. During the long hours as the ground crews ready the giant bombers, the 40th Combat Wing Field Order for Mission 115 comes in at 0130: the 92d Group will put up 21 B-17 aircraft and will fly as the lead group in the 40th Combat Wing Formation.

That's all; just the lead group. Prime target for the fighters.

At all the other stations the same orders, varying only in details of minutes and bomb loads and numbers of aircraft and positions in formations, are received, passed on, and generate their activity. Airdrome station names, unknown only a year ago or less, today mean "home" to thousands of men, enlisted men and officers, young and old. Alconbury, Bassingbourne, Grafton Underwood, Polebrook, Thurleigh, Hardwick, Great Ashfield, Knettisham, Ridgewell, Thrope Abbotts, Chelveston, Kimbolton, Molesworth, Bury St. Edmunds, Framlingham, Horsham St. Faith—and the others. Tonight they all have a great deal in common, and they are all also wet and cold and dank and uncomfortable.

Pick one station at random. A flat and grassy plain stretches two miles on a side, and it suffers the crisscrossing of its center by ribbons of concrete or macadam; the ribbons are the runways to send into the air, and to receive, the 30-ton bombers. Around these ribbons there runs a paved track, circling the field, a perimeter taxiway along which the big bombers trundle like great, ungainly winged whales. Then, farther out, along the edges of the crisscrossed area, there are the dispersal areas where the great birds squat, stolid and brooding, insensitive and mute to the ministrations of their ground crews.

Cavernous hangars loom like ghostly embattlements around the field; on the sides of these structures with their gaping maws that swallow 60,000-pound bombers whole are the clusters of administrative buildings, the closer huddling forms of workshops. Sometimes on the airdrome itself, but more often spilling out in a strange haphazard fashion across the plowed land and the thickets and the stinking, everlasting mud, are the mess halls for the officers and men. The paths to these oases of food and hot coffee rarely are visible in the mud, the snaking quagmire that works its way to the doors, but they nonetheless are always known.

Then, of course, there are the barracks. The barracks that are cold and dismal and wet. The barracks that *never* have had, or ever will have, coal sufficient to keep them warm and dry. The favorite pastime for the young officers at this station, it seems, is to steal sacks of coal from the unhappy British farmers nearby, and then to lead the shouting and irate citizens in wild chases under wet skies across the plowed fields. An odd way to keep physically fit, perhaps, but at this very station, the night before the Schweinfurt mission, this is exactly what happens. A first lieutenant, twenty-three years old, a pilot and veteran of two dozen bombing missions (also cited for bravery under fire), had to steal a 50-pound bag of coal to replenish the empty stock in his barracks. It is just another phase of life in the cold winter of 1943. . . .

Now, shortly after midnight, the stations in England are unlighted. There is the familiar haze overhead, the scud sweeping across the country only 300 feet high, the atmosphere sodden. You cannot say too much about this weather, because for the crews it is a curse that must be borne anew almost every day. Yet, even at those stations where the dispersal areas and the hangars do not yet give forth the rumbling thunder of bomber engines being tuned for their work, there is sound to be heard. It is a whisper, a bass drone. Somewhere "up there," perhaps in the murk or beneath the stars gleaming over the thick cloud tops, a coal-black night fighter cruises on patrol, the cannon and guns "hot."

The four-engine bombers squat and brood in darkness, but as a man's eyes become accustomed to the night, the Fortresses no longer are formless. Now they are grotesque, shadowy hulks in the gloom. Men stand beneath the winged metal creatures, guns slung over shoulders; perhaps they pace impatiently on their guard duty, or welcome the subdued slap-slap of mechanics' feet on the concrete approaching the mute aircraft. As each group receives the orders spreading through the divisions, the nocturnal stirring increases. The guards listen to the rumble of heavy trucks moving slowly, shifting gears whining in protest as they move around the perimeter tracks, splashing through black water to deliver parts to another shadow in the wet night.

The hangars are alive, the scene of many men hard at work, attending to the Flying Fortresses. Propellers turn slowly, they complain as starters move them around; smoke boils out of exhaust stacks, spits back angrily as the controlled explosions begin the internal frenzy beneath the cowlings, and then frays into wisps as the big blades revolve into blurs. All manner of work goes on: a new turret is eased into place, a new propeller is bolted to its shaft. Repairs large and minor, sometimes accomplished easily, but often with sweating, cursing labor . . . all to ready the 30-ton bombers for their rendezvous with the elite of the Luftwaffe.

At each group airdrome there is a windowless room, sealed tightly and guarded heavily. The entrances are gasproof, the blackout curtains double. Here is the Message Center and the Operations Room, drowning in brilliant light.

Between one and two in the morning the teletypes clatter suddenly across East Anglia, in 16 bomber groups with B-17's and three with B-24's; they trickle their messages into three fighter groups of the VIII Fighter Command, signaling preparations for the powerful P-47 Thunderbolt escort fighters. The sheets of paper snake upward beneath the viewing glass. At each base there is a virtual repetition of what occurs elsewhere.

It is a pyramiding effect, starting at the top and flowing downward, broadening as it moves. Command conceives the raid, and from here responsibility moves on to Bomb Division, which plans and schedules the "big picture." At the next level, Combat Wing further details and then directs activity. The groups receive their orders from Wing, and transpose the teletype messages to action. Within the groups there are the individual squadrons; within squadrons the flights. Within the flights, the individual bombers. And within each bomber we reach the level of flesh and blood. Ten men.

The entire vast machine rumbles into motion. Now, Command can only wait. Bomb Division is through; it files its papers, locks the files, puts the staff people on duty, and wearily goes to bed.

In the intelligence rooms of the nineteen groups at the bomber bases the duty officers pin large pieces of transparent plastic over the wall maps. They then carefully rule long lines in grease pencil on the acetate: the aerial pathways, routes to and from target.

The flak officers brush past the inner blackout curtains. With other officers they huddle in groups, studying reconnaissance photographs, peering at pictures of rivers, streets, smokestacks, gas and water tanks, power stations, factory buildings and workshops, bridges, hutments, airfields, flak gun positions, railroad sidings and yards.

At each group the intelligence officer bends over the target chart and carefully marks a small circle. This is the MPI— the Mean Point of Impact. Bull's-eye for the day for the thick, ugly darts with blunt noses and squared tail fins and innards of a thousand pounds of blasting hell.

Shortly before 0200 hours, at the average group, the commanding officer enters the intelligence room and walks to his desk. Waiting for him is a complete copy of the Combat Order. It contains the full details of the symphony in thundering motors and take-off schedules and assembly times and altitudes. It contains information on Take-off, Mean Point of Impact, Initial Point, Rally Point, routes, opposition expected, bomb loadings and weights—everything to accomplish the orchestral din of heavy bombardment in massed strength. The C.O. reads every word. He studies, makes notes, commits details to memory. The hands on the wall clock move, and the hours pass. . . .

Each group flying officer plots in exacting detail the assembly of all his forces. His task is to juggle dozens of pieces and then have all the pieces drop at specific time slots into their proper places. Each heavy bomber must be in its proper position on the perimeter track at a specific time. Each must move to the edge of the runway and each must take off at thirty-second intervals. Each must lumber into the air, wheel exactly on schedule, and reach its appointed place at so many thousands of feet in the sky, so that it may assemble with the other bombers. If the schedule is not met, the formations will be disorganized, the wings will straggle, the divisions will lack the complex interfiring defensive screen they will need so badly over German territory.

In the operations room the watch officer checks the crew lists with squadron commanders; this is the level of human beings under the flesh-and-blood cloaking titles of pilot, copilot, bombardier (or toggleer), navigator, radio operator, gunner—again this is broken down into TT (Top Turret), BT (Ball Turret), TG (Tail Gunner), LWG (Left Waist Gunner), and RWG (Right Waist Gunner).

The group navigators have their flight computers out, charts spread carefully on long tables. They are juggling into proper sequence take-off times, rendezvous points, altitudes to match positions, code names, colors, letters, and signals, "splasher" radio navigational aids, frequencies to use, check points—all to make possible the exact course in the sky.

There are haze and mist and rain over the runways; in the Briefing Rooms hang the thin and acrid smell of coal smoke, the gathering accumulation of smoke from cigarettes and pipes and cigars.

At Thurleigh, Colonel Budd J. Peaslee, who is to lead the 1st Air Division into battle, moves through several doors at

Wing Headquarters to the operations office. Here the duty officer has glued his ear to the red scrambler, a special telephone rigged for secret conversation. The words spoken into the telephone are snarled electrically into an unintelligible garble of sound that is so much static to someone who taps the line; at the receiver, however, it is rescrambled again into sensible sound. Peaslee watches the duty officer, who seems to be engaged in a one-sided conversation; his only contributions are curt, a "Yes," or "No," or "Twenty-seven" or "Fifty-two."

Peaslee walks to the wall containing the operations map, pulls back the curtain, and stares only at the German end of the black yarn stretched from England to the target. "One look was enough," he recalls today with distaste.

The duty officer says "Over and out," drops the red scrambler back on its hook, and looks up.

"Rough show," he comments flatly to Peaslee, "but with this soup outside they'll probably scrub it before take-off."

"Maybe," the colonel replies, "but we've gone before when it was like this. Remember the morning we lost·ten at the end of the runway?"

The duty officer doesn't like to remember it, and neither

Some ships never made the mission. "Something" went wrong with a bomb; ten men died in a terrible flash.

does Peaslee, but it isn't easy to forget. That particular morning ten bombers had piled up during take-off. "They all had armed bombs in their bays," Peaslee recalls, "and there were a hundred men aboard. It was the same kind of morning, wet and lousy, and suddenly it was lighted by a series of brilliant flashes, and then there was nothing."

One hundred men, and . . . *nothing*.

5

NOTES SELECTED AT RANDOM

"Fear came to some at the height of missions, while to others it was a cold shuddering aftermath experienced in the quietude of the darkened barracks. . . ."

From an official history of
the VIII Bomber Command.

Mission 115 had a hell of a lot of combat behind it. Once the previous missions went into the records, however, they became so many dry statistics of groups assigned, planes dispatched, planes aborted, bombers to target, bombers lost or damaged, and the statistics on the men. But it wasn't so easy for the men to forget. There was a strangeness about this violent air war so high over the earth that set it apart, away by itself, from all other aspects of the war. The suddenness of flaming death, of freezing in temperatures down to seventy degrees below zero, of choking because of a lack of thick air to breathe. There was no ground to hug, no feeling of solidity beneath a man's feet when his bomber lurched and heeled crazily through the sky.

The sky—perhaps that was the strangest of all, to fight a war five miles into the heavens, an arena separated by vertical distance from the rest of the human race. Except, of course, for the flak, which pursued the men in their planes hungrily, which filled the sky with dirty black splotches and flaming red cauldrons, and spat invisible shards of jagged metal in all directions.

The earth—miles below. A man can achieve peace of mind so far above his world, when his airplane functions properly and he has power and the machine imparts its solidity of lift from the wings. But to think—at the moment when bullets and cannon shells raked the guts of a bomber and its 10 men—of that horrible plunge to earth; this is what unnerved even the bravest. The parachute did not always promise succor. There were the ships that were torn in half, or had a wing blown loose to flip-flop crazily through space, while the bomber whirled in a tight spin, and centrifugal force pinned the men inside helplessly, like flies smashed against a wall. How long does it take to fall 25,000 feet inside the blasted wreck of a Flying Fortress? Whom is there to ask?

In their barracks, these men were not always quiet. Take at random from official histories the notes written by unsigned authors, one of whom wrote: "The men lived the battles in their sleep, with considerable mental disturbances. The other night the men went into the barracks and found Captain Fenton flying an apparently tough mission. Apparently his ship was hit and he exclaimed: 'Copilot—feather number four!' The lieutenant, sound asleep, answered him. Both of them, sound asleep, piloted the severely damaged Fort back home. . . ."

The living conditions in 1943 for the bomber crews were anything but conducive to high morale or to efficiency, but their effect on the men, all observers of the crews report, was but negligible. Above all else, though, they hated the mud, "the incessant, cloying, clammy, sticky mud." The blackout was a "constant pain; no matter how you sliced it—and sometimes you could almost slice it—it was a nuisance and a bore."

The bomber stations were by sheer physical necessity widely spread out, and the distances to be covered on foot meant often being plastered with the freezing mud of passing vehicles. The coal stoves in the Nissen huts—the grimy, hated Nissen huts—defied all attempts to keep them burning overnight. Much of the time there wasn't any hot water to be had, the sunlight seemed to have abandoned England for the duration of the war, and even keeping the latrines clean was a major task. This may appear as a startling note—but some stations went for five and six weeks at a time without being able to obtain mops, brooms, cleaning materials, or *any* implements.

And of course there was always the shortage of coal, and the "midnight requisitioning" by officers and enlisted men. At one station the commanding officer finally decided it was time to steal coal by the truckload; he had found a major and a lieutenant colonel digging through a slag heap, chuckling with pleasure when they came to large, unburned pieces of coal.

The men who lived on the more primitive stations took to jeering loudly at their luckier fellows who enjoyed the wonderful luxury of moving into Royal Air Force installations with permanent facilities. These men with brick barracks, hot water, sufficient heat, and other amenities were assailed—and envied bitterly—as the "country-club set."

On the official side of things the men were plagued with a serious shortage of supplies and maintenance facilities essential to keep the war running. "Many times," one report stated, "combat aircraft stood on the ground because there simply weren't enough maintenance men to get all planes ready in time for missions."

An official history recalls: "At one time the lack of equipment for cleaning machine guns became so acute that the gunners, having cleaned parts of their weapons with soap and

Last check of tail turret before take-off

water, *took them tenderly into bed the night before a mission to prevent them from rusting.*"

It was not long after the battles in the air assumed major proportions that the Germans evolved the trick of hammering away fiercely at a single group. This concentrated casualties among bombers that had taken off from the same base. The Germans were calculating in their move. When they were successful in these attacks, from 30 to more than a hundred men might be missing from the same station that night.

Morale inevitably took a beating. The reason was not so much that these men had been shot down on the mission, but the failure to replace them properly. It was a lesson we didn't heed soon enough.

These men knew that this was war, that people would be shot down and that they would be killed. But the facing of empty beds in barracks, of empty seats in the mess, of empty benches at the briefings—this was a constant, grating reminder that cut deeply into the souls of men.

At one station a gunner missed a mission when the surgeon ordered him to stay on the ground for the day. Every man in his barracks on that same mission went down over Germany. For several days the bewildered and hapless man would run suddenly to the other barracks in the hope that he might recognize one of his friends. He didn't, of course. Finally he could not stand the silence, the mocking, empty beds any longer. He was a seasoned and a brave man, but he broke. He fled the station and went A.W.O.L.

Even in World War I the lesson was learned that any unit could endure severe losses if the vacant seats in the mess were occupied by the following morning. This was the "full-break-fast-table" policy, and it was one that the Royal Air Force pursued with religious intensity. But the American stations did not fill up so quickly. The VIII Bomber Command in those days simply didn't have the men to bring in.

Often there were wonderful people to fill the aching gaps. And the chaplain was not the least of these people. "No one who watched the combat crews kneel to receive a final benediction before entering their planes," wrote a historian, "ever doubted the value of these sincere, quiet men whose job included everything from running errands for pipe tobacco to sitting beside a dying airman in a hospital plane."

Then there were the station doctors—the air surgeons. They did a tremendous job for the men. They were always present when the planes went out on the missions; they were always waiting when the crews returned. They were always ready, day or night, to meet the needs of any man, for any reason. Sometimes they went out on missions; they did not always come home.

"But when you boiled it all down," stated another officer whose name is lost to the records, "everyone agreed—in the midst of the misery where platitudes were nothing less than profane to these men—it was the men themselves who never allowed the morale to become a serious problem."

The men who stayed on the ground were, in the fullest sense of that badly overused term, the unsung heroes. No one ever focused the spotlights of publicity on the duty of guarding a Fortress in a freezing rain, or the men who packed parachutes long into the nights in rooms clammy with cold and dampness—and who dared not make a mistake in their precision folding of the silk and shroud lines.

No one ever paid attention, it seems, to the ground crewmen who had to struggle for footing in slippery, freezing mud, who had to take the bombs, which seemed sullen and brooding, from the mud, load them on carriers, and drive them to the stands where the hulking bombers waited. No one seemed to know, outside of the bases, that these men washed the bombs, cleaned the pregnant blobs of all mud, washed down the finned steel and the casings for the high explosives. The bombs could not have blemishes; even a single patch of hardened mud will keep a bomb from falling straight and true, from pursuing its desired ballistic trajectory. And maybe because of a patch of mud, a plane would go down and ten men would die in vain.

No medals were handed out to the men who suffered when a 1,000-pound bomb slipped, for no apparent reason, and crushed to a bloody pulp the hapless bomb loader's foot.

"Nobody wrote glamorous newspaper stories about the cooks," one gunner explained to me, "but those guys—at least on my base—never turned us down, day or night, when we wanted something to eat, or some hot coffee. And nobody seems to have counted all the cooks and the bakers and truck drivers and the guards and the clerks who said to hell with it, and who became gunners, and never came back to us."

And what did the crews think of the Germans? You can sum it all up with the statement of one man: *"You gotta hand it to Jerry; he's a beautiful flier, and boy, has he got guts! . . ."*

During the height of the period of disastrous missions over the Reich, an American aircraft firm, following the policy that Americans are better than anybody else, sponsored probably the most ill-received advertisement of the war. The advertisement was full page, and it showed a grinning gunner peering through the sights of a .50-caliber machine gun as he poured tracers into a swarm of Focke-Wulf FW-190 fighters. Beneath the heroic painting was the caption: "Who's Afraid of the Big Bad Wulf?"

One pilot who saw the page immediately tore it from the magazine and pinned it to his group's bulletin board. Beneath the page went a long scroll of paper with a red-ink headline that shouted: *"WE ARE!"*

Every combat officer in the group signed the scroll, and the group commander's name was at the top of the list. They mailed it to the manufacturer with their blessings.

What were these men like, who were to go out on Mission 115?

How do you describe Americans from all walks of life? In the VIII there were gunners wounded three and four times who refused to leave their weapons. There were bombardiers who toggled their bombs and died, coughing blood, as they slumped over the bomb sights. There was a pilot in the air who had been wounded, and flew with a foot in a cast, because he refused to stay on the ground. And he was not the only one. There were Nisei and Filipinos and Polacks and Irishmen and Jews and Italians and Germans and English and Danes and pure-blooded American Indians, and at least one Chinese who never stopped grinning and who was a real authority with a .50-caliber gun.

And what about the queen—the Flying Fortress? She was legendary, but the legends told about her were true. Take just one ship on the raid of July 14, three months before Mission 115.

This B-17 met a head-on attack by three Focke-Wulf FW-190 fighters. The gunners exploded two of them, and the top turret poured a stream of shells into the cockpit of the third. With a dead man at the controls, the fighter screamed in, and at a closing speed of 550 miles per hour smashed head on into the number-three engine.

The tremendous impact of the crash tore off the propeller. It knocked the heavy bomber completely out of formation as though a giant and invisible hand had swatted a fly. The fighter cartwheeled crazily over the B-17. It cut halfway through the wing, and then sliced a third of the way through the horizontal stabilizer. The top and ball turrets immediately jammed, the radio equipment was smashed to wreckage, and all the instruments "went crazy." Pieces of metal from the exploding, disintegrating Focke-Wulf tore through the fuselage, and a German gun barrel buried itself in the wall between the radio room and the bomb bay.

Crews of nearby bombers watched the collision. They saw a tremendous explosion, and the bomber hurtling helplessly out of control, tumbling as she fell. They reported when they returned to base that the Flying Fortress had blown up, and that the crew must be considered dead.

The old Queen hadn't blown up, and the crew was far from dead. The pilots struggled wildly in the cockpit, and somehow between them managed to bring their careening bomber back under control. The gunners shot down a fourth fighter that had closed in to watch the proceedings.

And they brought her all the way back to England, and scraped her down for a belly landing on the runway.

Postscript: not a man was injured.

The flak was rough, and the fighters were murder, and the Forts went down. But crews loved those airplanes.

Sometimes you can get an excellent glimpse of these airmen through the diaries of their medical officers. From a thick stack of files in the air force archives I extracted the diary of a medical officer of the 381st Group, one of the outfits that flew the mission of October 14.

This diary opens the door slightly to the lives of these men. The vignettes are pointed at times.

"Sometimes you don't need combat," wrote the air surgeon. "On the ninth raid of the group, on 14 July, 1943, a B-17 simply exploded en route to the target. The ship was over England when it tore to pieces in a blinding flash. Six men were killed instantly; the other four were blown into space, and were able to pull their ripcords."

On August 17, in the first Schweinfurt raid, the 381st Group sent out 26 of their big bombers. One aborted—and 11 out of the remaining 25 bombers failed to return.

"Morale was pretty low this evening on the return of the crews," the surgeon recorded, "particularly as soon as stories were compared, and total losses realized."

Two days later, on a raid to Holland—a "milk run"—one

B-17 went down. "The loss of this latest ship seemed to have
a depressing effect on the combat crewmen, presumably
because it was supposed to be an easy one. The line of
reasoning, I presume, is to the effect that if losses can be
sustained on the simple ones, what chance does anyone
have?"

On October 8, on the mission to Bremen (six days before
Schweinfurt), seven out of 21 bombers went down. Of the 14
that returned, several were shot to pieces. Then this addition
to the diary:

"B-17 *Tinkertoy* ground-looped just off the runway. *Tinkertoy* had her nose shot out and the pilot had his head blown
off by a 20-mm. cannon shell. There was hardly a square inch
of the entire cockpit that was not covered with blood and
brain tissue. One half of his face and a portion of his cervical
vertebra were found just in front of the bomb bay. The
decapitation was complete."

(On December 20, 1943, *Tinkertoy* was over the target
area when two enemy fighters rammed head on into the
airplane. "The ship," wrote the unknown surgeon, "has been
with the group since its third phase of training. It has a long
and interesting history and has been on many raids over
enemy territory. A number of people have been killed in this
ship and the group looked on it with mixed horror and
affection. . . .")

The report continued on October 8: "After this mission, in
visiting the many crews right after they hit the ground, the
tense excitement of many was apparent and in many cases
was border-line hysteria. This was the roughest mission experienced in some time and most of the personnel seemed to
feel the losses keenly."

The diary tells of a strange incident during one mission, of
which the 381st's air crews talked a long time. As the diary
records it: "Just as the formation was reaching the Danish
coast, a 20-mm. shell exploded in the cockpit of Lieutenant
Winters' ship, and Lieutenant Winters was temporarily
stunned or blinded by the flash. When he came to, the
bombardier and navigator had already left the ship, the
copilot was jumping, and one of the crew members gave him
a farewell salute—and jumped. The ship was in a steep
gliding turn and there was a fire in the rear of the cockpit.
Lieutenant Winters righted the ship, put on the autopilot,

went back and put out the fire, and brought the ship safely back to England. . . ."

The good lieutenant was not quite so dead as his crew believed him to be!

10 October 1943. "The mental attitude and morale of the crews is the lowest that has yet been observed."

Three days later: "Captain—, a squadron leader and a brave man, informed the commanding officer that he had no desire to continue flying."

The next day was October 14, and Mission 115. "Crews were briefed at 0700 hours and the target was the ball-bearing works at Schweinfurt, Germany. The mention of the word 'Schweinfurt' *shocked the crews completely* . . . [as] on 17 August this group lost so heavily on this same target. Also conspicuous by its omission was the estimated number of enemy fighters based along the route. Upon checking with the S-2 later, it was found that this omission was intentional and that the entire German fighter force of 1,100 fighter aircraft was based within eighty-five miles of the course. The implications are obvious.

"As I went around to the crews to check out equipment, sandwiches, coffee, etc., the crews were scared, and it was obvious that many doubted that they would return."

6

THE BRIEFINGS

Across more than fifty miles of England, on the cold morn-morning of October 14, the flying crews of the nineteen bomber groups committed to Mission 115 drift toward the briefing rooms. It is the flow of 3,000 men who will forsake earth and enter the high vaults. Their movement is in the form of small tributaries thickening into streams of air crews; these swirl temporarily in the backup before the building entrances. Outside each building there stand two guards, immaculate of dress, carefully checking passes and faces.

Thurleigh, the headquarters of the 40th Combat Wing, is also the home base of the 306th Group. Wing headquarters, a tenant on Thurleigh, is just big enough to tie three heavy-bomber groups—the 306th, the 305th at Chelveston, and the 92d at Alconbury—together in their combat operations. Colonel Howard M. ("Slim") Turner and Colonel Budd Peaslee, along with some operations and intelligence officers and some airmen, make up the staff. They have no administrative function; they are concerned entirely with combat operations. Peaslee's destination this morning is the 92d Group at Alconbury; he will fly the right seat in a B-17 that takes off from that airdrome.

Outside wing headquarters Peaslee's driver switches the jeep lights on to full bright, but they can barely penetrate the early-morning gloom and fog, and what is now a driving rain. The car rumbles along; the colonel has been over this road a hundred times or more, and he sinks back into his own private thoughts. "I think about home, about my motherless children, my own mother, the take-off, the assembly in the air, the German fighters, our escort, the flak." He smiles for a moment, seventeen years coming back clearly in his mind. "Those thoughts really weren't so special, after all," he

explains. "At times like that the same things always come into
my mind. I'm sure that 3,000 other men were thinking the
same things."

The car moves slowly in the murk toward Alconbury,
headquarters of the 92d Bombardment Group, and stops
beneath one of the few shielded lights glowing dully at the
entrance. There are little groups of men—"the sloppiest men
imaginable," Peaslee describes them—entering the building
under the watchful scrutiny of the usual two guards. No two
of these men, it seems, ever dress exactly alike. They wear an
amazing diversity of flying equipment. Some are clad in
heavy leather jackets zipped up, and there is about them a
semblance of dress. Many others have put on, of their flying
gear, only their outside pants, and when these are left un-
zipped they flop around sloppily like ragged blankets. Only
one item is common to all, *always*. This is the pair of clumsy
sheepskin-lined flying boots that will keep their feet warm
and dry.

Inside the building, under the glaring lights in the briefing
room, Colonel Peaslee joins the crews. Today, as the air
commander of the 1st Bomb Division, he will lead the Eighth
Air Force into the enemy heartland. The colonel is forty-two
years old. The "old-timers" usually stay on the ground, except
when their turn comes to "lead the show." For the moment,
however, Peaslee joins the rest of the 92d's crews like any
other airman attending the briefing. Let his own notes,
written so many years ago, bring the scene back to life:

"There is a heavy smoke haze now, and the temperature
has risen noticeably from the body heat given off. They sit at
all angles and postures on wooden benches and chairs. Some,
sitting erect, are sound asleep. Others engage in animated
conversations with their neighbors, and still others stare
ahead at nothing. They are getting in their thinking, as I have.
Bill [Colonel William Reid, 92d Group commander] and I
are sitting in heavy leather chairs that never appeared on a
supply order. I must ask him about them sometime.

"A neat major steps on the platform at the front of the
room and begins roll call. He sings out only the names of the
plane commanders. Each answers for his crew. There is some
screwing around in the front rows as a few commanders turn
to scan the faces in the back for their men. All are present.
The major moves to the rear of the platform and rips aside a

black curtain hanging against the wall. A large-scale map appears with the usual length of black yarn crossing it. There is no noise now as all lean forward, looking at the eastern end of the yarn.

" 'It's Schweinfurt,' the major says, and starts shuffling papers on the platform desk. He is giving us a few minutes to think it over. A buzz of talk breaks out instantly—wisecracks for the most part. One voice penetrates the others.

" 'Sonofabitch! And this is my last mission!'

"It may well have been."

All across the Midlands and East Anglia much the same scene is enacted, in the nineteen bomber group briefing rooms, in those of the fighter groups which will escort the bombers to the limit of their endurance. But it is only for the bomber crewmen that Schweinfurt has its very special meaning. The briefings are on the same target, but not all the briefing officers follow the same scripts—except for the security officers. At each base the security officer steps to the front of the room with his usual warning; today, October 14, it assumes special significance.

"Do not talk about the target once you leave this room. Report at once to the S-2 officer any person having knowledge of the target whose duty does not require it. This applies even more to a scrubbed target.

"Anyone flying this mission who has not had PW instruction report to an S-2 officer immediately after the briefing.

"Be sure you wear your dog tags, GI shoes, and do not—repeat—do not wear squadron insignia. Carry your rank, name, and serial number only.

"No one will leave this briefing until dismissed."

The Nissen huts and the brick buildings across England seem almost to be other-worldly, isolated as they are from the miserable weather just beyond their walls. In some briefing rooms there are not enough seats and the men lean against the walls or against desks. The conversation is a loud, ragged drone. The movement of the intelligence officer to the front has all the effect of a curtain rising on a stage. Silence erases all sound.

A long ruler moves along the wall map. It begins with a light tap at the home station where the briefing takes place, then slides toward the east. The ruler leaves England, eases across the Channel, into the continent, working its way toward

Germany. Deeper and deeper into the enemy land, until in the far southern reaches, near Frankfurt, the ruler stops. But Frankfurt is not the answer. The intelligence officer, still looking at the map, states flatly, "This, gentlemen, is your target for today. *Schweinfurt.*"

He pauses. At the 92d Group, Peaslee and the other men in the room wait for the words to begin again. *Why* Schweinfurt—again? The question is in every man's mind.

"I know what you're thinking," the intelligence officer at the front of the room continues. "That this is going to be a rough show. You are remembering the twenty-four bombers we lost on the first mission to Schweinfurt. You are wondering why we have to go back. . . .

"I must impress upon you that Schweinfurt is the most critical target in all of Germany. It is at the head of our list. We cannot really go ahead with other targets until Schweinfurt is practically destroyed, or, at the very least, seriously crippled."

The men listen attentively. There is no longer any "screwing around," for these are words of life and death. The intelligence officers at these bases are not assigned regularly to combat missions, but they command the respect of their men. Most of them have volunteered for and flown combat missions because they were self-conscious and sensitive about briefing combat crews on flak and fighters they had never seen.

The intelligence officers all across England explain why it must again be Schweinfurt. They discuss the importance and the relationship of ball bearings to industry, to planes and subs and tanks and guns and all sorts of equipment. "Half of all Germany's ball bearings are produced at Schweinfurt," drones the voice, and there is not a man who does not immediately reach the same conclusion. The Luftwaffe is going to turn not only Schweinfurt, but the route to and away from that target, into a vicious hornet's nest. A shudder sweeps, almost perceptibly, through the briefing rooms. The men try not to look at one another, but many think the same thing. "Who will be missing from here tonight? How many crews will get it today?"

Move across England into the area of the 3d Bomb Division area, the wave that will follow the force led by Peaslee. Here a group intelligence officer concentrates on target details: "Our target—the VKF Number One Plant—is one mile to the east of two other larger ball-bearing plants. It consists of a ball shop and a heat-treatment building surrounded by assembly, testing, and storage buildings where a six months' supply of bearings is stored. These buildings are of old construction with wooden floors—they are pretty well soaked in oil. In the raid of August 17, the 1st Bomb Division did most of its damage to the west of our target, and only one or two bombs fell on the lower left corner of our target. Photos are on the wall and you can study them after the briefing.

"There are camouflage and smoke screens. The plants have probably all been camouflaged by disruptive painting since the last raid. Elaborate, double-ringed smoke screens, the inner taking in the target and the city. The outer ring forms an elongated pattern including an airdrome and the bend of the river, and enveloping the inner ring."

In the briefing room of the 92d Group Colonel Peaslee studies the faces of the men around him. Until the target was announced to the combat crews, only he and a few briefing officers knew the eastern terminus of the black yarn stretching across Europe.

"Such a decision—selecting this target—was a terrible thing to have to do," Peaslee recalled recently. "Not only were hundreds of lives involved, not only the fate of a nation, but the fate of many nations. Day after day, as the target decisions were made, the history of the world war changed. And a general who made one of those decisions knew it only too well. He has feelings like you and me, and when he was aware that hundreds and even thousands must die as a result of his order, his sleep became troubled and his food was tasteless. He had no choice but to inject steel into a heart as soft as yours and mine. He killed the enemy physically if we carried out his orders. He killed us emotionally if we turned back showing a white feather. And he killed himself a little all the time."

At the 92d Bombardment Group, the intelligence officer— a schoolteacher in civilian life, whom the crews call "Dad"— is explaining, as recorded in Peaslee's notes:

"Flak will be light to nil along the route, but you will get a few rounds as you pass south of the Ruhr. According to our last flak information, the target is defended by 300 heavies— 88-mm. guns—and the gun crews are excellent. Your route will take you through the lightest concentrations and you will be under aimed fire for seven minutes. Your IP [Initial Point, where the bomber formation is committed to its specific target] is twenty miles southwest of Schweinfurt. You will turn right at 'Bombs Away' and get back into tight defensive formation for the return flight. The air commander [here he refers to Peaslee] will execute a series of slow turns to aid you in tightening up your formation. Your return route is over France, of course, and direct to the Channel. It is possible that the enemy may muster 300 fighters along your route [this was seriously underestimating the total], as he can draw from all of north Germany and France. . . .

"The enemy fighters are persistent and aggressive. They will probably try to break up our formations with head-on attacks. You new crews—don't panic and try to dodge. You'll leave yourself wide open to get picked off if you straggle. You play into their hands and leave your comrades without their best defense, and you're sure meat alone. Freeze into defensive formation, and if someone ahead gets out of tight formation, move right up into his place, for he has either been hit and will go down anyway or he is straggling. Don't hesitate—it's your neck.

"You tail gunners"—the major emphasizes this point— "keep a sharp watch for twin-engine 210's sneaking up on vapor trails to blast you. Most of the day fighters are FW-190's and Me-109's, and it's possible for some of them at least to hit you twice—on penetration and withdrawal. They will expect us to return across France, so the chances are that they will land in France after the first interception to rearm and refuel for your return. Consequently you must maintain defensive formation until you recross the Channel. The P-47's, P-38's, and Spits will cover you on the return to the limit of their range, but take no chances."

They didn't; the big P-47's never got off the ground because of clouds that closed in the fields. The twin-boomed P-38 fighters didn't become operational until the next day. No Spitfires showed up.

The major turns to the side and gives a quiet order to an aide, who grasps a rope and lowers a screen that has been folded on wooden arms against the ceiling. The lights blink out, and an operator steps up to a projector in front of the platform. Several pictures flash in succession on the screen while the major taps the pictures with a long pointer, and explains carefully the details the crews must know. The plane commanders carefully jot down notes. They follow the pointer as it touches on flak positions, on the aiming point for the bombs. They study schematic views of the city, stare at photographic blowups, mark down details of the RP—the Rally Point, where they will reassemble the formations after the bombs are gone.

The lights come on, and the screen disappears. The major known as "Dad" steps down, and another officer stands before the crews. The new speaker concentrates on escape and evasion. His talk is somewhat more grim, for he operates on the assumption that he is speaking to crews who are definitely going to be shot down. He discusses the escape routes available, and the procedures to follow in the event a crew reaches the ground alive in Germany, or France, or perhaps Holland or Belgium. (Many will.) If the airplane is under control while it is descending, the officer tells the pilots where to go—if at all possible.

He points to an arc of red yarn on the map. It is like a fence; inside the yarn there is protection. Outside the yarn—beyond the reach of friendly fighter escort—is No-Man's Land. The yarn, unhappily, is much less than half the distance from England to Schweinfurt, where the black yarn ends. The officer tells in detail where the rescue boats are located in the North Sea to snatch up the crews of planes that must ditch in the water (one will). He emphasizes strongly the value of the escape kits, and explains the reception to be expected if the men parachute into the occupied countries. He spends little time on Germany itself. Most of the men in the room listen with impatience to this briefing, for they have heard it many times before, and they are bored; the briefing officer knows this, but there are new crews in the room, and even the older crews may hear something which this very same day will save their lives.

The cast on the stage changes, and the group navigator steps to the front. He punctuates his briefing with numbers and times and schedules, and the flying crewmen and navigators afford him absolute attention. He completely covers the take-off plan. He details individual planes into squadrons, the squadrons into groups. He assembles groups into wings, wings into divisions, and divisions into Air Task Forces.

These Air Task Forces will consist of the 1st, 2d, and 3d Air Divisions. They are intended to form an unbroken stream of four-engined aerial might that stretches a length of twenty miles. There should be more than three hundred heavy bombers in that stream.

No one knows it yet, but their actual number will be much less. Not just in numbers of aircraft, but in machine guns, in formation slots, in defensive boxes and fire screens needed desperately, but unavailable.

The group navigator continues with information on fighter routes, timing, and escort positions.

Finally he calls off the time "hack." Each man in the room sets his watch at a selected minute and second. They listen carefully as the group navigator drones off the seconds— "five—four—three—two—one—*hack!*" At the final word every man in the room presses in the winding stem of his watch. Thus every one of the watches of the more than three thousand men assigned to the mission is correct and coordinated down to the second. Each briefing officer then announces H-hour; this is the take-off time for his group. The crews will man their aircraft exactly sixty minutes before H-hour.

The group bombardier announces data on bomb loading, fuse settings, the aiming points, and the bomb interval of the various squadrons. Next comes the armament officer, who specifies the amount of ammunition to be carried. Each airplane will carry for this mission an extra supply of .50-caliber shells. It means a tricky take-off in an airplane heavier than usual, but no one minds. They're going to need every shell, and they are well aware of that need.

The weather officer takes the stand in front of the group, and his is the least assuring of all the briefings. The weather, to put it bluntly, stinks. Outside the briefing room, out on the runway of the 92d Group, and at the other twenty-one groups, the visibility is down to a quarter of a mile. The weather officer promises one mile at take-off time; that is vastly better, when you are rolling down a field no more than five thousand feet in length and the belly of the airplane is pregnant with stifled hell. Further details: the planes should break out and be in the clear at 2,000 feet. Along the assembly route there will still be a solid overcast beneath the bombers but, assures the officer, the Channel is clear and it's just about perfect over the continent. The weather for return does not look good at all, but the picture is changing almost by the minute.

Do they go, or stay? No one truly knows, and the decision to take off, or to scrub the mission, will not be made until the very last moment, when the bombers are at the runway, engines idling, waiting for the signal to roll.

The first briefing officer, the major from intelligence, returns to the front of the room. "Colonel Peaslee is here from Wing," he announces. "He is air commander today and will be in the leading aircraft as copilot. Colonel, will you say a few words?"

"I knew this was coming," Peaslee groaned in recollection. "I had been trying to think of something to say all during the briefing. My mind is a complete void as I stumble to the platform. I have talked to these men, or men just like them, many times before. I want to break their tension, to get them to laugh if possible. I can't think of a thing that's witty or funny in connection with what we are about to do. Finally I just start talking. I tell them how to fly their formation—as though it were an exhibition, a presidential review or inauguration. I tell them to anticipate the turns, to conserve their ammunition, and not to fire at fighters that are out of range; to move up at once if they see someone straggle. I caution them to keep their guns loaded until they land, and remind them of the time we lost ten bombers when the crews started cleaning their guns over the Channel and got jumped, and the time we lost eight when German fighters invaded the landing pattern over England. The story of one of our own fighter boys on his first sweep pops into my mind, and I pass it on. He worked into a German transport formation in a landing pattern and came home an ace, with six transports to his credit, then found out later that all the German pilots he had shot down were women.

"I use plenty of profanity. For some reason these boys enjoy hearing the Old Man swear in public. It doesn't matter much whether you swear at them, or at higher headquarters or at the enemy, although they seem to enjoy most hearing you cuss out higher headquarters. I guess it puts you on their side and makes them feel you belong to them. I've been on a good many of these outings and they know it. That, too, gives me a membership in their lodge. They are receptive to what I say, and when I make some inane remarks about the Germans of Schweinfurt walking on roller skates tonight as a result of all the balls we are going to scatter around, they laugh—a good hearty laugh. I sit down."

The intelligence major comes back just once more. "Well, fellows, that's it," he says to wind up the briefing. "This *could* be a milk run! When you land, come immediately to the debriefing rooms. I'll have a man there for every crew and plenty of doughnuts and coffee. We won't keep you but a few minutes."

The major, of course, is lying. He knows it, Peaslee knows it, the pilots and gunners all know it. They are all too painfully aware that at this stage of the game a milk run into Germany, this deep into Germany, just isn't in the cards. They all know that in just the last week, in a three-day period alone, nearly nine hundred men went down before the German's guns and his cannon and rockets.

The major is a liar, and no one blames him for it. His briefing has been honest in every respect but this one, that he has played down the mission as routine. This is not a routine mission and it cannot possibly be anything but hell for most of the people who are leaving England for the east.

From every mission like this one there will be more than one debriefing officer who will sit at his table, waiting vainly for a crew, feeling guilty as hell even though he didn't have anything to do about his empty table, about the gunner report sheets that will never be filled in, the pencils that will stay clean and sharp, the chairs that will stay in their places. He will sit there alone, unhappy and morose, and against the background of chatter from the other crews that have returned he will have time to think about flame and a wing torn off and the screams of men and parachutes that don't open. The coffee will grow cold and the doughnuts will become stale and lifeless, and just what the hell can he do about it?

So with the lie hanging in the air, unquestioned and unopposed, the men start to leave. Some of them wait, and they assemble in little groups that collect silently in the corners of the room, where men slip to their knees before their chaplains—Protestant, Catholic, and Jew.

7

"A BRIGHT GREEN FLARE..."

This is the hour when the execution of Mission 115, target Schweinfurt, passes into the hands of the combat crews. All over England the planners have done their job. Except for General Anderson, at the highest level, one man who will decide at the last moment whether or not the murky skies will permit the risk of massed flight, the planners clear up their papers, and walk to breakfast where, most of all, the hot steaming coffee will be welcome.

The crews spread throughout the nineteen bomber bases have work to do. Navigators and bombardiers gather to work out final details of their mission. All crew members pick up survival kits, and they shove their way into the equipment huts, or first hurry back to the barracks to attend to a last-moment chore. By now they are wearing, or carrying, their flight gear.

The clothing the airmen wear is bulky and weighs heavily on them. Each man wears closest to his skin either a pair of woolen long johns or an electrically heated suit. On top of that is heavy OD clothing. Next, a flying suit to be zipped up, and a leather jacket over that. There's room on top of the jacket for the Mae West, the individual life preserver which will keep him afloat in the Channel just in case that's where he ends up during this mission. And of course there's room on top of the Mae West for the parachute harness and the bulky chute itself.

The airmen wears his bulky sheepskin-lined flying boots; he carries a pair of GI shoes just in case he is shot down and has to walk out of enemy-occupied territory. In combat he wears a flak suit, a modern front-and-back attire of armor to keep pieces of shrapnel from flak or bursting rockets away from the center of his body and from his groin. He will don a lined leather flying helmet, and he will also wear an oxygen mask with dangling bladder and hose line. And if you could crawl into the cockpit of a B-17 in battle, you would see the men there wearing their "tin hats"—heavy metal GI helmets. And after everything else, the airman dons a heavy, thick pair of flying gloves which extend well back over his forearm.

It's a lot of equipment, but the high vaults are filled with savage cold, and many a plane has come home, unscarred by enemy bullets, but with a man inside whose fingers or feet have been so badly frozen at sixty-five degrees below zero that they must be amputated. And it doesn't feel one bit easier because it wasn't a bullet or a cannon shell that made a man legless for the rest of his life.

On the ground, however, wearing even part of this equipment is uncomfortable. Despite the cold and the dampness, the men perspire freely. They crowd into the equipment huts, they jam together and jostle one another and in just a few minutes the sweat beads on their foreheads, greases their hair, and runs in itch-maddening rivulets from beneath their arms and down the backs of their necks, and it stinks; it stinks of the smell of freely perspiring men. They don't give a damn about the smell, but all that sweat is going to freeze up there if they don't dry it first. . . .

The crews collect in jeeps and trucks, some walk, but they all move out to their bombers. The husky Fortresses squat on their dispersal "hardstands," small asphalted areas that are scattered at irregular intervals in the woodlands and thickets. Colonel Peaslee's car moves slowly toward his bomber, its broad wings looming through the mist.

This airplane is distinctive for today: it will be the first off the ground in all three air divisions, the first over the continent, the first over the target, and the first of the attackers to return home. Whether it will be the first to land is a moot point, and not one of the ten men who will man its positions hopes they are first. The planes with the wounded always have the green light to hurry back to earth.

Peaslee sees more than twenty men in or about the bomber, and they all are busy. The combat crew is already attending to its own responsibilities, and the ground crew nears the finish of its grueling all-night task. They have worked the night through in the cold and the rain and the miserable dampness that cut through to their skin without benefit of a hangar overhead or a dry place to work, and only the occasional visit of a truck with tepid coffee to break the long hours.

There was battle damage to repair from the last mission, when this ship was thoroughly chewed up by Focke-Wulfs. The crewmen removed the propeller from the number-three engine, and replaced it with a new one. They jacked up the airplane and changed a main gear tire. The directional gyro—gyroscopic compass—hadn't been working well, so they replaced that. They patched up holes and cuts and tears in the skin, spliced wires, and they made every known ground check of every piece of operating equipment.

They didn't do it completely without interruption, for the crew chief, who is a "maniac for perfection," accepted nothing that didn't satisfy *his* standards. He wasn't to fly this four-engine monster into Germany, but ten men were, and in his opinion anything less than an attempt for perfection would be criminal. Now, after the crew has made a dozen adjustments, he still isn't satisfied, and he climbs up the rig to an engine himself and then, after descending and signaling a mechanic in the cockpit to wind her up, he steps well back. So do the rest of the ground crew, because the mechanic's life isn't all dull and too many times in the past a tired man, bleary eyed, has slipped on a patch of oil or grease and—well, he slipped his life away as he fell into the reach of the whirling blades.

It takes only a split second for it to happen, and when the whirling buzz saw of the propeller is given a chance, it sprays blood and flesh and bone around. Not only does it make the other men sick, but it kills—instantly—the hapless soul who is flayed into pulp, or is decapitated, or sliced in two with that whirling knife. They don't give out Purple Hearts for this kind of accident, and no one's name gets in the papers, and there aren't any communiqués, but the man is just as dead and his wife is just as much a widow as the grieving wife of the pilot whose plane blew up beneath him over Germany.

But finally even the chief is satisfied, and the bomber is as ready for flight and combat as any dozen men can make her. Peaslee climbs out of his car to be greeted by Captain James K. McLaughlin. "We're in good shape, sir," McLaughlin reports quietly. "Want to take a look?"

The colonel nods assent, and the two men walk around the 30-ton bomber, poking and prying as they discuss the various phases of the mission. McLaughlin will be flying in the bomber's left seat as first pilot; the copilot, whom Peaslee has displaced, in turn displaces the tail gunner (who will sit this one out), and from this vantage point will report to Peaslee during the flight many details the air commander will need to know on attacks, target, formations, and other matters. During their discussion Peaslee says nothing about *how* this lead bomber will be flown. McLaughlin is a veteran of a good many missions, he is sharp and experienced and the operations officer for the group.

As they walk by the bomb bay, they stop to watch the ground crew winding the last thousand-pound missile into its place. On its side a mechanic has chalked the cheerful words: "Greetings, you bastards!"

Peaslee and McLaughlin, with their tour completed, have five minutes left until it is time to "man stations." In twenty minutes they will start their engines. In thirty-five minutes they will begin to taxi the airplane to its take-off position. In one hour, if the mission is not scrubbed, they will start their roll down the runway.

The rest of the combat crew moves up; with their arrival a gas truck starts up and pulls away, disappearing into the gloom. The crew chief reports to McLaughlin, announces that the fuel tanks have been topped to take the last possible drop, and that the B-17 is ready for flight.

The pilot calls his crew. "Relieve yourselves and get dressed." It is amazing that no one who has written of the saga of the bombers remembered to include this "pre-take-off ritual." Before every take-off the same words are repeated, and before every take-off the crewmen walk beyond the hardstand to the thickets or the open grass, and urinate. One might say that this is a formal process before embarking on a mission, and while the crews joked about how the bombers were filled to the last drop and they did just the opposite, it was not at all humorous at 26,000 feet and sixty degrees below zero, when a man began to ache with the pain of not relieving himself. The cold affects the bladder, and what might be cause for a good laugh in another situation is murder at high altitude.

Getting "dressed" is a simple procedure. The crewmen zip up the dangling ends of their heavy leather jackets and their flying suits. They slip on their parachute harnesses, and check their oxygen masks for leaks. Now they walk around like great shuffling bears, their movements sorely restricted. But you don't have much room to walk around in a B-17.

At more than three hundred hardstands in the dispersal areas the scenes are much the same. The maintenance crews complete final checks and adjustments of equipment. Inside the Fortresses the gunners have assembled their weapons, doted upon them with a final cleaning, reassembled parts with precision and with loving care. For to the gunner aboard the Flying Fortress the heavy machine gun is the same as the rifle to the infantryman lost in No-Man's Land. It is his passport to life, the most important thing on the whole planet. To be sure, there are as many as thirteen heavy guns aboard the B-17, and the men have positions of crossfire, and there are other bombers in the big formation boxes. But when a Focke-Wulf comes screaming in, barrel rolling with superb precision, the cowling and the wings flaming with the firing guns and cannon, that airplane is coming straight in at the individual gunner and no one else.

Ask a gunner, *any* gunner who has come home from one of these missions. Every German pilot had it in for *him*. . . .

You think of the superb aerodynamic machine that is the Flying Fortress, and you think at the same time of flight and beauty and the cleanliness of the crisp space so far above our heads. But to the pilot and copilot cleanliness is something else again. The base is muddy and so is the field, and it's almost impossible to keep the windshields clean, or the side windows. And like many other things that are commonplace in peacetime they are life and death in war. The bulletproof screen in front of the pilots may be dirty. "Dirty" is just a few specks. But there may be fighters coming in for a head-on attack, and when you're peering through thick glass into the sun in a ship that bounces and shakes and vibrates, and you're tired and sweating in all your gear, can you tell those specks from the specks of fighters far out but closing swiftly?

More than one pilot peers through the windshield this morning of October 14, and because he likes to live, he either cleans the glass himself or gives the crew chief absolute hell for the specks of dirt.

And so 3,000 men prepare themselves. Copilots are in the cockpits, checking instruments, engines, controls, and gauges. Pilots and squadron leaders huddle in groups, checking the infinite details that enable a swarm of four-engine giants to fly as one tremendous machine of destruction wheeling beautifully through the skies.

For some time the bases echo with the sputtering and roaring of engines. Through the countryside the British people listen to the noises, the subdued hums, the abrupt pounding of engines, the strange and invisible piston-created symphony that tell them the Yanks are preparing to have another "go at it." Then the sounds begin to fall off, like a waterfall that is dammed slowly at its source. There will be a period of relative quiet, and when the sounds rumble through the wet morning air again, they will continue until louder roars, the songs of B-17's under full power and rushing down the runway, rumble across the countryside.

Pilots at nineteen airdromes check their watches; again and again the involuntary reflex of tension mounting as the final moments rush along with the sweep of a second hand. "All right, let's go." Those may be the words, or perhaps a pilot will call, "Let's get aboard," and the men will move purposefully to their airplanes.

The ground crews are still on the scene; indeed, they will not leave for some time. They call after the departing crews, "Good luck!" and "Bring her back in one piece, you jokers!" or perhaps, with a bit of wistfulness because they know the odds are that it won't be so, "Hope you guys have a milk run." No one really looks closely at their faces, and this is a shame, for mirrored in their tired eyes, on their oil-spattered skins, are the looks of anxious and caring men, and not a few are emotional at this point.

They are tired, dog-tired. They will not leave for bed, the blessed oblivion of the slumber of exhausted bodies, until every airplane is off the ground. At least one hour before the bombers are scheduled to return to the airdrome, they will be clustered together at the hardstand, waiting. Waiting, and looking into the eastern sky many, many minutes before a bomber can possibly come within sight. Waiting and wondering. Thinking of the crew—*their* crew, *their* airplane, that is their sweat and toil and the utmost skill they have to give.

Some of them, in this fall of 1943, have already done this more than a hundred times. And there are hundreds and hundreds of missions yet to be flown.

Seventeen years later Budd Peaslee remembers clearly the ground crews at his base. "They got few pats on the back when things were right and many kicks in the butt when things went wrong," he recalls. "Their bomber and its flying crew made up their home-town ball team, their entry at the county fair. They groomed their entry and, in a way, pampered its crew. The night their team came home from its twenty-fifth mission called for a wild and glorious binge. It meant graduation for the team—completion of its tour of duty—and the beginning of a new class for the plane itself and the ground crew. The league was tough and only a few graduated. When a ground crew and its bomber turned out two classes, they became standouts—extremely rare cases. There have been as many as four graduation classes from a single bomber, and its ground crew then became celebrities.

"Too often, however, the ground men watched the eastern sky in vain, and there was little conversation between them. Finally they walked slowly back to their bunks, looking down. Maybe their toes scuffed the ground a little. They were sick, deep inside, and they never saw the hilarity at a neighboring hardstand as another crew greeted its team and someone painted another bomb or a swastika or two on the nose of the B-17. The next morning, or even that same night, perhaps, there would be another bomber on their hardstand, and they would start another battle for a standing in the league, with their new team. They used to wonder if they would like the new team. They always did."

The pilots have called the men, and the crews climb into their bombers. Each Fortress accepts its men as it has always done. Now something is different. The airplane is *alive*. An airplane is made for men, and it is never complete, it is never what it was built to do in the air, until the men are inside.

The men move to their stations. The B-17 sits on her two main wheels and tail gear, nearly seventy-five feet long, and while she is on the ground, wings not yet grasping at the air, the body of the airplane follows a gentle incline. The pilot at the left and the copilot to his right, despite the size of the heavy bomber, seem almost to be cramped within a cage of steel, glass, controls, and instruments. A wedge of compartmented glass in front of them is their forward windshield, with side windows for both. Directly in the center of the windshield and at its lower edge is a metal container with three instrument dials; in the center is an accelerometer, flanked by carburetor air-temperature gauges. If the men behind the controls lean forward in their seats, they can just make out a small plexiglas dome through which the navigator peers from time to time.

In front of the two pilots are three main clusters of instruments: one before the pilot, one before the copilot, and a third panel in the center, the latter composed mainly of flight instruments. Directly behind this panel, and bordered by the control columns with their wheels, are the stands with power controls and accessories: there is also the AFCE—the Automatic Flight Control Equipment, or autopilot for short.

There are controls and switches, dials and gauges and handles and buttons and toggles in front, to the sides, between, above, below, and behind the pilots. More than one hundred and fifty of these in all, running the gamut from navigational equipment and controls to the directional gyro, airspeed indicator, artificial horizon, turn indicator, turn and bank, rate of climb and descent, altimeter, and others. There are controls and switches for the bomb doors, for hydraulic pressure and electrical power, for lights and oxygen, for the engines, fuel supply, and pressure and feed, for the flaps and landing gear, gauges to read vacuum pressure, oil and cylinder head temperatures, propeller pitch, turbo-supercharger regulators, mixture—it is a long list, and one thoroughly bewildering except to the experienced and the trained.

Forward of the leading edge of the wings, the B-17 is arranged in split fashion. Below the pilots is the nose compartment, where the bombardier and navigator have their stations for their particular duties—as well as manning the nose armament of the Fortress. The very tip of the Fortress is conical in shape, a formed wedge of plexiglas; the older B-17E models have metal stripping that laces the nose for added strength; the B-17F's have eliminated the stripping and the plexiglas is clear except for gun ports. Below the horizontal center line of the plexiglas wedge is a flattened plexiglas panel through which the bombardier peers. There is added visibility in the small half bubble above the navigator, and also through several windows on each side of the nose. The bombardier has his Norden bomb sight and controls to work the bomb-bay doors, switches to set the bombs to drop in sticks, in a salvo, or individually at specific time intervals of so many seconds for each bomb.

Behind the bombardier sits the navigator, surrounded with radio and electronic navigation equipment, and all the other complex gear required to maintain accuracy in the high journeying across England and the less friendly continent.

Originally the Flying Fortress had only a single .30-caliber machine gun in its nose for forward armament; by the time the B-17's were arriving in England, the healthy respect for German fighters had increased this to two and three .50-caliber guns, and often the crews said to hell with the book, modified the nose, and installed four guns, and even as many as five, although the latter arrangement cramped sorely an already restricted space. The gun ports in the nose are actually set in the glass in a nipple-like mount, not only in the forward plexiglas, but in the side mounts as well. During a running fight, the bombardier and navigator often switch from gun to gun as fighter positions snap out over the intercom.

Swinging one of these 65-pound guns by hand in the teeth of the powerful wind created by the Fortress's flight is no easy task, especially when a man is encumbered in his heavy and bulky flight gear, when the airplane may be rocking or pitching violently, and there is little enough space to begin with. But all things considered, the "big fifty" is just about the most versatile and flexible weapon of the air war, firing bullets that leave the muzzle at 2,900 feet per second and that can penetrate most parts of an enemy airplane, including the engine. The official book says that the bullets will penetrate "any and all parts of an airplane," but the man who wrote the book hasn't seen .50-caliber rounds bouncing harmlessly off the thick belly armor of the FW-190's.

Immediately aft of the pilots' compartment—so close that when the twin guns fire the sound is like that of exploding cannon shells—is the upper or dorsal power turret of the B-17. It is an electrically operated mechanism, and within the steel and glass turret the gunner manages to squeeze his head, shoulders, and arms. Actually the turret is a completely independent unit. Hand controls turn it in azimuth and elevation and fire the guns; there is equipment for oxygen and interphone communication, gun sights, ammunition belts, and containers. The turret is armor protected, and it has a plexiglas dome, or curved plexiglas panels fitted into the steel mountings. The B-17 engineer works this position, and his is the best position in the crew for sight-seeing, if that is his inclination. He commands a full forward view, and to both sides, and can look back along the glistening curved metal of the Fortress; he will see one or two guns sticking upward from the radio compartment, and then the towering tail. He can also look straight up, and that is a good thing, for sometimes the fighters like to come hurtling down in vertical power dives, raking the bombers from nose to tail in sustained fire.

To move farther back into the Fortress, a man must traverse a narrow catwalk spanning the bomb bay, and then into the radio compartment. The radioman fires in a limited upward arc, defending the bomber against diving attacks. Originally the B-17 had only this station for dorsal protection; the crews who think of the early B-17C and D models in the Pacific without an upper power turret shudder when they imagine themselves flying those early models against the Luftwaffe.

Unquestionably the loneliest position in the Flying Fortress—or the Liberator—is that of the ball-turret gunner; the turret is like some grotesque, swollen eyeball of steel and glass and guns that seems to hang precariously from the belly of the B-17. It is a hellish, stinking position in battle; the gunner must hunch up his body, draw up his knees, and work into a half ball to meet the curving lines of the turret. The guns are to each side of his head, and they stab from the turret eyeball like two even splinters. Jailed in his little spherical powerhouse, the turret gunner literally aims his own

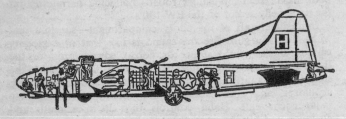

B-17G; crew positions

body at enemy fighters, working both hands and feet in deft coordination, spinning and tilting, and then depressing switches atop the gun grip handles to fire the two weapons. It is the most unenviable position in the bomber, *any* bomber, the man most unlikely to escape from a blazing B-17 is that lonely soul in the ball.

The two waist gunners of the B-17 live in a tubular world, with the walls, floor, and ceiling made of thin metal skin and its supporting heavy ribs that completely encircle them. Wide hatches on each upper side of the fuselage yawn out into space, and it is through these hatches that the single guns point, swinging on their mounts. By the time a B-17 returns from a running fight, the floor is almost impossible to walk upon, flooded as it is with the dense rain of empty shell casings.

It is here, too, that the paradox of Fortress structural strength can easily be understood. This is the bomber that absorbs punishment like no other, that can be cut and slashed and torn and holed, and that will continue to fly. You might, then, think of the Fortress as a nearly impregnable machine with powerful ribs and frames and thick metal skin. It is not that at all, for with an easy push a man can jab a screwdriver right through that metal. It is the brilliant interlocking of its main structural members that provides the Fortress's great strength; the skin is only a surface membrane.

In the very stern of the heavy bomber, a cramped wedge that forms the blunt tip of the Fortress, is the tail gunner's compartment. The gunner—who fires his twin machine guns in a kneeling position, with his knees on soft pads—actually flies beneath the trailing edge of the high rudder. His view of the world is not always the best; although he and the ball-turret gunner—if the time is available—can observe with satisfaction the results of bomb strikes, the tail gunner also has to face German fighters boring in, wings and noses alive with firing guns and cannon. And when the bombers stream the thick, white contrails far behind them, the tail gunner is liable to get bad eyestrain, for the German pilots have the clever trick of flying hidden from sight in the midst of the thick vapor trails, and breaking out at the last moment at point-blank range to open fire.

The B-17 is interlaced with control cables, heating lines, communications lines, and the oxygen system. In the air, the vairous parts of the big bomber become as a single entity, the connecting links acting as blood vessels and nerves, sinew and bone, eyes and ears, until the bomber is no longer a collection of many parts and her crew, but a single, living, breathing, flying, fighting creature. If it is not, if it is subjected to balky communications and rendered unable to function in this manner, survival in the most bitter arena of aerial battle is seriously compromised and perhaps lost beyond redemption.

As the rest of the crew move to their stations, the bombardier moves to attend to his own critical task on the ground. He climbs out on the narrow catwalk that spans the bomb bay. In one hand is a container that he handles with extraordinary, almost painful care. In that container are the fuses, the tiny little items that make bombs come alive. Without the fuses the bombs are inert chunks of metal and chemicals. They can be kicked, pounded with hammers, or even dropped onto hard concrete—as they often are—with no further result than the crushing of a man's foot if the bomb loader is unlucky.

Now the thousand-pounders are being transformed by the magic of those little fuses. The bomb-bay doors are open, and the thick missiles hang by shackles in their racks. Beneath each airplane stands an armament sergeant. The bombardier hands down the box of fuses, and the sergeant in turn hands up a wrench. Then they go to work, patiently, carefully. A fuse is inserted in the nose of a bomb, and tightened. Then another fuse is inserted in the tail, and that one, too, is tightened, until finally all the bombs are armed. Now they are horribly sensitive, and their steel casings have become the thinnest and weakest of eggshells.

No one *ever* bothers these two men. They are priests beyond the touch of mere mortals. Shortly before this mission, during the preparations for another raid, a Fortress on its hardstand suddenly disappeared. Instead of the bomber a

Emergency landing; six men got out. . . .

searing flash of light existed, and then a shattering roar. Twenty-three men disappeared with the airplane, and the shock waves tore two more bombers on neighboring stands into pieces.

Outside the control-tower rooms, on the railed balconies, the operational staffs congregrate to stare out across the field. The overcast no longer seems quite so thick as it has been all night. The flying control officer at each field studies his watch. It is not time; not yet.

In the bombers the crews complete all preparations. Now they wait. This is the buffer period, the time for waiting in the airplanes when there is nothing left to do but wait. The second hands move around across the dials, and the men fidget and squirm in their uncomfortable clothing.

And then it *is* time. The flying control officer watches his second hand reach the exact moment, and he nods to a man standing nearby.

A two-pronged green flare arcs into the sky, sputtering and gleaming. It is the signal to start engines. At each dispersal stand the bombers come to life. Engines wheeze and grind and the propellers spin faster and faster; there comes the deep, coughing roar before the final clearing blast of smoke. Soon the bombers vibrate gently with the energy of four motors idling. It begins as a ragged, loose sound, and then ascends into a rich cry of power. For several moments the engines are pushed to full throttle. The pilot and copilot, and the engineer behind them, in each plane, run quickly through the final check list.

Across the turf at each airdrome bounces an ambulance. It takes its position meaningfully at the far end of the runway. Soon another joins it, and another. More vehicles move out along the runway where the bombers will rush into the sky. Wreckers, radio-equipped jeeps, fire trucks—every man hoping his time will be wasted.

In the lead bomber of Mission 115, until the moment that the Fortresses have assembled in group formation, Colonel Peaslee assumes the duties and status of copilot. He is three grades higher in rank than the man seated on his left. But as copilot in this particular B-17 Peaslee from now on does exactly as he is told by the captain. He can override McLaughlin only in the event that he thinks the airplane cannot take off.

The heavy bomber rolls forward; at the edge of the

hardstand McLaughlin tests the brakes. Exactly at H minus thirty minutes the B-17 rolls onto the taxi strip and turns. Ahead of the bomber, in the drizzle, a jeep cuts across the perimeter track. The jeep drives exactly in the center of the strip, which is 75 feet wide. McLaughlin pays strict attention as he skillfully maneuvers the airplane down the strip.

The B-17 is a hulking shape in the light mist falling from the low clouds. Behind the Fortress is another bomber, a large ghost; another is right behind it, and another, and another. Nose to tail, brakes squealing in protest, engines advancing and throttling back in power, they proceed in an ungainly and elephantine fashion. There comes a final squeal of brakes that punctuates the roar of engines and propellers, and the lines of bombers, each approaching the runway from a different direction, drag to a halt. Now the planes wait, engines idling.

Well behind the lead airplane with Peaslee and McLaughlin at the controls is a bomber that will never make Mission 115. The pilot has failed the test of taxiing his giant machine in the grayness along the narrow taxiway, and the 30-ton bomber rests ignominiously in the mud, its gear hopelessly mired. For these ten men, the mission is already over in an unhappy and swift anticlimax. Soon the ground crews will

Taxiing out . . .

swarm over and around the stricken Fortress. They will defuse the bombs, unload the finned cylinders and truck them back to the depot. The airplane will be jacked up and hauled away, to be returned to its hardstand where it will wait for the next mission.

Strangely, to those who have not flown these penetrations deep into the enemy's country, the crew is far from elated at what potentially is their good fortune of assurance that Schweinfurt will not mark their final resting place. Rather, the ten men walk back to their bunks unhappy, ashamed at having let down their friends.

"They left a gap of a dozen defensive guns in the formation, and several tons of explosives would be missing from the target," explains Peaslee, recalling the incident. "There is a terrific sense of guilt associated with the failure to make a mission, whether failure is avoidable or not."

For the rest of the crews in the bombers poised for take-off in England there is now another period of waiting as H-hour approaches. Everything is now resolved to the second hand of Time. The many airdromes are seemingly immobile, yet they are charged with a tension that is almost electric. Each airfield waits, impatiently, prepared and overanxious to disgorge a swarm of winged creatures of destruction.

The fate of 3,000 men is committed to one man.

In Pinetree, VIII Bomber Command Headquarters, General F. L. Anderson is surrounded by a glare that boils off bright lights overhead. He does not feel the cold and mist in which the Fortresses crouch; not with his eyes, perhaps, but clearly with his mind. In his mind he can see the thousands of men in the rain at the end of nineteen runways.

It is irrevocable. He must pronounce sentence at any moment. He must send the thousands out, knowing hundreds will not return. But there is still time, a little time in which to be sure.

The operational staffs pause almost to a man at their breakfast, glancing at the wall clocks, at each other. The ground crews wait fretfully; they will sweat out every plane, every take-off. All across the many airfields the cooks and the bakers, the motor-pool drivers and the mechanics. Doctors and technicians, clerks, the crews who are not flying this day. The British who work at the fields and nearby. The fighter pilots, the crews of rescue boats. All of them do one thing concurrently: *they wait.*

There are several colonels with the general. They walk up to him quietly, and speak briefly. They tell him of the weather conditions at the many bomber bases, and the weather is still lousy. It is border line; touch and go. That alone is a bitch; how many planes will be lost and how many men will die because of 30-ton bombers that skid, or drop a wing too close to the ground, or plunge into the trees? Once before, and not so long ago, 100 men disappeared in a blind flash. . . .

The general waits for one final report. Hundreds of miles from where he sits, hundreds of miles from the bomber bases, high over the continent, a fighter pilot in a weather reconnaissance ship takes a last look around. He presses a button on his radio microphone, and speaks a few words. *The* words.

Over a secret channel, into the room where the general waits, comes the message:

"The continent is in the clear."

This is what the general has needed to know. He raises a clenched fist, and his hand turns, and his thumb slowly turns to point upward.

In the shadowy cockpit of the lead B-17 of the 92d Group, with the visibility barely more than two thousand feet, Colonel Peaslee stares across the field. The radio jeep comes alive, and a bright green flare hisses into the air. At the same instant, from the control tower, another green flare, dimmed by distance, sputters through the mist.

Mission Number 115 is ON.

The throttles in the lead bomber move forward. The propellers spin faster and faster as fuel flow increases, and the roar becomes a bass scream that claws through the air.

Peaslee glances at his pilot, and the two men nod.

The lead bomber begins to roll.

8

AIRBORNE

The Flying Fortress gathers speed to itself like an enormous boulder accelerating down a steep mountainside. With each passing second of take-off the propellers bite through an increasing volume of air, imparting to the wings of the heavy airplane the lift they seek. Faster and faster, recoiling with the shocks of the uneven runway surface.

The runway border lights stretch as far as the eye can see, but in the distance they fade into a fog-created limbo. Magically, as fast as the bomber gains its speed, new lights glow into being to replace those racing past the wings. The air-speed indicator needle creeps around the dial, and pauses momentarily at an even 50 miles per hour. The second bomber is already wheeling into position on the runway. Normally the Fortresses roll from their standing positions at thirty-second intervals; this morning, however, it is necessary to make full instrument-condition take-offs, and the interval is extended to one minute for each B-17.

Peaslee stares out into the murk, when McLaughlin's voice comes crisp and clear over the interphone. "I'm going on instruments. Keep her on the runway and pick up the wheels when we're clear."

It's the captain talking to the colonel, but the voice is sharp and meaningful, and it is a direct order. McLaughlin is the aircraft commander, and the colonel is the copilot, and there is absolutely no doubt as to who issues orders, who commands the machine.

The B-17 creeps toward the left of the runway, and with the barest touch of pressure on the right rudder, Peaslee overpowers McLaughlin's foot on the pedal, and the bomber swings back where they belong. McLaughlin is taking no chances, he's making a move that reflects excellent judgment. Right from the runway he begins his instrument take-off,

85

adjusting his senses to instrument flight while he is on the ground. From this moment on, while everything is under full control, he will fly the artificial horizon, the air-speed indicator, and the other flight instruments without any reference at all to the earth. It is an excellent move because it *always* takes several seconds for any pilot to adjust to the transition from visual to instrument flight, and there are more dead pilots than the living want to remember who failed to snap fast enough from visual conditions to the world of instruments at the end of the take-off run. If the wing dips and the bomber slides off on that wing at this altitude, the trees and power lines and buildings and even the earth are too close.

When this happens, the take-offs continue without interruption, for there's a war waiting to be fought in the high arena over the Third Reich, and every gun available is needed. The bombers continue to roll, but the ones still to take off are handled with more care, more precision. When they have all gone and are climbing for altitude, for the problems of rendezvous and assembly, the intense flame is dying in the woods behind them. There remains, perhaps, as has happened so many times, little more than a glowing light and a pile of twisted, blackened junk in the English woods. The rescue men gasp and fall over the undergrowth as they fight their way toward the light and the stench of burning flesh. They expect they're all dead, but there's always a chance that one in ten is alive, or half-alive, and it is their job to save that life if at all possible.

But on this morning, October 14, on Mission 115, it does not happen. A total of 383 four-engine bombers leaves the haze and wetness of England, and of the more than thirty-eight hundred men who are in those bombers, not one dies because the pilot has failed so near the earth.

Not too far ahead of the first of those 383 bombers the runway lights turn red, and Peaslee cannot help but feel a sudden stab of apprehension. Red means the end of the runway and a blinding explosion on the other end if the bomber does not raise itself, but even as the thought half-forms within his mind, he sees the needle reach the figure of 88. This is what he calls his moment of eternity, and at that same instant eternity stays its comfortable distance away. The rough feeling of the runway vanishes. That is the only change that Peaslee feels, but to the thousands of hours a pilot accumulates it is the same as a warning bell clamoring insistently in his ear. The B-17 is off the ground, and in one swift motion the colonel grasps the gear to bring up the wheels and tuck them away.

When he looks up again he sees nothing outside the airplane. The sky is heavy gray and except for the pounding of the engines, lessened because the ground no longer blasts the sound back into their ears, the heavy bomber is in limbo. Peaslee glances at the instruments; everything registers normal, the air speed is an even 100 and is still increasing. McLaughlin has made this take-off, from this runway, many times before, and he is not greedy for altitude—not yet. He is just high enough to clear all the obstacles he cannot see but knows are there, and he holds the heavy bomber flat as he waits for speed.

At 120 miles per hour he has what he wants. The air-speed needle glues into place at 120, and two other instruments become active. The altimeter is still a scant 300 feet but the rate of climb rises slightly above the zero point. Then there is 500 feet of air beneath the Fortress, and without looking at the artificial horizon, Peaslee senses the start of a turn. McLaughlin barely touches the wheel and his foot nudges the rudder pedal with infinite sensitivity, but the bomber responds.

The pointer of the radio compass starts a crawl around the face of the dial, edging toward zero. The airplane is turning under McLaughlin's sure hands for the splasher, the pulsating radio signal on which the bomber centers its initial flight.

As the lead Fortress cleared the edge of the airfield, the sound boomed out from the accelerating machine, rushed through the trees and thickets; the airplane climbed slowly, and the sound spread out, an invisible wash of shock waves heralding the birth of new flight. Even as the echo reverberates into the homes of the countryside, the second ship is on its way. The lead aircraft emits its trail of thin blue smoke, sign of engines under full power. Then the third, and the fourth, each movement the juggling of 30 tons of bomber rushing into the blurred mist at the far end of the runway.

Each new take-off is more difficult, it seems. The lead bomber at least enjoyed an air space untroubled by the passage of another machine in front. Now the runway is alive, charged with the slip stream and the wake turbulence of the Fortresses that have rushed away into the leaden mists. The pilots fight the controls, muscles responding to the feel of pounding as the bombers rock on their wheels, accept the broadside slap of air, the uneven ocean into which they rush. The bouncing stops; there is the rumble of wheels coming up into their recesses, and then smoother flight.

In the lead bomber exhilaration sweeps over Peaslee. It is a sensation not uncommon to the crews, this wonderful experience of having completed a hazardous—and successful—take-off. The two men at the controls grin at each other in the dim light, and the feeling pervades the entire crew. It is a sense of joy; Peaslee describes it as an urge to break out into song. Abruptly the interphone crackles with a sudden burst of chatter from the crew. They're calling to each other, wisecracking, snapping out jokes, and one man bellows happily in what is supposed to be singing.

The feeling passes quickly, for there is work to do; precise, careful, vital work. At 2,000 feet, for the first time this day, the heavy grayness begins to recede. It is the most grudging of retreats. Operations briefed the crews on a cloud deck at 2,000 feet. Instead, the lead Fortress has climbed to 6,000 before Peaslee and McLaughlin can detect the top of the overcast by the brightness above them. At 6,500 feet the bomber rushes through the last vestiges of cloud and breaks out into full daylight.

It is a dazzling world into which they ascend. Having lifted the gleaming machine from the earth and its mantle below, suddenly they are above a spotless sea, a vast and unending ocean of white that stretches in every direction, as far as their eyes can reach. With a rush that overwhelms them, they have been flung from the planet into a space that is strange and awesome, no matter how many times it is visited by men. But at this moment all that exists below is a distant thing, and this is *their* domain in which to drift. There is no sense of movement, no feeling of rushing through the air.

The four engines pound dimly in the recesses of the men's minds; heard so often, they are prosaic and then no longer heard. The sky stretches up and up, right out beyond all sight into the edges of space beyond. There is a star 93,000,000 miles away, but it is now terribly close, and it blinds the men. They put on their dark glasses, and there is some relief, but still the star sends its needles of light to stab through the eyeballs and to dance on the wings, until the glistening silver metal shimmers and becomes liquid pools of wavering light. It is beautiful, and the men for the moment are silent as they drink in the new world. But later many of them will curse the sun, because it is a haven, a place of ambush for fighters, and how the hell do you see a Messerschmitt or a Focke-Wulf when it screams in, straight from that blinding glare?

The lead Fortress is not alone for long. Peaslee turns cumbersomely in his seat and tries to look back through the side glass. The second bomber is 500 yards behind, shedding wisps of clouds as it breaks through into clear air. McLaughlin continues to climb until the needle reads 8,000 feet. This is assigned cruising altitude for this splasher, and he throttles back to cruising power. Over the source of the pulsating radio emissions, McLaughlin swings into a wide circle. For the next sixty minutes the Fortress turns tediously, one wing slightly low, as the other bombers seek the company of the early arrivals. From Peaslee's ship bright signal flares rush into the air, a call for Fortresses far from the splasher to slide in, to join in V's, to create triangular-shaped elements of bombers in the sky.

It is a tiresome procedure, it burns gasoline with frightful insistence, but it is absolutely necessary. This business of rendezvous and assembly is one of the most difficult phases of a bombardment mission, but it is tossed off with little enough consideration by armchair strategists who never seem to consider the thousands of gallons of fuel the bombers must burn to achieve formation before they can ever enter enemy skies. The procedure works well, except in isolated cases. Then there is the problem of an instrument failure, or inexperience, or weather that overcomes the best of instruments and piloting ability. Mostly in these cases, the airplane of one formation will run to join wings with any other available formation.

Peaslee has a specific problem. As commander of the 1st Air Division, he must assemble in a massive body in the heavens a huge pyramid of bombers. Before he moves into enemy air space, that pyramid must be properly built up into specific formation, so that it may gather strength from the unique positioning of the many guns; strength in numbers of aircraft, in bomb weight and pattern, and above all in the defensive fire screen that will provide their only protection against the enemy.

At H plus one hour Peaslee orders McLaughlin to break from the circling maneuver and take up a new course toward the second splasher, climbing slowly as they proceed. Twenty-one bombers, as scheduled for the mission, have taken off to form the strength of the 92d Group in the air. The initial splasher, where the bombers assembled, was over Thurleigh. Now they move toward the second splasher, which is the Combat Wing Assembly Line. Here Peaslee is to rendezvous with the 305th and the 306th Groups.

As Peaslee moves the formation through the sky, its strength accumulates steadily. Other groups have assembled over their splashers, and they fall into a ragged shape behind the first, slowly beginning to dress into the larger wing formations. The plan is for three very large formations, made up of the 92d Group (19 bombers), 305th (16 bombers), and 306th (18 bombers), to form into the 40th Combat Wing, with a combined wing strength of 53 Fortresses. There will be three combat wings—the 1st, with 91st and 381st Groups (28 bombers); Peaslee's Wing, the 40th; and the 41st, with the 379th, 303d, and 384th Groups (51 bombers)—which in turn will make up the 1st Air Division. The Air Division constitutes the opening wedge of the aerial armada to invade Germany.

Unfortunately, it does not work out so well on this particular morning. Mechanical aborts and other failures that force bombers to return to their bases cause an immediate depletion in strength. And then Peaslee, despite all his uncomfortable squirming in the cockpit, cannot find the low—the 305th—Group. Frantically he calls the lieutenant in the tail gunner's position:

"Where the hell is the low group? Can you see a loose group anywhere?"

The answer is a strained "No, sir."

Because of poor visibility, and layers of clouds that stretched far above the 6,500-foot level where Peaslee's bomber broke into the clear, the 305th Group commander found it impossible to assemble with Peaslee's formation. The 305th's different arrival time at the assembly point meant that the two formations never actually sighted each other.

Making the best of a worsening situation, the commander of the 305th wisely proceeded, once he determined assembly with the 92d and 306th Groups was impossible, to the next assembly area, where the radio beacon marked the position of Daventry. Here the 305th Group commander again searched in vain for the rest of his wing. Failing to find the 40th Combat Wing, he contacted the commander of the 1st Com-

bat Wing—these B-17's were in visual contact with the
305th—and then assumed the trail position in this wing.

Colonel Peaslee, to his extreme discomfort, knew nothing
of all this; since he did not monitor the channel of the 1st
Combat Wing, and his own calls to the 305th had produced
no answer, he had no way of knowing the position of the
305th Group, or the decision that placed it with the 1st
Combat Wing. All this time his own formation was climbing
steadily, it had passed the successive splasher beacons that
marked the assembly areas, and now the 40th Wing was
almost at 20,000 feet as it neared the final beacon that
marked the edge of the English Channel.

He has time for one final circle, when the Air Division will
tighten its formation before taking the final plunge into
Germany.

Bitter disappointment fills his mind, for now the entire
mission is jeopardized, and it is definitely possible that all that
has happened this morning will be to no avail, and he must
scrub the mission. Peaslee, like every other commander, is
under standing orders that no force of only two groups is
ever to attempt penetration of the German defenses; there
is every chance that in such a weakened force *every* bomber
will be shot down.

There is still one last chance, and as McLaughlin leads the
two groups into their final circle, Peaslee orders the bombardier to fire a signal flare every twenty seconds. It is a futile
gesture, for there is not another lone group in sight. At least,
however, Peaslee has a few minutes in which to struggle for a
solution to his problem.

As the circle runs to its finish, Peaslee makes up his mind.
He orders the formations to assume their course for Germany. Captain McLaughlin looks doubtfully at Peaslee; he
never says a word, but there is no need for words. He is as
informed as the colonel on emergency procedures, and he is
fully aware that Peaslee is forbidden to order the groups to
continue.

"Maybe the 305th is circling over the Channel; there's a
good chance that they'll meet us there," the commander tells
McLaughlin. Both men know the hope for this is so slim as to
be almost nil, but for Peaslee again it is a matter of time, or
staving off the dreaded decision to abort the attack.

Below the climbing bombers the earth appears. The overcast begins to dwindle, and soon it becomes a ragged and

shredding line. The sun slams down into the cockpit, and ahead of the B-17's nose Peaslee stares out glumly at 100 miles of French coastline. The land comes closer and closer, and all the searching Peaslee and the rest of the crew go through is useless, for there just isn't that missing group anywhere in sight.

Time has run out for the colonel. He has in his formation 42 giant bombers and that means a hell of a lot of bombs. It also means some 500 defending machine guns, and the other people in the air are going to need those guns, desperately.

Peaslee makes his decision glumly, and switches the VHF radio to a common channel. He calls the wing leader immediately behind his own position. This is his first order of the day as the air commander of Mission 115.

"I am short one group," he calls. "You will take over the lead and I will 'S.' I will fly high—high on you to Bombs Away. I will retain air command from that position." Peaslee is referring to an unorthodox position just above and to one side of the top group in his wing formation.

It does not trouble the colonel, indeed he never thinks of it at the moment, but his order can lead to a court-martial with the most dire consequences; he has violated procedure, he has ordered an unorthodox formation, he has passed on the lead position of the raid. If he had not done so, it would have meant an abortive mission for two groups, and a seriously weakened force would have gone on into Germany.

"What the hell was I air commander for?" he shrugged later. "I didn't even think of the people in my formation then. I was passing sentence on my own neck as well as theirs. Besides, we were up there to hit the Germans, not to waste a lot of gas and come home again without doing our job."

At that moment, seventeen years ago, the only approval for Peaslee came in the look of McLaughlin's eyes above his oxygen mask. Without a word said, without any instructions from Peaslee, the captain slowly swung the formation of the 92d and 306th Group into two long curves of an S. The bombers gain in altitude; one S is enough, and as the mass of B-17's crosses the French coast the 40th Combat Wing— Peaslee's force—comes out just above to the left and nearly abreast of the top group of the new leader.

By the time the 1st Air Division strikes into enemy territory, however, the Mission 115 force is already depleted from that at the start of the mission. The three wings that consti-

tute the 1st Air Division were assigned at take-off a total of
164 bombers. One Fortress, at Colonel Peaslee's field, became
mired in the mud adjoining the runways and never left the
ground.

Behind the 1st Air Division, headquarters planned for two
additional forces. These groups constituted the remainder of
the 383 aircraft assigned to Mission 115.

The 3d Air Division dispatched 154 B-17 bombers plus six
spares. The 2d Air Division, flying B-24 Liberators, sent 60 of
these four-engine bombers into the air.

Trouble began from the outset. The B-24's found it impossible because of heavy clouds to assemble properly. After all
attempts to join forces, only 29 of the 60 planes, less than
half the assigned force, managed to form in two units. Their
assignment: to fly a longer route into Germany, to the south
of the B-17's of the 1st and 3d Air Divisions, and accomplish
a specific time rendezvous just before the IP, so that the
Liberators could join in the long bomber train which would
concentrate strikes on the target.

If they could not assemble with the B-17's to strike the
ball-bearing works, they would hit the secondary target of the
day—the center of the city. Mission 115's "last resort" target,
in event of clouds or other difficulties, was Ludwigshafen, and
the alternate last resort the city area of Saarbrücken.

Wisely, the commander of the depleted force of only 29
B-24's refuses to take his small formation deep into enemy
territory. Instead, with the Thunderbolt fighter escort flying
over the Liberators, the two units swing in a diversionary feint
in the direction of Emden. Over the Frisian Islands the
airplanes wheel in a wide sweep, and return to England.
There are no incidents.

Score: 60 four-engined bombers immediately cut from the
strike to Schweinfurt.

Two bomber forces struck out toward enemy air space,
crossing the defense line thirty miles apart. In the 1st Air
Division was a total of 149 B-17's, and in the 3d Air Division,
a total of 141 B-17's.

Grand total breaching the defense line: 291 heavy bombers.

Many of the Flying Fortresses assigned to Mission 115
failed, obviously, to join in the attack. Of the 1st Air
Division's 164 assigned airplanes, only 149 crossed into
German air space—a loss of 15 bombers to mechanical and

engineering difficulties. Eighteen bombers of the 160 Fortresses that took off as part of the 3d Air Division also turned back.

Examples: In the 92d Bomb Group, 21 B-17's took off. Three aircraft aborted. B-17G, Number 42-3494 of the 407th Bomb Squadron, turned back after three hours of flight when the number-three supercharger ran away, leaving the airplane unable to maintain altitude with the rest of the formation.

B-17F, Number 42-30711, was also flying for three hours when it dropped out of the formation. Without warning, the manifold pressure of the number-two engine dropped sharply. Back at the home field, an investigation disclosed a large crack in the induction pipe of the engine.

Take the 388th Group of the 3d Air Division. This force took off between 1005 hours and 1042 hours, with a total of 21 bombers, and formed as the low group of the lead combat wing of the 2d Air Task Force (3d Air Division). The entire group proceeded on course. One by one, however, five bombers dropped out.

Three B-17's suffered engine trouble, one experienced serious leaks in the oxygen system (fatal at high altitude), and the fifth became lost in clouds. This latter ship, finding itself alone in the sky, was flown back to its home field.

Fortresses aborted for all manner of problems. Engineering failures included rough engines, runaway superchargers, tachometer oscillation, leaking oxygen regulators, sluggish superchargers, generator malfunctions, weak brakes, insufficient oxygen supply, engine oil leaks, engine instrument failures, oil cooler failures, creeping flaps, cracked exhaust stacks, cracked air ducts, flat tail wheels, propeller governor failures, over-boosted engines, leaking fuel tanks, and inoperative fuel pumps.

The crews found trouble within the airplanes as well. On some ships the power gun turrets froze and jammed into position; these came home. Radio transmitters went out, and communication with other airplanes was impossible. Heated gloves burned out; electricity heated suits shorted. Oxygen masks froze up, and interphones refused to work. Not all of these problems brought the planes home; only where the difficulties encountered were so severe that the continued flight of a plane endangered its survival did the pilot turn back for his home base.

But whatever the reason—weather and assembly problems,

engineering difficulties or trouble with equipment—a total of 93 bombers failed to continue as part of the combat force that plunged into Germany.

Figure it out with an average of three tons of bombs per airplane. That makes 558,000 pounds of bombs that never reached the target because of such failures. As well as more than twelve hundred heavy machine guns missing from the defensive fire screen.

There is so much more to a mission than the communiqué that bleats that "a maximum force of heavy bombers struck today at a German city . . . !"

9

"YOU WORK UP THERE...."

The B-17, for all her years, hasn't fallen from her reputation as a machine that is beautiful in the air and graceful as a swllow in her flight. Nearly two decades ago her crews bestowed upon her the title of the Queen of all the bombers, and not an airplane since has intruded upon that accolade born of combat.

Alone in the high blue, the Fortress was a dream for her pilot to fly. She was famed for being as steady as a rock in the air, she was renowned for this steadiness which made her one of the most superb bombing machines ever built for war. The Boeing engineers have a saying, "If she looks good, she'll fly good." And the B-17 was a sweetheart to look at.

There is a vast difference, however, in a pilot's concern with only his one airplane in the heavens, when he can slide off on a wing and trace a graceful line through a sky flecked deliciously with soft clouds, and maneuvering from twenty-five to thirty tons of bombing airplane in perfect step and timing with a mass of other B-17's.

Quite another thing entirely, especially if the observer could *feel* all those rocks in the sky. And the sky sometimes is very hard. There's turbulence, of course. Turbulence found in clouds which comes unexpectedly and almost always, if the clouds are high enough and thick enough and broad bellied at the bases, with shattering violence. No one ever wrote about trying to hold formations when the rain crashes down against the windshields and sometimes becomes sleet, and it freezes and it's almost impossible to see, and everyone is scared, because just outside that line of vision there's all hell waiting. A Fortress then isn't a graceful thing sliding through the sky.

It's a bomb—a bomb made up of metal that can slice like some enormous and terrible buzz saw through your own airplane. It has four whirling blades, it is explosive with fuel tanks and bomb loads and just the sheer explosiveness of impact in the air. The Fortress then is an enemy, and a pilot fights like all hell against his ship—and the others—to survive nothing more than formation.

Formation charges the air with snarling thunderbolts in the form of air energy. There's normal turbulence to contend with, but the turbulence created by a bomber, and a stream of bombers, drives pilots crazy. There's prop wash, the air screaming invisibly back from propellers. If you could see the air, there would be a whirling, corkscrewing funnel that strikes a trailing airplane with devastating effect. It's air that doesn't slide off a wing, it rolls and rotates and spins, and gives a pilot muscles he never thought he'd get just by driving a big airplane in a straight line through the sky.

Besides the prop wash there are wake turbulence and vortex effects. The air that streams off the wing tips of a bomber goes crazy. Like prop wash, it has a corkscrewing effect, only it's more concentrated, and it's worse. Then, of course, the whole airplane throws back a steady stream of air that's been disturbed and shaken up and joggled. You don't push thirty tons through the air at 150 to 200 miles per hour and not create an effect that pilots just don't like.

All the rules of flying tell you to stay away from that air. Let the vortexes and the prop wash and the wake turbulence become great enough, and they'll tear at an airplane with invisible fingers that can rip metal open and slam an airplane way up on its side and terrify the crew—especially the gunners in the back, who wonder just what the hell is going on now.

To lead a bomber formation takes great skill: the leader must think constantly of those behind him; he must be most considerate of their capabilities. A leader can ruin a formation with a simple error, and must be ever precise and gentle in his leadership.

Yet the lead bomber of a combat formation has one great advantage over all those Fortresses that follow. Despite his vulnerability in battle, despite the fact that he is sitting way out there by himself when the fighters come rolling in for their head-on atacks, the pilot doesn't have to fight everybody else in the formation.

Ask any bomber pilot who has flown missions with a sky

full of airplanes in front of him. The air isn't soft; it's hard and it's stiff, and it's savage. It doesn't even flow in a stream. The other bombers have churned it into an impossible rapids in the sky, a tornado funnel that grabs hold and doesn't easily let go. When the air is churned and whipped up like this, the Flying Fortress isn't an indomitable war machine any longer. It's a flimsy creature made out of balsa wood and tossed into rapids that rage and pound and thunder. The bombers don't even fly any more. They bounce and flop around, they slide crazily, they are smashed under the nose, and they bob up and down like corks in a stormy sea.

The more they do this, the greater the danger of collision. It's bad enough to fly an airplane when the air is violent. It is a full-time job and it takes constant attention to the controls and a pilot literally works like hell. After an hour or two of fighting his airplane, a man gets tired, and he sometimes gets a little careless. That is a stupid thing to do, because when a pilot is mixed up in a sky full of airplanes, two machines sometimes try to occupy the same air space.

It doesn't happen too often. When it does, the two bombers cease to exist as the Flying Fortresses they were just an instant before. There is a great blinding flash in the sky. The flash disappears quickly enough, although it is impressed deeply on the retinas of all the eyes watching the scene in stunned disbelief. Sometimes the blast doesn't even create much smoke. But there is always the sight of a wing or two flip-flopping crazily in the sky, and a lot of wreckage, and fire, and sometimes in that brief but timeless moment the other crews can see a body twitching as it falls.

The blast also releases frenzied activity on the part of all the other pilots, because a shock wave rips out from that brilliant light. The shock wave is steel hard, and it throws Fortresses around like chips at sea. That means that more collision is breathtakingly imminent—unless the other pilots are really on their toes.

In all this crashing air the Fortress isn't quite the same agile and lithe creature as the fighter airplane. In a fighter, you can flick the stick, and the response is immediate and effective, and the horizon whirls very satisfyingly. You don't "flick" the Fortress, *especially* when you're in that sky overflowing with other airplanes all around you—in front, in back, on top of you, below you, on all sides. You're wing tip to wing tip, everything is preordained. It's height to height, speed to speed, turn to turn. A pilot pushes and pulls and heaves and strains. In short, he *works*.

Hollywood has managed to create some memorable impressions of bomber pilots. But they don't really show the discomfort and the stinking sweat of the cockpit. How do you manage on a celluloid screen to show how damned uncomfortable an oxygen mask can be when a man wears it for hour after hour, when the sweat collects near his eyes, and stings, and he can't wipe it away, because it was trouble enough to get that mask to fit properly to begin with? You get hotter and hotter, and there's a cupful of sweat collected underneath your chin where the mask is full and round, and damn, but that itches! The sweat beads on your nose, and it collects on your upper lip, and it's possible but not at all pleasant to try to wipe it off with your tongue when you're flying that airplane and worrying about collisons and trying to stay in formation.

It's cold in the high reaches where men have fought over Germany. But even when the needle drops far below zero, a man gets distressingly hot. The sun beats in at this high altitude with vicious intensity, and there's no closing any curtains to grasp shade, because the pilot and the copilot and everybody else in the airplane need every inch of space through which they can look out. Bundled up in all his gear—the boots and gloves, the electric suit which grips a man's shoulders like a vise, shoved into his mask and helmet—and wearing that tin hat over his head, a pilot sweats—and he can lose several pounds on just a single mission. Underneath the flying helmet and the steel helmet his hair is sloppy and caked and glistening with sweat, but he can't do anything about it. It has to stay that way, even if he could wipe it off, because who wants to expose a head soaked in sweat when it's thirty and forty and fifty below zero, and even lower!

From a distance, it doesn't seem possible that the pilots are working so hard, that the physical labor is constant, that the labor itself is nothing without skill and finesse and experience behind it. A mass of bombers in the high blue is majesty itself. The thunder booms in deep resonance from the very heavens; it is a rich cadence of machines marching off to war in a measured step all its own. There is procession among the clouds, and the bombers slide forward with ponderous and majestic grace.

It isn't that way at all, of course. Listen to an explanation of the work given by a leader of a combat wing to his pilots who were soon to leave for Mission 115 on October 14. It is stripped of all but its essentials:

"There's this business of relative speed. If you are behind anybody, you will have to pull a lot more speed than he does to catch him. If you are behind, you will have to go faster. Time once lost cannot be regained. Obviously, it means you will have to go faster. It does not mean he is trying to get away from you.

"Don't worry if you have to fly a little faster. Use your manifold pressure, your extra rpm. The wing man is always indicating more than one hundred and fifty-five miles per hour, especially if the squadron leader does not stay in formation, and they are all jockeying, and the speed will vary from about 130 to 190 miles per hour. The element leader and squadron leader should stay in position; the second and third element leaders likewise. If your wing man falls back let him fall back. He will have only one thing to do to catch up—open the throttle. The trouble is always after the target. You can help that sometimes by swinging beyond the rally point."

The bomber box in the skies is not nearly so rigid as it seems. It is a creature of fluidity, naked to pilot error and turbulence and vortexes from other airplanes. It means constant attention to the rudder pedals, to the elevators and ailerons and the trim, and working always with a hand on the throttles. After a lot of experience of being kicked around the sky, a pilot learns the knack of his trade. It is the mark of finesse of the man who's become skilled at wrestling a giant bomber through the storm of air that has become a very real and tangible enemy. He leaves the throttles of the two inboard engines strictly alone; he forces himself to forget that these even exist. They remain at constant revolutions per minute, and the pilot then concentrates his attention on the two outboard engines, and two is much better than four under these circumstances. By working the two throttles with the skill of a musician, he can juggle his machine with expert touches in its assigned slot, and he flies a better formation and is not so absolutely dog-tired by the time he reaches the target.

The business of rendezvous and assembly is wicked. The two following passages, taken from official histories, were recorded during critiques of Mission 115. They refer specifically—and again in basic and clinical terms—to assembly and formation. The first is from a captain, a pilot:

> At the start of the assembly, we checked the clouds. As we had a few clouds about 15,000 feet and assembly was planned for 20,000 feet, we decided to rendezvous at 11,000 feet, giving you that much time to climb as individual groups. This is easier on the group. We rendezvoused at 11,000 feet from Bury to Swaffom to Wisback to Cambridge. We assembled as a combat wing until reaching the Division Assembly Line, making two turns of ninety degrees.... The rendezvous was not at altitude. We had to give you thirty minutes to get a good combat wing formation. Sometimes we cannot do this, but this time we gave you time to go from 11,000 to 20,000 feet. You were to stay at that point until reaching the coast.
>
> We always allow about a minute extra on each leg. That takes care of wind changes and will not affect your rendezvous with the Air Division. In a wing assembly, if you ever find yourself at a point one or one and a half minutes ahead of time, you can figure the leg was flown exactly as it was planned. You should always take this into consideration. You can lose one or one and a half minutes without interfering with the rendezvous.

The second excerpt is from remarks by Colonel Van DeVander, who commanded the 385th Group, which led a Combat Wing.

> The radio contact was perfect, and that made a good mission. I always had perfect radio control. We swung on the outside of the 94th Group and kept about 1,000 feet below them. We then climbed to 9,000 feet. Then they called us again. We had a little trouble because of a cloud layer; however, we made our times and course good. We were about two minutes early at the division assembly. We could see several groups. Groups began coming in ahead and forming wing assembly....
>
> There was a layer of cirrus where we were to start climbing. We were in good formation. We started climbing early; then I went down to 19,000 feet. Some of the groups went right ahead into the cirrus. I thought they were abandoning the mission; however, we pulled back into fairly good assembly. By the time of reaching the French coast we were in good formation. The 94th Group was always tucked

in well. We were on the inside at Turn One. At Turn Two, we decided to lose a little distance, as we were running close.

In these terms it is all the matter of a day's work. But some of the airplanes that turned back over the Channel and aborted the mission did so because rendezvous and assembly and tired engines proved too much for their limited fuel consumption. Mission 115 was a raid that promised to be met with unrestrained fury by the Germans; it was not, however, a suicide attack or a strike on which we could afford to lose bombers we *knew* would not return. So some bombers with unhappy pilots were forced by fuel shortage to turn back and abort the mission. When they did so, it was only after the engineer stated flatly there would not be enough gasoline to complete the mission and return to England.

The attack, as can now be realized, involved far more than flying 460 miles from England and returning in a straight line. Instrument conditions take-offs and climb out, difficulties of rendezvous and assembly, maximum bomb loads, extra ammunition, the long distance of the raid, plus the necessity of turning after target and following a more circuitous route back to England—all these factors drained the limited fuel of the bombers.

Many of the B-17's carried additional bomb loads. With some bomb-bay space taken up by auxiliary fuel tanks, the armament crews slung 1,000-pound bombs beneath the wings on external racks. This meant not only extra weight, but a penalty of drag that slowed down the bomber and demanded more power to keep up with the other Fortresses. Some pilots over the Channel still had sufficient fuel to reach the target and return, but only if they jettisoned the bombs hung from the external racks, and at the earliest possible opportunity.

Over the Channel, then, even as the bombers vibrated from the test firings of the heavy machine guns, several aircraft released the black shapes. They plummeted four miles through space, and then sent up their geysers, soundlessly from the Forts, to mark the point of impact.

Thus all the factors combined to write the story of the formations: weather, fuel, engines, propeller pitch, weights and bomb loads, rpm, fuel mixture, turbulence, turns in formation for assembly—they are all vital, and they inject doubt and compromise into every mission.

A recording of the chatter of the pilots and the copilots talking to one another, bitching and cursing, would quickly enough bring formation flying down from its lofty pedestal in the sky to its equivalent in labor and sweat and fear.

They bitch mostly about the prop wash and the wake turbulence, which make their airplanes jiggle constantly, and turn the entire formation into a thing that ripples through its length and breadth and height, that reacts without warning with a shuddering spasm, leaping from plane to plane, from squadron to group to wing to division.

Flying Fortresses at this stage of a mission are especially tricky to fly. They are heavily loaded and too often overloaded. Turbulent air and the slow speed of formations mean the constant fear of a stall, and this is *murder*.

"Just let the lead ship slow down," explains Peaslee, who has flown all the positions in the formation, "and the effect is a chain reaction through the formation. If the first airplane loses speed, then the ships right behind must slow down to keep from running into him and chewing him up with their propellers. And the bombers behind them must slow down. The whole formation suffers a spasm that can shake it loose and jiggle the airplanes all over the sky. And more than one Flying Fortress has gone down over Germany, cut right in two, from the blades of another ship that for some reason or other—sometimes it can't be helped—moved out of its slot and reared up.

"When these Forts are loaded to the limit, as our planes were, and they must slow down in the turbulence that shakes them up, they're literally hanging on the edge of a stall. So the pilot has got to shove his throttles forward and get the most out of his propeller pitch, because if he slows down any more with all that turbulence raising hell with his lift, he *is* going to stall.

"The trouble is that he may need more air speed than the plane in front of him, and if he comes in too close, he doesn't dare chop power, or he's smack in the stall. So he must keep his throttles forward or, maybe if the wing suddenly gets thrown up high and he loses lift, he has to slam them forward even more. But then he's too close to the ship in front, and he has to swing sharply to the right or to the left, or stick his nose down, or skid if possible—he has to do something; he can't go forward, but he must move where another plane isn't. In a sky filled with planes.

"And if this poor bastard can't do this, then the *other* planes must get out of his way. *Fast.* Because with the bombers loaded the way they are with all their fuel and bombs, it's doubtful if anybody is coming out of the collision that will result.

"Pretty soon the formation is all shot to hell. It's ragged and the planes are bobbing and weaving and everyone is trying to get back again as fast as he can into a nice, tight defensive formation. If this happens over England, or well before the Germans show up, then things aren't too bad. But if the Jerries ever catch sight of a formation like that, they go berserk and rip into the Forts with everything they have. That's the basic key to their tactics—break up the formations. Our people knew it, too, and that's why everyone stayed on their toes all the time."

There's one more man to talk about, the unlucky pilot who's got to fly the worst spot of all—Ass End Charlie. This is the pilot in the Fortress that tails everyone; the very last ship in the formation. Not only does he—or the flight of three bombers—have to contend with all the miseries inflicted by wake turbulence, but he goes out of his mind just trying to stay in the right place in terms of speed. That man is the most overworked pilot on the whole mission.

He must—almost constantly—kick rudder back and forth, skidding to stay behind. His throttles are always being adjusted, and the wear on the engines is enough to make the crew chief weep. He skids and slips because he doesn't want to run into the bomber directly ahead of him, and he's even more frantic not to fall behind. He has a constant choice of staying in the worst heat of the frying pan, or falling back into where the fire blazes the hottest. If he falls back, he loses all the benefit of the bomber formation's defensive fire screen, there is no protection of gun for mutual gun, and the fighters just love *that.*

"When you look back from a lead bomber and see the formations real tight and in the groove," explains Peaslee, "it's more than watching a tremendous feat being enacted. You know those men out there in all those bombers are in the groove and they're ready to protect each other in the face of the most vicious and determined air opposition in the world.

"You know that the bombs are going to come out of airplanes all in the position where they belong, that they are going to fall in compact groups, and that if the lead bombardier has done his job well, absolute hell is going to erupt in the crucial factories the Germans need so badly.

"And because it is all second nature to you by now, you do not think in detail of all that this requires. You accept the skill and the courage of these men, just as they accept them from you. It is a wonderful thing to experience the calm and deep confidence of the air crews, the trust these men have in one another.

"Not just the pilots, of course. When the Fortress vibrated from the gunners testing their weapons, I felt the vibration only subconsciously. It was nice to know that, headed for Schweinfurt as we were, there were no complaints over the interphone. This is one of those moments when silence is golden, for it means that everything is all right, that everything is working properly. It means that all the guns are firing cleanly and well, that there are no jams, that the top turret with its twin guns just behind me is swinging freely and the ball turret under the belly is ready for action.

"The operator of the ball turret deserves countless words of praise, and he rarely receives them. He rides for hours on end curled up in a three-foot ball of plexiglas and metal, with about half the inside space taken up by two machine guns, his ammunition, and the turret mechanism. He is wide open to attack, he hangs suspended in space, and it's grim and lonely down there. I have never ridden in a ball, but I accept without question any complaints from that station."

The interphone in Peaslee's airplane, as in many others at that moment, comes suddenly to life. "Bogies at eight o'clock high."

There they are, a long file of Thunderbolts to the right, trailing a silver vapor far behind them. The "little friends," the most welcome companions in the sky to the bomber crews. And many a man in the Fortresses wonders to himself: how did they get here? There is only one way, of course, and it meant that those pilots, alone in heavy and high-performance fighters, had to climb *in formation* through more than six thousand feet of solid overcast. This is a magnificent feat, and it demands the very utmost in skill in a fighter which, given half the chance under blind-flying conditions, will drop off on a wing and spin crazily to earth. There are more occasions when this has happened than any pilot likes to remember. Such as the time when, caught in a violent and far-reaching storm, 22 out of 30 fighter planes, *and their pilots*, disappeared forever.

The heavy Thunderbolts are right on time, meeting exactly their scheduled rendezvous and altitude. Effortlessly they float past the bombers and swing out, far in front and to the flanks, loafing behind their giant engines. Peaslee sees, far ahead of the moving wall of bombers, a Channel sky quiet and peaceful and nothing in sight over the occupied countries.

But there *are* black-crossed fighters out there waiting. . . .

The colonel calls the lieutenant in the tail and asks for a reading on the rear formations. The evidence of skill is wrapped up neatly in the tight defensive boxes etched against the bright sky. The rear wing of the first division—Peaslee's command—is in solid ranks as is the following division. There is nothing to find fault with, and for this Peaslee is grateful. He is not alone in this feeling.

"Take off! Take off!"

Even as the bombers cross the English coast, the enemy's Radar Warning Service and the Radio Directional Finder Screen are in opeation. The unseen tentacles of the locator system are plotting course and height and speed. No German yet knows the target, and because fighters are already taking off for interception, it is vital to determine this information. The B-17's will fly over cities already struck—Zeebrugge, Flushing, Ypres, Woensdrecht, Antwerp, Bochum, Hamm,

and others—and no German knows whether these cities will
again be struck, or whether a city unvisited by the Fortresses
will receive its first bombs today.

The European coast line moves beneath the B-17 formations, and the beaches stand out clear and sharp even from so
many miles in the air. The fields are still green, and the pe-
culiar mosaic pattern of farms stretches out into the distance
as the Channel is left behind. From so high it is difficult to believe that this is a contest of war. Canals and roads bisect the
land in neat squares and rectangles.

And then come the signs that destroy the illusion of peace.
Sudden bright flashes on the earth, tiny splinters of red flame,
and seconds later there are black and white puffs in the sky,
miles from the Fortresses, but the warnings of thicker flak to
come later. Gradually the occupied countries pass beneath
the bombers, and Germany moves into sight, far ahead of the
lead plane. From the air it is impossible to note where one
nation ends and another begins. Not until the industrial belts
of Germany are clearly identified—with their heavier flak and
the first approach of the black-crossed fighters—will there
come that feeling of "invading" the enemy's homeland.

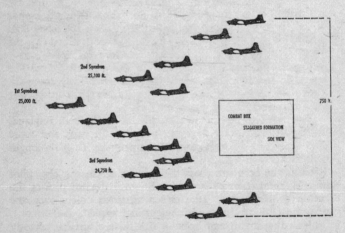

The bombers thunder into Germany in precise formation,
stacked into their defensive positions. Each combat box—a
staggering of three squadrons—is so positioned that the

formation has the maximum mutual protective fire of the bombers' guns. From top to bottom a box stretches 750 feet. It is actually an intricate thing, the squadrons fitting into groups, the groups into wings, the wings into air divisions. The vertical wedge of a combat wing stretches 3,000 feet from top to bottom, and it is made up of three separate combat boxes: the lead combat box in the center, with one higher and one lower. No matter how a fighter plane comes in to attack, it must pass before the crisscrossing fire of the defending heavy machine guns.

The bombers approach the Ruhr Valley, and the formation with infinite care follows a course that leads them out of flak range to the south. The Germans on the ground behind their superb 88-mm. guns and their *Grossbatterien* of the Ruhr—Happy Valley, to the air crews—would like nothing better than the opportunity to pour a withering fire into the massed bombers. On the charts in front of the pilots the Ruhr is a blob of red arcs that scream of danger. The guns are the best in the world and the gunners know no peer, and the wreckage of American and British bombers scattered across the valley provides grim testimony to their quality.

The bombers flank the southern tip of the Ruhr, and the sky to the left no longer is clean. Perhaps a hundred rounds of flak erupt in the clean blue, and the dirty splotches drift behind the formations. The shells are not aimed at the bombers; trying for any targets, the Germans reach out—fortunately without any hits—for the Thunderbolt escort. The fighter pilots have strayed, and they know it only too well. They pour on the coal and streak across the sky, cutting over the Fortresses, ranging ahead once again.

Near Aachen, more than two hundred miles from England, the fighter formations begin to thin out. In twos and fours they bank their wings, and peel off to return. They no longer have fuel enough to continue.

Peaslee watches the last fighter swing closer. The pilot waggles his wings and turns to the west. Peaslee presses the button to his throat mike and broadcasts blind over the common radio channel: "Thanks, little friends."

The colonel does not know it, but first blood has already been drawn.

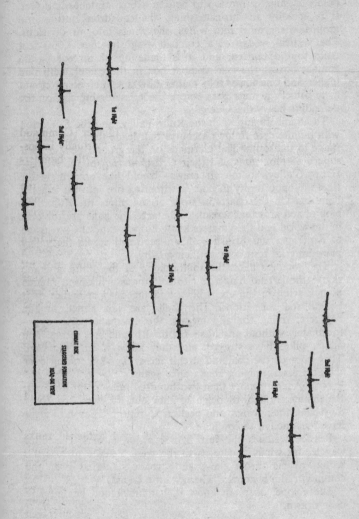

10

FIRST BLOOD

The historical archives of the VIII Fighter Command record the morning of October 14, 1943, as "virtually impossible for operations." What was hazardous for the bombers was murder for the heavy single-engine P-47 Thunderbolts. Despite a forward visibility of barely 1,500 yards, and the ragged cloud ceiling that hung down to 200 feet over their fields, no less than 196 of the big-bellied Thunderbolts howled into the air.

No pilots this day were more frustrated and angered than the men of the 4th Fighter Group who took 51 of the P-47's into the thick soup blanketing England. The planes took off in rain that totally obscured the ends of the runways. Because the bombers reported clouds extending as high as 15,000 feet, the fighter pilots decided to stick it out on the deck, and run for the coast where breaks were reported.

"Only a miracle," reported these shaken fliers, averted what might well have become a terrible disaster. The route forced upon the Thunderbolts was a No-Man's Land of balloon cables and the big barrage balloons, drifting invisibly just above the clouds. Maintaining formation as well as possible, the pilots swung and turned and skidded frantically to avoid plunging into the steel cables that swung ominously in their path.

Somehow they eluded the obstacles, and tightened ranks into a mass wedge of Thunderbolts. In this superb formation they reached the area where a break in the clouds had been reported. There was none; indeed, the visibility had worsened and the clouds were pressing closer to the earth. There was only one way out, and the heavy fighters drifted slightly from each other—except for flights of four airplanes, which stayed glued together—and bored into the overcast.

Several miles into the skies brilliant sunlight greeted the

planes. But that was all. Not a single bomber was in sight, despite a climb to high altitude and a wide orbit to permit the maximum search. The 4th Group aborted the mission and busied itself with the task of groping its way back to earth.

The 352d Fighter Group, which sent a force of 53 Thunderbolts into the thick clouds over England, enjoyed no good fortune. At 1314 hours the fighters spotted 25 B-24 bombers of the 3d Air Task Force, and swung into trail position behind the Liberators. For the next thirty minutes the force of 78 planes orbited the assembly group. Without any other bombers in the sky, and with reports of all fields closing in owing to weather, the bomber commander elected to abandon the mission.

The other two fighter forces hit pay dirt. First to see action was the 353d Fighter Group, whose 44 Thunderbolts rendezvoused with the 1st Air Division midway across the English Channel. At this point the B-17's were approximately ten minutes behind schedule.

The three squadrons of Thunderbolts came in from a wide turn to assume escort positions. In the front and working over the top of the Fortresses was the 351st Squadron. The 350th Squadron took up escort position on the right, and the 352d Squadron swung far out to the left.

The top squadron, directly over the top of the 1st Air Division force, split into two sections in order to cover the entire front of the bombers and maintain a position where they could direct the other two squadrons flying off to the sides. On the left the 352d flew at high altitude, weaving along off to the side and well out in front of the bombers. This provided a flank against any enemy attacks that might come in from high and above. On the right, the 350th fighters flew at the same altitude with the bombers, weaving along the side of the formations and ranging to the front. Thus the two side squadrons were in position to block any German aircraft that would be moving into position for attacks.

These were the escort positions of the 353d Group as the mass formation made landfall over Walcheren Island. At that moment, at two o'clock high, the fighter pilots warned of twenty-plus contrails moving in from above 34,000 feet. One flight of six German fighters led the others, with a flight of five, and several flights of four fighters, all mixed in close.

At this moment the 352d Squadron was at 31,000 feet to the left of the bombers, with a second Thunderbolt echelon staggered in trail at 32,000 feet. Immediately the Thunderbolts went to full power. As one man, the pilots pulled back into climbs and turned directly into the enemy force—now identified more clearly as 16 Messerschmitt Me-109 and four Focke-Wulf FW-190 fighters.

At once eight fighters—the four FW-190's and four of the Me-109's—broke from the attack. The eight fighters immediately half rolled onto their backs, and disappeared in vertical power dives for the coast line. It was an invitation for the Thunderbolts to follow and to deplete their force—leaving the bombers wide open—but the pilots weren't buying the move.

Within seconds the mass of Thunderbolts spread out and scattered after the German fighters. Wherever possible, the P-47's remained in flights of four, providing each other excellent support, and breaking apart further into two-ship elements—leader and wing man—as opportunities for close attacks appeared.

There was no question but that these Germans had come to stay and fight, and they hammered at the Thunderbolts with everything they had. The American fighters had an excellent advantage; the big Thunderbolt was designed to fly and fight at extreme altitude, and this fight was above 30,000 feet, where the P-47 was in its prime. The pilots used that advantage handsomely.

During the fight, which lasted for twenty minutes—an extraordinary engagement for fighters—the Thunderbolts set aflame and exploded four Me-109's and poured bullets into four more, inflicting major damage. While the 352d engaged the black-crossed planes, the other two squadrons went on with the bombers. As the mass formation drew away from the fierce air fight, two Me-109's raced in at high speed for the last box of Fortresses. Eight Thunderbolts turned to meet them head on, but the Germans wanted no part of this. The two Messerschmitts broke off and dived for the deck.

The Germans used this engagement to test new combat tactics. When a Thunderbolt raced in to the tail of an Me-109, the German flier immediately snapped over into a half roll, and plunged almost vertically on his back. Watching the P-47 behind him break off the attack—the pilots were under orders not to pursue for any distance any German plane—the Messerschmitt rolled back to normal flight and came back to the fight with the great speed gained from a zoom climb.

Unhappily for them, the new tactics proved ineffective. The Thunderbolt pilots simply waited until the Me-109's were committed to the zoom, and rushed in. Two of the four fighters destroyed went down in this fashion.

Every Thunderbolt pilot lauded the performance of the big and heavy fighter above 30,000 feet. The Germans were convinced that the swift and light Me-109 was far more than a match for the P-47 in the swirling combat of the dogfight, and they endeavored constantly to get on the tail of a Thunderbolt. But this was 30,000 feet, not close to earth. Not only did the P-47's outclimb their opponents, but they dangled the bait of what seemed a perfect kill in front of the Germans. Here is an excerpt from the official record of the engagement:

All reports from our pilots who engaged in combat above 30,000 feet with the Me-109 agree that the P-47 will outturn and outclimb that airplane at that altitude. In several cases P-47s maneuvered into position on the Me-109's tail by letting the enemy aircraft come down from above and get into a Lufberry [tight horizontal circle] with them, then reef it in and outturn them.

"Little friend"—Thunderbolt escort fighter

Far ahead of the dogfight the lead boxes of bombers approached the vicinity of Düren, in the Rhineland, when the pilots of the 350th Squadron sighted 30 enemy fighters. These were quickly identified as yellow-nosed Focke-Wulf FW-190's, climbing up from about eleven o'clock and splitting into two groups as they neared the Fortresses. One half went to the left side and the other half swung to the right. As this latter force came about in a fast, wide turn to hit the B-17's, the Thunderbolts raced in to attack—coming in fast and from above. One look was enough, and the Focke-Wulfs at once pushed over and dived inland at maximum speed. Red Flight snapped out several long deflection bursts but without visible effect as the German fighters rushed away.

The 350th Squadron came around in a rapid, climbing turn, rushing under full throttle to reach the other force of Focke-Wulfs that had split off to the left side of the bombers. As the German fighters came around for dead-astern attacks against the Fortresses, the Thunderbolts hit them in the middle of their turn.

It was over in seconds. Concentrating on the bombers, the enemy fliers never even seemed to see the P-47's. The big fighters scattered the German formation. Three FW-190's were set aflame, a third was hit heavily, and the remainder fled for the deck without getting in a single shot at the bombers.

The second section of the 351st Squadron, then flying top cover for the lead bomber units, had an even better time. More than twenty mixed Me-109's and FW-190's rushed in against the Fortresses from three o'clock at 24,000 feet. As the Thunderbolts turned to meet them, the enemy fighters flashed by, to the right and beneath a P-47 section. And this made for a perfect setup.

Sticks all the way forward and rudder pedals tramped down, the Thunderbolts clawed around in a diving right turn, putting the sun directly behind them and blinding any enemy fliers who glanced black. Apparently none did, anyway, for the Germans never had any warning until the P-47's were right on their tails, each Thunderbolt scoring heavily with its eight .50-caliber machine guns. In less than ten seconds the 351st Section destroyed four and damaged one. The remainder of the enemy force dived headlong out of the fight.

Score for the mission for the 353d: ten fighters shot down, one probably shot down, and at least three heavily damaged. For this victory the Thunderbolt force lost one of their number in combat; the pilot was listed as missing. A second plane, with its gear shot out by a cannon shell, landed on one wheel, and the pilot walked away. A third P-47 crashed near Hornchurch, killing the pilot.

To support the 2d Air Task Force (3d Air Division) the 56th Fighter Group put up a force of 48 Thunderbolts. These rendezvoused with the bombers at 1305 hours over Sas van Gent, and provided support along the bomber track to Düren.

In the vicinity of Dison, the Thunderbolts wheeled in a wide turn and headed for home. But the Germans provided some unfinished business, and at the same time showed the promise of what the B-17's could expect once their fighter escort was on the way back to England.

Four Focke-Wulf FW-190's cruised at 17,000 feet near Aachen, waiting patiently for the Thunderbolts to depart before opening their attack. At the same time, 1335 hours, another eight fighters were spotted west of Aachen, at 5,000 feet, heading to the northwest. North of Aachen, and flying due north, was a force of 20 single-engine fighters. Then one of the Thunderbolt pilots called out 12 twin-engine Messerschmitt Me-110's at 15,000 feet, following the rear bomber box and climbing. White and Blue Flights, of the 61st Squadron, hit these airplanes in a screaming dive. On the first pass two Me-110's went down in flames, and another was crippled. Several Me-109's passed nearby, headed for the bombers, and the Thunderbolts swerved long enough to explode one of these planes and to scatter the German formation.

But now their fuel was at the critical mark. It was either run for England, or ditch the fighters in the Channel.

The Thunderbolts flew into the west. For the loss in combat of one Thunderbolt the big American fighters had shot down 13, probably destroyed one, and damaged five of the enemy. Despite this ringing success, however, their last sight of the bombers was not a reassuring one. Two Fortresses were spinning, wrapped in flames.

PART III

ATTACK

---

*Germany heard a clashing of arms all over the sky;
the Alps trembled with uncommon earthquakes....
Never did lightnings fall in greater quantities from a
serene sky, or dire thunders blaze so often.*
    Virgil—*Georgics*, **Book One**

11

LINE PLUNGE THROUGH CENTER

Prelude to Schweinfurt: "The German fighter raked us the length of the Fortress's belly. It was like sitting in the boiler of a hot-water heater and being rolled down a steep hill. The right wing was shot to hell. There were holes everywhere. A lot of them were 20-mm. cannon holes, and they tear a hole you could shove a sheep through. The entire wing was just a goddamn bunch of holes."

> *Report of a B-17 pilot after a raid against Meaulte on the French coast.*

Share the thoughts of a B-17 gunner, 384th Bomb Group, Mission 115: "You try to remember what the target will look like. A sprawling plant, cluster of vehicles . . . a river for identification, then there's smokestacks, marshaling yards. Sometimes it's all a blur; something for the pilot, the navigator and the bombardier to worry about. . . .

"A long time ago I should have known Chicago like a book. But when I walked around to find an address, I had to ask a dozen people where the hell I was going.

"Now we're moving directly to an address in a city none of us have probably ever seen before. You don't ask anybody down there about it, and you're coming in without knocking on the door. Instead, you're going to blow it in, with the walls and everything else.

"The pilot makes a routine check of positions . . . like everyone else, you glance at your oxygen indicator, and in turn add your 'okay' to the comments passing back through the bomber.

"From this high, Germany is beautiful. Greens and browns. Peaceful and serene. You think about it, when suddenly someone cries: 'Fighters at eleven o'clock!'

"The whole airplane begins to shudder and shake through its length. Tracers spill through the air like crimson fireballs, arcing lazily, hiding the hidden four bullets between each flashing blur. You kick out some short bursts, leading a black-nosed shape swinging in fast from the three-quarter stern position. They're Focke-Wulfs; one screams in from above, a beautiful swing through the air, and just as his wings and nose blink brilliantly, you squeeze and hold down for a long burst. The guns shake and shudder, hammering sounds, the wind tearing in at you . . . and goddamnit, but your bullets smash into the cockpit! She whips over crazily, starting a cartwheel, and your bullets keep at him until suddenly flame appears, the stress of the wild tumble tears a wing off and the fighter disappears in a flash.

"Then, suddenly the Fortress shudders, a quiet groan, but louder than the motors and the calls on the interphone and the hammering guns. A groan, and magically, a jagged tear appears in the left wing. And you're scared; oh, God, how you're scared. . . ."

"Bogies at six o'clock climbing."

These are the first warning words that Colonel Peaslee and the rest of the crewmen in their Fortress hear of the German fighters closing in. It is impossible to record the terrific Schweinfurt battle in complete running continuity; impossible because so many things happen at once, happen too quickly, explosively, and violently. Missing from this narrative, of course, are the reports of all the crews of heavy bombers that fell to the enemy. This, from a historical standpoint, is infinitely regrettable, for theirs would be the stories to reveal in all their grim horror the terror and pain of air battle. Yet there is more than enough to tell. . . .

"Bogies!" the tail gunner cries again. "Many, all climbing on our tail. My God, I count 60 of them, some twin engine!"

Bedlam explodes through the interphone system; not only in this aircraft, of course, but in all the others to which the German fighters are drawn. Everyone in the crew sees German planes—for they are coming in from all directions, from all points of the compass, from high and from low—and tries to report. This is the moment when the initial flush of the combat about to detonate sweeps the men in its particular excitement; the words babble from their lips, and they shout out the positions of the approaching fighters.

The moment there is a lull in the shouting and Peaslee can make himself heard, he curses the crew, emphatically and with every choice bit of profanity he can jam into several seconds, for their breach of discipline. He admonishes them to keep calm, to break their silence only when necessary. Efficiency and discipline in a Fortress of the sky are indispensable to survival.

Because of the furious speed, and the wide arena of battle, it is necessary to report all fighter positions by the clock-sighting method. The nose of the bomber represents twelve o'clock. Directly off the right wing is three o'clock. Dead astern is six o'clock, and off the left wing is nine o'clock. "Six o'clock" high represents an attack made from high above and directly to the rear of the bomber. "Seven o'clock level" indicates a fighter coming in from just to the right of the tail (looking aft), and at the same altitude as the bomber.

"All right, you men," Peaslee snaps. "You're all aware now that attack is imminent. Concentrate only on those fighters that come in to us. And for God's sake, don't waste your ammunition on fighters that are out of range! We didn't expect these people to show up this early. It's a hell of a long way yet to the target, and it's going to seem a lot longer going back home. Stay on your toes...."

The Germans swoop in from the vast air space surrounding the bomber boxes. To the Luftwaffe pilots the formations of Flying Fortresses seem to be exactly that—a giant box in the sky bristling with death from every single bomber. They know the staggered formations give the Americans an excellent defensive fire screen. They know that no matter from what direction they attack, the defending tracers will erupt toward their airplanes. They know that it is a hellish thing to ask a man to rush headlong into a great space in the sky that literally comes alive with flame, with bombers twinkling and sparkling from nose and tail and sides and belly and top with heavy machine guns. They know this, and more than one German pilot is frightened before he makes his move to attack.

Who wouldn't be? But the fighters still move in for their firing runs, and no one ever accused the German fighter pilot of being anything but a skillful, courageous, and dangerous foe.

The men in the bombers look out—it is just past 1333 hours, and the Thunderbolts are on their way home now—

and see the black-crossed airplanes everywhere, closing in. Now, we share these moments with Colonel Peaslee:

"There are enemy fighters on both flanks and at the rear now—how many I don't know, but many. So far they have made no hostile move. We sit in dread, for we know there will be unlucky ones among us when they start their play. I happen to be looking dead ahead when the first break comes. Suddenly out in front appear flashes resembling continuous photography multiplied a hundred times. I recognize it instantly—I have seen it before. Just as quickly I make out the approaching silhouette of the fighters—and flashes are coming from their 20-mm. cannon.

"The opening play is a line plunge through center. The fighters whip through our formation, for our closing rate exceeds five hundred miles per hour. Another group of flashes replaces the first, and this is repeated five times as six formations of Messerschmitt Me-109's charge us. As each group of flashes appears our nose guns break into sound and the vibration shakes the bomber. After the first wave, they are joined by guns of the top turret and the ball turret as these guns swing around to bear. The tail guns join in occasionally as the gunner takes a quick shot at the fading targets.

"The shock of the first attack is over, and I start to get scared. How the planes ever miss collision is a mystery. It depends on the enemy fighters alone, for we are unable to dodge. That is probably our salvation. If we were able to, we might possibly dodge into their paths, and the results would be sensational. There are few things more spectacular than a head-on collision of bomber and fighter.

"As soon as I get a grip on myself again, I strain to find out what has happened to our formation. It seems a miracle. As far as I can see, all are in position. I call the tail gunner. He reports the aircraft to the rear still in position, but two are smoking—one badly—and another appears to be drifting back. More damage than that has been done, I know—inside our bombers there are dead and dying. The gunner adds one bit of cheerful news—a trail of smoke far to the rear arcs away toward the ground. It is not very much to be cheerful about, of course; the sky is absolutely filled with German planes.

"I yelled into the throat mike—I curse the long machine-gun bursts. I condemn the crew for wasting ammunition. We have hundreds of miles to go yet—if we are among the lucky.

Even as I yell, my earphones become bedlam once more.

" 'Here they come! Fighters attacking! Fighters at nine o'clock high! Fighters at four o'clock low! Fighters at six o'clock!'

"I try to look simultaneously in all directions. I can see the fighters on my side. They've half-turned and are diving toward us in a continuous string, their paths marked in the bright sunlight by fine lines of light-colored smoke as they fire short bursts. It is a coordinated attack, the finest I have ever seen. Their timing is perfect, their technique masterly.

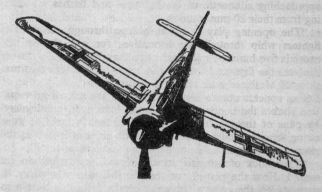

Swift, agile, heavily armored, and four cannon, two machine guns and rockets. Focke-Wulf FW-190

" 'B-17 going down in flames,' the tail gunner reports. 'No parachutes yet. We have two aircraft lagging badly—back about three hundred yards.'

"The damage is beginning to show. The tail gunner continues: 'Formations of twin engines approaching seven o'clock high. They're back about six hundred yards. My God, they've fired rockets!'

"I look back, my face against the ice-cold side window, and barely see them as they dive away in a turn. When I face front again several great black blobs of smoke appear, and we fly through the smoke almost instantly. There is a slight jar. That was close. Fleetingly I wonder how those rockets were able to strain through our formation without hitting anyone. The whole procedure is repeated a few seconds later, and this time I see it all—the bursts are only fifty feet off our left wing. They are big—about four times as big as ordinary flak, with angry, shapeless blobs of dirty red flame in the centers. I hear them over the roar of the motors, and they sound like someone throwing a handful of heavy stones against a tin roof—*hard!*

"Now we have fighters above us, below us, and to our flanks, all attacking or climbing back into position to attack again. Their coordination, however, is gone. Momentarily I am aware of our own guns. The bursts have become short, but the sound is almost continuous as it bounces at me from the various gun positions. Our gunners are finally aiming, not using their guns like garden hoses.

"As the rocket attacks go on, the action around us continues at such a pace that I see only fragments of it from the corners of my eyes. I try to look everywhere at once to absorb reports from the gunners. For the most part they have fallen silent. There is little use in reporting fighters that are everywhere. There is no way of counting them.

"I feel McLaughlin's hand on my arm. It's a hard grip and I see he is looking down and ahead. I lean over, craning my neck, following his eyes. A few hundred feet in front of us a bomber has been hit by a rocket. I catch sight of it just as the right wing starts to fold upward. The fuselage opens like an eggshell, and a man dressed in a flying suit spins clear out in front. I see the pilots still at the controls, then the plane is swept with flame. The right wing breaks free, and with the two engines still spinning it drifts to the rear, flaming at the ragged end. The shattered mess disappears under our left wing, and the sky is clean again. It all happens instantaneously, but to me it is like a slow-motion movie scene.

"As I look around again I notice our right-wing man, my deputy formation commander, is out of position. He has drifted back a few feet but I can still see him in the cockpit. I call him on our wing channel. There is no reply. I know he is not out of position voluntarily, and I have a premonition that he is not going to be with us long. Our formation has become ragged. Many gaps are left by missing bombers, and our gunfire suffers.

" 'Close up formation, close up formation!' I call it into the mike, then shout the words. *Formation;* it means everything to us now, it is the road to some salvation, some defense against the men in the black-crossed planes.

"Yet it is a futile order, and I know it. But at least it distracts me for a few seconds, and Christ! I want to be

"We didn't see any chutes...."

distracted from the carnage around me. Captain McLaughlin glances at me. In spite of his concentration on keeping our formation in position, little has escaped him.

" 'Colonel, I don't think we're going to make it.'

"His words are incredibly calm; a matter-of-fact statement. They are nonetheless grim and biting. I agree, of course, but I refuse to commit my thoughts to words, and as our eyes meet above the oxygen masks, I just nod.

"I get a report from my tail gunner. One of our aircraft has pulled out of formation and is turning back. I take a look. I know that if the pilot is trying to reach England he is condemned. Fighters will pick off his aircraft like a sitting duck. There will be a patrol out looking for such as he. I cannot guess the reason for his action, since the plane appears to be in good shape, but he may have a ruptured fuel tank, or wounded aboard who could not survive the full mission. Or he may have become mentally unbalanced by this fight. Whatever it is, he is lost.

"My deputy has drifted farther back, now he has lost the protection of our massed guns. The fighters jump him, but he plugs ahead by himself—he is trying to make the bomb-release line, if no more. That is pure guts.

"Another bomber leaves us. He is smoking and his wheels are starting down, a signal that he is going to land.

" 'My God, please take some evasive action!' someone in the crew begs over the interphone. Yet he knows as well as I do that evasive action in formation is futile—less than futile. 'Jinking' is all we can possibly do—moving suddenly a few feet up or down. Even that serves only to disturb the aim of our gunners, and we are just as apt to jink into a burst as to avoid it. Its only accomplishment is to give some mental relief to the crew. The men feel we are at least doing *something*.

"I suppose this feeling of being caught in a hopeless situation is far from new. Men must always have experienced it. I think of the Middle Ages. I see myself strolling across an open plain with a group of friends. Suddenly we are beset by many scoundrels on horseback. They come from every direction, shooting their arrows. We defend ourselves as best we can with slings and swords, and crouch behind our leather shields. We cannot run, we cannot dodge, we cannot hide—the plain has no growth, no rocks, no holes. And it seems endless. There is no way out—then, or now.

"I have been studying the tactics of the rocket attackers. They make the same approach each time and fire from the same range. I can tell within a few seconds when they are going to fire. I decide maybe there is something that can be done—that I can contribute a little to this fight. There is nothing so useless as being an air commander in an air battle. You just sit there and watch what goes on, for command is lost in the fog of battle and all depends on the training of your crews.

"We will try an experiment. I talk to McLaughlin. As the next rocket formation approaches the firing point, we will start a shallow turn to the right—almost a drift. It will give the enemy an increased deflection shot and will not disturb the formation. As soon as the rockets have been launched we will slide back to our former position.

"I see the rocket planes coming into position. Now! I give the signal! The maneuver works—or maybe it's just luck, or just poor shooting. Anyway, the bursts are to our left. We continue the practice. The bursts still miss.

"We are approaching the Initial Point, the point at which we commit ourselves directly to the bomb run on the target. Schweinfurt, here we come! As we turn, I take a hasty reading on our formation. I have eight aircraft left and my other group has been reduced to six. Fourteen planes left, and we still have so many miles to go! I call the captain leading the other bombers and tell him to close in on me and to drop on my command, 'Bombs away.' He does not respond, but his formation moves in near to ours as we start the sighting run. The fighters know what our intentions are and they come at us like tigers. . . ."

12

THE UNNAMED

The sky over Germany is alive with energy so violent as to be almost beyond belief. The heavens are a world alien to men, a sorcerer's nightmare blazing in angry flames. They leap into existence without warning. Sudden flashes of light, frightening and angry, blinding, revealing in their intensity a spectrum of red, orange, yellow and white. Cannon shells and bombs, aerial mines and rockets exploding, each intent on skewering a winged machine with its pregnant bomb bays and the ten vulnerable men inside.

No longer do the Flying Fortresses progress in a stately march through the upper heavens. The majesty has vanished, the crisp efficiency of tight formation is desperately sought but impossible to achieve in that raging hurricane of air. The bombers slog their way through the thickening mass of exploding flame and smoke. They are forced onward not merely by strength of motors and whirling propellers, but equally with the determination of grim men in the cockpits. The bombers drive ahead through a whirlwind of steel splinters and flame and jagged chunks of red-hot metal. The steel is everywhere: it crashes into wings and engines, slams into bulkheads and airplane bodies. And into the bodies of men, spewing out blood, tissue, intestines, and brains.

Through the carnage there leap spears of bright flame, each portending a shocking release of energy, a mind-stunning slap of concussion. Sometimes the spear strikes the heart, and death and destruction come with explosive suddenness. The flame lances directly into the core of a 30-ton airplane, it reaches cunningly into the bays in the stomach of the Fortress, and the blast strikes eagerly at the fuses. Six 1,000 pounders are in there, and they can take so much punishment and no more, for they are intended to react to this type of attention.

Into German skies...

They do, and here the ten men who are to die forfeit their lives in merciful fashion. It is an instant thing, a thing of only a millisecond. Nothing drags out, there is no time for the pain to turn a human being who is an intelligent creature, the father of children, a citadel of pride and ethics and morals, into a shrieking animal. The rocket releases its energy into the bombs, and three tons of high explosives react just as the miracle of science, the pride of civilization, designed them to react.

Just a few thousandths of a second, no more...the blast from the exploding rocket strikes the detonators of the bombs, nose and tail. All receive the punishment at the same instant. They, in turn, react. A shock wave, a shudder of energy flashes through the mass of explosives in the bombs. Their molecules are unstable, and the shock wave seizes upon this instability. The molecules become excited and they churn furiously as they seek a path of stability. There is nitro and hydrogen and oxygen and carbon. They suffer their rearrangement, and the solid mass within the bombs is no longer what it was just an instant before.

The mass crumbles within itself. It shreds and cracks, suffers an internal turmoil. Unseen by any man, it pulsates with a flashing of weird light, the warning of gases under fantastic combustion. They boil and seethe into a terrible heat, and in these microseconds, beyond all human ken, the six bombs are no longer solid masses, but gas that is appallingly hot. The pressure is explosive, it hammers at the steel casings, and not even the steel can resist. The powerful metal crumbles like tissue paper, collapsing before the irresistible surge of the gases within.

In a fraction of a second after the flame spears into the B-17, the entire airplane and its 10 men vanish. In its place there is a searing ball of fire, a terrible glare of the explosives releasing their energy. Even as the concussion smashes into the neighboring bombers, hurling them from their formations, the volatile fuel within the tanks is consumed, and this liquid also erupts into flame. As the formation continues on its terrible flight, there is behind them a monstrous smear, churning angrily within itself.

The fighters are through the heavens, swift and merciless and terribly efficient. They assemble far ahead of the battered formations, climbing slightly. The pilots are excellent, their coordination is superb. They heed carefully the guttural commands of the leader, and suddenly a haphazard group of Focke-Wulfs slides into an even formation, wing tip to wing tip, woven into a single engine of destruction. Eight fighters; there are eight large rockets to be released first, and then the massed firepower of 32 heavy cannon and 16 machine guns will erupt to exact its toll.

They come in *fast*, and they scare the hell out of all those people in the bombers. They close with a speed up to six hundred miles per hour, and they do not flinch or waver or tremble as the gunners hose streams of tracers at them. The B-17's are alive with lights. Two guns on top of the fuselage, two guns in a turret below, and as many as four guns in the nose, all spitting defiance and fire and an avalanche of bullets. But the German pilots hold their formations, and the eight fighters sweep forward like a great flaming scythe.

It is, each man who survives the attacks swears, the most

helpless feeling in the world. The German planes reach within the range of their weapons. The rockets streak out first, and they distract the gunners, and sometimes a pilot just cannot sit there grimly plodding along, and he jerks on the control yoke. The bomber twitches, it moves spasmodically from its slot in the formation, and that is exactly what the fighters hope for. A man with his eyes glued to a sight notices this weakness; he nudges a rudder pedal with little more than a trace of pressure, and his Focke-Wulf responds.

The gunners look out and the pilots stare helplessly as the wings and noses of the line-abreast formation, the scythe, all flame into life with orange and yellow flashes. They are surprisingly brilliant, and they mean cannon shells and bullets spraying the sky with a rain of death.

Within a bomber the noise is deafening. The gunners shout the positions of the incoming fighters, there is the pounding roar of the four powerful engines, the background bass hiss of the air rushing by. The machine guns hammer and bark and cough deeply, their vibrations ripple through the Fortress, and there can be heard the terrible *whump!* of a rocket exploding nearby. There is the heart-stopping sound of metal clashing against metal, of cannon shells exploding against wings and fuselage and engines, the staccato impact of bullets and steel fragments ripping through aluminum and steel.

The sounds of air battle are numberless, and they join into a crashing cacophony, a singular sonic shriek. The world itself plunges into insanity in these moments. It reels and shakes wildly, it careens with sickening sensation. Earth and sky blend into a vibrating spasm of movement and recoil and impact. If the sky is cloudless, then air battle spews forth its own rain. Shell cases erupt from the shadowed bellies of the bombers above as well as the fighters, and they splash downward in a metallic hail, banging against metal skin, chipping windshields, sending lightning-fork cracks through the plexiglas. The waist gunners especially hear their keening sound, the singsong, high-pitched chime of the cases as they whirl through the propeller blades.

And there is *the* sound, the one that grates deepest against the nerves, that is hellish and hated, that knifes into the brain and makes a man wince through and through. A scream, metallic, thin, and high, a slender file blade cutting through the nerves. Above all else there is this cry of the fighter racing in close, sounding a scream that can be none other.

Out of the whole armada, out of that frenzied maelstrom, take just one bomber, described anonymously in the records of Mission 115.

To her crew she has always been a graceful and beautiful creature. They have often talked about this 30-ton craft, of the manner in which she slides through the air in the clean sunshine high above earth. Under her glistening belly the ball turret turns slowly as she moves into German territory. In her transparent nose the bombardier prepares his equipment, checking for the run over the target of thirty to sixty seconds, the meaningful justification for this airplane and all the others to be plunging into Germany. He kneels before his bomb sight like an acolyte before an altar, just as intense, equally as concerned for proper obeisance to the delicate equipment. The livid yellow of his inflatable life jacket, the dark green of his oxygen mask, stand out sharply against all his bulky attire.

The Flying Fortress does not seem to be occupied by men. They are beings from some other world, alien creatures with strange breathing systems dangling from beneath their faces. The rubber diaphragms of the oxygen masks expand and contract regularly like living lungs, delicate membranes exposed outside the body, fragile to puncture.

Outside the airplane the sun is intensely bright, but the temperature is forty-three degrees below zero. It is an enemy, that cold. It never for a single moment relaxes its vigil, always preys upon the hapless man who exposes his sensitive flesh to the jagged teeth of frostbite. Golden sunlight and vicious cold, an acceptable and normal paradox of the high arena. Frost forms on the transparent nose through which heavy machine guns bristle, and the bombardier opens a panel to let the icy air shrill through, clearing the glass.

Germany is below the transparent nose, and there is a wisp of clouds maybe a thousand feet beneath the bomber. The bombardier glances down and smiles beneath his mask at the sight of the pilot's halo he sees—a tiny circular rainbow on the cloud with the shadows of his bomber and two others as they rush into the enemy land. A good omen, maybe.

The first black specks appear in the distance, and there is the barest feeling of a gentle skid as the pilot closes in, tightening up his Fortress's position in the formation. The long minutes pass, the gunners sing out, for the moment they have nothing to fire at, and wait, as spectators at the opening act of the drama, as the rockets and cannon rip into the planes of the initial formations.

And then the waiting is over, the black spots are closer and closer. A man cries out in astonishment: "The whole god-damned Luftwaffe is out today! Look at those bastards come in. . . ." He is right: the sky is a vast circular bowl, and from the edges of the bowl the fighters swarm down in incredible numbers.

Everything happens so quickly that it is blurred and chaotic. Movement and action are more instinctive than deliberate. Around this particular ship the bombers accept their punishment. Some die in violent agony; others absorb the death blow with seeming stoicism, drifting out of formation, easing toward the earth far below, and never coming out of the long, gentle glide, dead airplanes before they smash into the earth.

The fighters come back again and again, and the fourth or fifth time around, or maybe it is the seventh or the tenth—no one is sure—they find the range they want, and then this is *it!* The blazing coals hurled from the fighters crash and bang through the ship, and the Fortress convulses with the force of the impacts. The machine writhes and protests in metallic cries of despair.

When a cannon shell smashes into a Fortress, the way it sounds depends upon where you are. If you're not too close, it's a kind of metallic *whoof!* like a small bark from a big dog—and you feel a jar that shakes the whole ship. It is a tremor, it reaches and leaves you quickly. But if the shell explodes nearby, then there is nothing gentle or distant about what happens, and it sure as hell isn't a momentary tremor.

It sounds like some giant smashing his cupped hand down on the surface of still water. A double sound, really—the first from the impact and the second when the shell explodes. *CRAA-AASH!* Like that. Like firing a shotgun into a bucket, so that the sound and the blast all come exploding back up into your face, shaking you up and stunning your mind. For the moment you're not scared, because your senses are knocked silly, and you don't know how to be scared or anything else. Your bowels seem weak and watery and your stomach shrivels up until you know how much damage has been done.

And this happens all the time through the fight; *all* the time, if they pick your airplane and they find the range. Many a man has come home off these raids without a mark on the outside, but cut up pretty thoroughly beneath the skin.

Now there's good reason for the weak bowels and the shriveled stomach, because the Fortress *is* hit. Its inner walls are covered with a green insulation that is thick and heavy. The shell has hit right in the middle of the stuff, and the fire moves quickly along the shredded edges. *Fire!* The most dreaded thing in an airplane loaded with fuel and ammunition and bombs. Fire that can easily rush away from all possible control, that licks and sears and burns at men and metal alike. In a moment the green insulation is blazing fiercely, and the smoke gets thicker and thicker. It chokes and stings the eyes, it's hard to see a goddamned thing, and hell yawns wide just outside the hatches and doors of the airplane.

The fear is so bad now that, surprisingly, it freezes inside the men. It's worse than before, but the need for action, the long training, the coordination of the team that makes up the crew, the concern for the others, all these take precedence.

All the time the fire spreads the Germans are still hammering away. The fighter pilots also see the smoke, and this is what they eagerly seek. It is the sign of a crippled airplane, one they have hurt, and they close in with the blood lust at its peak to finish off the cripple. The Fortress reels and shakes and pounds; another fighter comes in from the front, a Focke-Wulf, barrel rolling with extraordinary grace and precision, wings and nose ablaze with the terrible orange light. A bullet from its nose guns races into the airplane. It creases an ammunition can in the radio room and it also scatters incendiary material from one of the tracers in the belt. The insulation is burning even worse than before, and there is new fire, and by now, in most planes, half the crew would have been over the side.

Already the sky looks as though the Fortresses were in the midst of a mass parachute invasion. At one time the crews estimate there are up to one hundred and fifty parachutes in the air. White ones and brown ones, each of the latter signifying a German pilot whose fire was met with concerted gunnery from the bombers and who flung himself away from a blazing coffin.

The Fortress is now in serious trouble, and the navigator and bombardier abandon their guns to fight the enemy which is closer, far more deadly, than even the Focke-Wulfs and the Messerschmitts.

The navigator crawls through the widespread legs of the top turret gunner. The man in the turret knows there is fire, but he pays no attention to it. He forces himself to remain oblivious to the flames just as hungry for him as all the rest, and he will stay this way, beating out a thundering symphony with his twin guns, until he hears the fire is out, or sees the airplane breaking into pieces in the sky. He feels the man crawling between his legs, and he ignores the movement.

The navigator squirms through and reaches the catwalk that leads across the bomb bay. He is 23,000 feet above the earth, where the air is thin and cruel, but he has no mask. He has taken it off. He tries to worm his way into the narrow passage between girders, but his parachute jams and holds him fast. If the parachute had not jammed, he would have been several feet away from where he is at the exact moment that a cannon shell comes in through the airplane just behind him, and explodes. The flash is blinding, the roar brings blood to his ears, and he cannot feel the fire extinguisher in his hand. He tastes blood—it trickles from his mouth as well as from his ears. He ignores it; the fire, the fire, must get to the fire.

He grasps for the extinguisher again. It is a useless motion, and it is not until this moment that he discovers that the exploding shell has broken his arm. He cannot do a thing. Despair floods his face and the bombardier, struggling through to join him, sees this and something the hapless navigator does not even yet realize. Parts of his chin and nose also are missing.

The bombardier brings the navigator out and moves in first. By some miracle that no one will ever understand they struggle into the radio room—the one that is wounded and with a piece of chin chopped out and a piece of nose shot away and the broken arm and all—*and they put out the fire!* They tear the burning insulation loose and throw it out of the ship through the hatch; to the crews of nearby airplanes it looks as though the Fort is coming apart at the seams.

Not yet. A B-17 resists death with a grim hold on its mechanical life, and this is one reason why her crews, with religious and loving fervor, call her the Queen. This Fortress is not yet dead, but her ordeal is not over, not so long as the Germans see the flame and the smoke that mark her as a cripple.

An engine goes wild, and the vibration shakes hell out of the airplane. The gunners curse a blue streak; they curse the fire and the fighters, the terrible vibrations that throw off their aim. They are wild with anger, besides being equally scared, and everything they hate is out there in the form of airplanes with black crosses on them.

The fire is out, but the engine is sheer murder, and out on that wing strips of torn metal flap and clash like a rain of bolts crashing to the top of a tin roof. And just when they sigh in relief because the engine has quieted down a 20-mm. shell goes directly into the top turret and makes a bloody hash out of the gunner. Someone said that God smiles on those who die instantly; if that is true, this man has been so favored.

The Fortress struggles valiantly to hold her place in formation; she still has her bombs, and she fights as fiercely as any of the rest. But the airplane is sluggish, the two men at the controls are working like madmen to get her to respond, and they don't know what's happened until a waist gunner calls in: "Lieutenant, there's a bunch of goddamned cables slapping me in the face!"

His voice is more irritated than frightened; intent on working his heavy machine gun, he has not yet realized that the cables run to the controls and that if just one more cable comes loose to maul his face, this airplane is going to become absolutely uncontrollable and everybody is going to have to get the hell out. No one thinks about that. Not because bailing out means almost certain capture, to say nothing of possible death on the way down, but how is the navigator going to haul on the parachute D-Ring when his arm is broken?

The cable, by some miracle, doesn't break. The engine manages to pick up at last, and they do not fall out of formation to be picked clean by the vultures waiting to pounce on the cripples. They stay in formation, they make the bomb run, the six heavy missiles smash into the target.

They bring her home, a wreck. She is a flying sieve, battered and pummeled and, according to a few of the more important laws of aerodynamics, absolutely unflyable. But they haven't told this to the pilot and copilot, so they bring her home, with one dead, one wounded.

And this is only one of the many Fortresses struggling

Mangled, torn, shot to pieces, the Forts came home

through the skies over Germany, grimly bent on bringing Mission 115 to its conclusion of target runs and the more personal run for home.

The clean air synonymous with high altitude might never have been. The sky is diseased with the signs of aerial combat, the splotches of rockets exploding in their deep, angry flame, erupting in the upper air in dirty, shredded patches, oozing down an invisible surface in greasy smoke tatters.

There is misery, agonizing pain on the part of German and American alike, their flesh ripped open by bullet and broken steel, the sightless groping of cannon shell. Amid all this the screaming of men who burn alive or hover near death is mostly silenced by the tumult of the enormous amphitheater filled with its roaring sounds of engines and the thunder of unremitting explosions.

The air is thick with the flotsam of the savage air war. Not merely the erupting rocket explosions and the smoke of burning airplanes, the shower of shell casings, but also with the minor debris of so vicious a conflict. There are shining silver objects, main exit and hatch doors of Fortresses and of twin-engine fighters. Men hurtle through this congested, moving block of contested airspace. They sail through the formations, barely missing the knifelike propellers. And sometimes they do not miss. The blood and flesh and bone and gristle spray outward like a minor rain. It happens many times, for there simply is not enough room for men dropping in the air and the swirling mass of aircraft.

One man—seen by many crews—escaped immediate death by a miracle. Knees clasped to his chest, spinning like a high diver gone berserk, he is flung through the formations. He whirls through two separate bomber boxes, through a line of fighters racing in, Indian file, and he emerges through all this without having swerved an iota in his incredible flight through space. He does not open his parachute quickly, and no one knows for certain whether or not the silk really did blossom above his head.

Many men do not fall far before death strikes in its own sardonic fashion. Bombers are crippled; they burn, or suffer a collapsed wing, or a red smear lines the inside of the cockpit windows and the living still in the crew hastily abandon their stricken machines. Too often, much too often, the crewmen crawl from their bombers, hang on desperately so they may drop at the right moment to clear obstacles, and then release their grip, only to smash into the tail surfaces of their own bombers. They are flung aside, broken and crumpled, not even twitching as they begin the fall that will last for five miles before the earth accepts the lifeless forms.

The flak, the rockets, the shells, and the bullets do strange things; they make war in the air absolutely unexpected in its sudden personal impact. A bombardier catches the full brunt of one FW-190 attack. Thirty-caliber slugs stitch a dozen holes in a neat line across his chest, and pieces of exploding shells from each side shred his ears and the side of his face. He dies without making a sound; looking at him from straight ahead, with his flying helmet still on, the boy seems almost unmarked.

Sometimes it is possible to follow the trail of a single rocket, and to note its effect in detail. As in this case ... The crew reports a twin-engine Ju-88 far behind, setting up a rocket barrage. One large flak rocket rushes ahead of its brilliant flame on a three-quarter converging course, and in its weaving path is flung through an entire formation without bothering a single bomber. It passes through and moves inexorably toward another Fortress, as the crew watches helplessly. Some fifteen feet above the B-17 and slightly to one side, the detonator rams home and the rocket's charge explodes.

In the same instant as the blossom of dark red flame appears within its black shroud, a chunk of steel finds its way to the skin of the Fortress. It tears through thin metal, rips through a control cable, and very neatly clips off the whole front of the top turret gunner's knee. Helpless, the gunner is hung up in his turret, unable to work his guns, and cursing terribly in a grim, low voice.

"Someone come get me the goddamned hell out of this sonofabitchin' thing," he grates, as the blood pours in a bright scarlet stream down his leg, and he remains upright only by bracing himself with his arms and his other leg. They ease him down carefully, slipping on the blood, and quickly fashion a tourniquet around his leg. He disdains the morphine, and lies there in the belly of the bomber, through the bomb run and all the way home, cursing without a moment's letup.

The men get hit and some of them die, but more, by the dozens, are wounded. Their fellow crew members rip off oxygen masks in the biting thin air and rush to their aid. Sometimes it is useless; more often it means that a man goes to the hospital that night instead of to the morgue. Attending a wounded and helpless man is often incredibly difficult in the midst of such a battle. There is the cold that sometimes aids the unfortunate by helping to freeze the blood, a strange sort of coagulation. The bombers shake and rock and slide and slip and bounce, and first aid is almost impossible. Sometimes several men are wounded at once, and the inside of the airplane is spattered with blood and gore, and only the fact that a man will die if he does not get help at once keeps his friends from being sick.

One man who went through the entire Mission 115 without a scratch was not fit for duty for weeks. He was not injured, but his best friend, a buddy of many years, suffered a tremendous blast in the face. He fell to the belly of the bomber, writhing, hands clasping a bloody, mangled mess that a moment before had been a normal face. The other gunner, hurrying to his aid, slipped, and fell heavily. He glanced down, and in horror noted the crushed eyeball that had been gouged by the explosion from his friend. . . .

This was the clean air war many an infantryman coveted.

13

A QUEEN DIES HARD

"I had accepted the fact that I was not going to live through this mission. It was as simple as that. I was calm; it was a strange sort of resignation. I knew for certain that it was only a matter of seconds or minutes. It was impossible for us to survive. . . ."

Post-mission debriefing of a B-17 pilot, October 14, 1943.

There is a terrible feeling when a bomber dies. Not just among the crewmen who, if not dead, are abandoning their machine in frantic haste before it becomes their tomb, but among those men in accompanying bombers who watch, helpless to assist, as a tongue of flame licks hungrily from a tear in a wing, feeds on fuel streaming backward, gathers strength, and throws itself through the rest of the airplane.

"These are the sights that tried our souls the most," a pilot once explained. "To watch from your own bomber as a sister ship suffers the flame and begins to fall off in her opening death throes, to know that within her blazing heart the men are your friends and buddies, and maybe you know the pilot's wife well, and know the kids, too.

"It involves more than the men. You don't fly a Fortress for months and years without coming to know that gallant lady in the most intimate respects. You know her, and you place in her sturdy construction, the manner in which she flies, in everything about her, not only your life, and those of your crew, but all the life to come—if we survive this stinking war, that is.

"But one thing I'll tell you. A Queen dies hard. She doesn't want to go, no more than any man inside her. You may not believe this. If you don't, it's only because you haven't been there, and you haven't watched combat-hardened men cry as a ship goes down; cry as much for the machine as for the men. Because, you see, when 10 men claimed her for their own, she was no longer just a machine. She was *their* bomber. That made her special, and made her come alive."

Again, select one of the 60 Flying Fortresses that went down over Europe on Mission 115. This story was pieced together over a period of time. It is authentic, and the result of the reports—after the war, when they were freed from prison camps—of the navigator and the tail gunner (their names, unfortunately, are not given in the documentary records)—the only two to survive. The story is also based on the accounts of crewmen of other bombers, who watched it happen. . . .

In the midst of the savage opening attacks one B-17 eases out of formation. The other pilots wonder at this, for there is no flame, no jagged metal showing. The heavy bomber begins a graceful slide on one wing, a lazy and gentle maneuver, but she does not stop her motion as her wing approaches dangerously near a neighboring Fortress. Frantically, the other pilot tramps hard down on his rudder, and skids crazily out of the way with barely a second to spare.

The Fortress keeps in her slide, beginning to pick up speed, and everyone stares hard at the big ship, and still not a mark shows. They are too far away to see a single bullet hole in the side of the B-17, near the cockpit. The hole testifies to a single armor-piercing bullet that entered the Fortress and without losing momentum struck the pilot in the head. Slicing in at an upward angle, the lone bullet entered the pilot's skull just below his eyebrow. A spray of brains, tissue, bone, and blood spattered over the copilot and splashed over the controls and against the glass and the instruments. At that moment the lifeless body of the pilot slumped back.

The shock froze the copilot in the right seat. Eyes bulging, he stared in horror, his mind and senses numbed. Unfeeling, unseeing, just numb, as though all his nerve endings had been clipped with a sharp blade. He did not move, did not close his mouth within his oxygen mask, yet he began to choke, his respiration paralyzed. Now the great bomber, controls untouched, answers the tug of a shock wave and one of her wing tips drops. The B-17 slides out of formation.

This abandoning of the formation bewilders other crews who witness it. They cannot, of course, see what has happened inside the aircraft.

The navigator, feeling the slide, watching the other bombers receding, fights his way to the cockpit, afraid that either both pilots are dead or the control cables have been cut. It is the former possibility that frightens him most, for not a word comes over the interphone, despite the repeated calls of the crew.

Leaning between the two pilot seats, the navigator shouts at the copilot. It is to no avail, and the shock retains its grasp on the horror-stricken man until the navigator in desperation strikes him on the side of the face. He begins to shake off the numbness, but it is a slow process, and his mind stays frozen from what he has seen, from the brains and blood spattered on his gloves, his arms, on the control wheel. With a gasp that rattles deathlike in his throat—heard by all the crew—he draws back in revulsion.

Now the Fortress loses altitude quickly. With every passing second the heavy bomber picks up more speed; she is in the beginnings of a death dive. Frantic, the navigator reaches over the body of his dead pilot to grasp the wheel. With all the strength at his command he hauls back, a desperate struggle to bring up the nose of the bomber from its steepening descent. But this is no way to fly a heavily loaded Fortress with three tons of bombs still in the bays, with the wind screaming past the hatches from the great speed building up. It takes more than sheer strength to regain control.

The navigator is successful in his struggle and the nose of the Flying Fortress responds to the back elevator movement. She comes out of the curving dive with a brutal force, punishing the crew and the airplane alike, imparting nearly triple weight to the men. At once, with her dangerous speed and the elevators still hauled in the back position by the navigator, she lifts her nose high and begins to rush upward. The navigator has done the best he knows how, but it is far from enough.

Then she is shuddering. The nose points at the blinding sun and the effect of the pullout vanishes too quickly. The big ship hangs on the edge of a stall and buffets in warning of potential disaster. She buffets, and then she vibrates from nose to tail from the recoil of her guns. The stray is the quarry of all the fighters, and immediately the hapless Fortress with her dead pilot and frozen copilot moves into the lonely airspace away from the formations, the black-crossed fighters come whipping in to cut her to pieces and to scatter the pieces over German soil.

Facing death, the navigator does everything he can to right the airplane that hangs almost on her nose, lift nearly destroyed, the last vestiges of aerodynamic balance vanishing. He throws his weight forward on the wheel, his feet slipping in the blood still pulsing from the pilot.

But the bomber answers sluggishly. You simply don't fly with the elevators alone; you must coordinate the ailerons and the rudder and the throttles and the trim and match everything with the demands of gravity, air resistance, angle of attack, power, and a lot more. The navigator can't do it, it is impossible for him to force the Fortress to respond. The ship doesn't receive the control she needs, and she ignores the hysterical mauling of the wheel by the sobbing man who struggles for balance over his dead pilot.

The nose drops, but it is not a smooth maneuver that will bring the heavy ship about. The B-17 slews to the side, wallowing in an almost helpless skid, like a man trying desperately to climb up a steep, slippery embankment when he has no handhold and the embankment keeps shifting beneath his frantic movements. It is impossible, of course.

The German fighters see the signs, and the Focke-Wulfs rush in, eager for the kill. Their guns and cannon blaze, and within seconds the bomber is cut and slashed to ribbons, her skin and wings punctured, two engines spitting oil and smoke, and two men already hammered to the belly of the ship, lifeless. The gunners are swinging their heavy weapons about, screaming out the positions of the incoming fighters, begging the pilot to evade, to maneuver the big airplane to give them better firing positions. The Focke-Wulfs know what they have, and they do not let go. Their noses and wings sparkle brilliantly as the shells and bullets spray out in a torrent. The gunners are frightened men; not from the fighters, for these have been faced many times before. It is the yawing, sloppy motions of the airplane that speak of slashed controls or a dead crew behind the yokes. Yet there are the fighters, and the bomber still flies, and they are gunners. Despite the fear welling up like nausea in their throats they concentrate on the fighters, and squeeze out short, steady bursts.

The nose comes up again, but the wings are banked dangerously near the vertical. The Fortress slews around in a helpless bank, shuddering as the air burbles off the wings and lift spills away. Gasping for breath, the navigator fights helplessly against the weight of his dead pilot. He screams at the copilot wrapped in his protecting shell of shock, and then he can scream no more, because the air is too thin to begin with and he cannot gasp enough oxygen into his starving lungs. He slumps down, spots before his eyes, desperate for air. It comes without warning, a mask slapped onto his face by another crewman he never sees, never recognizes. A man has saved his life, and he doesn't know—and never will know—who it was.

Now it is too late. The nose of the bomber keeps coming up as the wings continue to roll, and then the Fortress has had it. Caught behind the deadly effect of the raised nose, the diminished air speed, and the near-vertical bank, the big airplane seems to groan, and then she simply . . . quits. The lift is gone, the controls are useless, and the B-17 falls over on her back, wallowing and shuddering, the last convulsive movements before the final death plunge.

The fighters are still in there, and the navigator's fear sweeps over him. With the world reversed and gone crazy, the terrible drumbeat of cannon shells exploding through the airplane, he rips open the pilot's escape hatch—now at the bottom of the airplane—and squeezes through. The air blast throws him back and away from the Fortress and he falls gratefully through space, counting to ten slowly before yanking the D-Ring.

Within the dying, battered B-17 the guns fall silent as the crew feels the horror of a totally helpless airplane. In that moment of the inverted stall, as the bomber shudders again, the final gasp of warning, the tail gunner—wisely—scrambles through his escape hatch into space, following the navigator whose body has fallen free, unseen and unnoticed.

They are the only two men to leave. No sooner does the gunner fall away than the Fortress claws around in a sudden, fierce, inverted spin. She whirls crazily, spinning like a dervish as the earth rushes upward. Centrifugal force pins the men into the aircraft. In their heavy clothing, their parachutes and flak vests, the shrieking B-17 becomes their final tomb.

No one can ever say for certain, but it is likely that the frozen gaze of the copilot never left the face of the man next to him . . . not until that last terrible instant when the bomber met the soil of Germany, and disappeared with her eight imprisoned men in a flaming explosion.

The bombers did not often give up without a valiant struggle. With engines shot out or burning, with a wing cut to pieces, or a vertical fin and rudder ripped into tangled wreckage, with oxygen systems ablaze, with pilots smeared in their own blood and steel in their bodies, with control cables shot to ribbons and writhing like deadly snakes, still they fought to survive in the teeth of the most murderous gauntlet of the skies in all our history.

And there were those bombers that could have been abandoned by pilots and other crewmen, and were not. This scene of carnage and horror is perhaps the brightest page in the history of the VIII Bomber Command: the great bombers that fell from their protecting formations with gaping tears and wounds that revealed the skeleton framework within, that careened and tumbled with gunners hanging lifelessly over their weapons, with bombs still in the racks, turning red hot with the fire of hydraulic fluid or fuel whipping violently through the bays. Bombers dying, their death assured, but not abandoned. Still with a pilot and copilot at the controls because within that battered, torn fuselage there was a badly wounded crewman who could not leave the airplane, or if this were possible, would never survive the wrenching shock of an opening parachute. Sometimes men were unconscious or their parachutes had been shot to ribbons. Whatever the reason, they could not jump.

So the pilots stayed at their controls. Sometimes they made it down, and most or all of them survived, and the injured received the medical attention to keep them alive.

More often they did not succeed. They met death together, reaching the end of their last flight as fire tore open the fuel tanks, or the earth leaped up to consume machine and men in a final terrible caress.

14

SCHWEINFURT BELOW

Colonel Budd J. Peaslee: "We are right behind the leading formation as the bomb run starts. They are in good order, but one of their groups of 21 bombers has been reduced to *two!* The unit has been devastated, and it's more than a little pathetic to see those two lonesome guys plugging along as though all were intact.

"McLaughlin is all concentration now. He ignores the tigers completely and talks to the bombardier. They are hooking the controls to the bomb sight. From now until bombs are away the bombardier will fly the Fortress by remote control. The pilot rests his hands on the wheel. He can overpower the bomb-sight control if it becomes necessary. The controls move in little metallic jerks.

"Down below us, in the nose, the bombardier is searching for his aiming point. When he finds it, he will push a switch and the bomb-bay doors will grind open. The trick is to move the sight indices together; and to do this the bombardier controls the flight of the airplane by moving a knob on the AFCE. This swings the Fortress slightly to the right or the left.

" 'Let's make it good,' I call to McLaughlin. 'We've come a long way for this.'

"The fighters come at us from all directions. It will be almost a relief to get into the flak zone. They will break off there, to pick us up again as we come off the target and out of the zone.

"We begin to get a few bursts of flak. It is inaccurate. They are scared, too, down on the ground 23,000 feet below. They are firing while we are still out of range. We rapidly move into range, and the ground fire changes from meager and inaccurate to accurate and intense. The sky around us is filled with black bursts. Some of it we hear—the handful of rocks on the

tin roof again, when the bursts are within 50 feet. The men
handling the guns at Schweinfurt are no amateurs.

Queen of the bombers ...   B-17F Flying Fortress

"It is past time now for the fighters to leave us, but they do
not. They stay with us, fighting in their own flak. This is very
strange. Their orders must have been to defend Schweinfurt
at all costs.

"I have never seen braver men than these fighter pilots, our
mortal enemies. If I were the German in command of men
and machines like these, I believe I could stop the daylight
bombing of Germany—at least up to this point. But Hermann
Göring is their commander, and he has chosen to violate a
simple principle of war. He should have ordered total annihi-
lation of the first formation of each attacking force. Our
commanders live in fear that he may one day do so. Today he
has come the nearest to achieving that principle, for his guns
allow only a few of our leading aircraft to escape. But he
does not know—and at the moment neither do I—that soon
the Mustangs will come, the fighters that can cover us anywhere in Germany. Thank God for Hermann—he is our
friend.

"The determination to keep us from reaching the target has
been futile, but they have made us pay a terrible price, a price
that we cannot afford to pay. The stakes in this game have

been terrific for both sides, and the devil took the pot. Below us Schweinfurt is rapidly going to hell as the bomb strings ahead of ours walk through the city. Its dead will outnumber our own by fantastic figures, and the machinery that has made the ball bearings is literally beginning to fly apart.

"The bomb run is good in spite of the fighters and the flak—the kind we refer to as 'flak you can walk on.' It seems as though our aircraft will never reach the bomb-release line —the seconds drag by. Finally, just as we are thinking the bombs must be hung, we feel the bomber lighten in regular little jerks and we know the halfway point has been passed.

" 'Bombs away,' the bombardier reports.

"McLaughlin releases the controls from the bomb sight, and we swing into a right turn toward France. It's a slow turn for reassembly, but there is little need to reassemble. Those left of us are already huddling close.

" 'Primary bombed.' The strike message flashes back to England. It is a simple statement, nothing more.

"As our right wing dips in the turn, it reveals our approach route, both on the ground and in the air. At our level I can see the rear formations approaching Schweinfurt. They look ragged and are under intense attack. The fighters have left the empty planes for the time being to charge those still carrying bombs toward their city. Our formations do not waver as they crawl across the sky. It is as though they were being pulled by an invisible chain into the thresher of flak over the city, and there they will disgorge their heads of grain, the thousand-pounders.

"Far below them on the ground I see part of our ante to the devil's pot. Our course is plainly marked by rising columns of smoke. I know what those columns mean and I count them—nine, ten, eleven. They represent 11 bombers, with 110 men aboard, punctuating the line from the Initial Point to the target.

"Behind our dipped right wing I can see the city, and it is smudged with smoke in the sunlight. As I watch, and as more bombs splash down, the smudge is renewed and thickened. From now until long after the war is over there will be no windows in this city, and the cold winter winds will sweep unchecked through the homes—all the homes, rich and poor alike, for there will be no window glass at any price.

"We are pulling away from the target toward the French border when there is an unexplainable occurrence. One of our bombers climbs out of formation. He does not appear to be damaged and has plenty of power left in his engines. There are no fighters near us at the moment, and I wonder what his object can be. I broadcast an order for him to return to formation, but there is no acknowledgment. Then parachutes begin to blossom behind and below him. They come at regular intervals until there are ten—the full crew.

"What in hell is this? I will never know. The bomber continues momentarily to fly beside us, then slowly noses over and, gaining speed, disappears below. I cannot fathom it. Did the crew hold a caucus—decide there was no future in this business, decide to quit the war? I wonder.

" 'Well,' McLaughlin tells me over the interphone, 'we have done our flying for Uncle Sam for the day. Now we fly for *us*.' "

The two combat divisions of Mission 115—the 1st and the 3rd —lost 21 bombers shot down before they reached Schweinfurt. Of the total force dispatched, 228 Fortresses reached the target area; a force, notes the army air forces' official history, that was "sadly mauled."

Despite the terrible casualties and the battering received by the Fortresses, an official army air forces' study made after the war was able to report that "the bombing was unusually effective." The sudden course change near the Initial Point proved an unexpected source of relief to some Fortresses by confusing the formations of attacking German fighters, and their blows diminished greatly as the bombers wheeled into their runs.

The first force enjoyed excellent visibility, and the immediate result of the run was "a high concentration of bombs in all the target areas. In all, the 228 B-17's that succeeded in bombing dropped some 395 tons of high explosives and 88 tons of incendiaries on and about all three of the big bearings plants. Of the 1,122 high-explosive bombs dropped, 143 fell within the factory area, 88 of which were direct hits on the factory buildings. The incendiaries, as usual, proved somewhat less accurate."

There are discrepancies and conflicting reports of the bomb run, which is to be expected considering the brief time involved, the savagery of the fighter attacks and flak, and the exhaustion of the men both physically and emotionally. The official army air forces' historical report states that "the second-force bombardiers were handicapped by clouds of smoke caused by the preceding attack." Many of these bombardiers were affected, but not all, as Colonel Peaslee explained: "I sat only a hundred yards behind the 305th on the bomb run and only 100 feet from the 306th.

"The 306th and the 92d had each lost two squadrons at the bomb run, so we joined together and bombed as a group. The 305th had been reduced to two aircraft and was bombing with the lead combat wing commanded by Lieutenant Colonel Theodore Milton. We had no mixup at the Initial Point and everything went just as it was supposed to.

"It was a real good bomb run and the targets were in the clear as the bombs of the lead formation had not hit the ground when our bombs went away. We certainly had no problems of visibility from smoke, although some trailing bombers might have encountered some."

It was gratifying to note, stated the official report of Mission 115, 1st Bombardment Division, that the 40th Combat Wing, although greatly depleted in force from previous operations, was able to place all of their bombs "squarely on the designated Mean Point of Impact."

Crippled badly, and suffering from many disabled planes in its formation, the 40th Wing turned in one of the most excellent bombing runs of the entire war. Fifty-three per cent of all its bombs dropped, photos revealed beyond question, fell within 1,000 feet of the aiming point of the primary target.

There is no contesting the fact that the lead division suffered a terrible beating by the time it was in position to drop its bombs. The case of the 305th Bombardment Group is most striking. Major G. G. Y. Normand of the 385th Squadron led the formation, and grimly held his wing position through the worst attacks of the entire mission. When the target finally was reached, the bombardier, dissatisfied with the approach, called for a bomb run separate from the remainder of the wing.

But Major Normand, knowing what the bombardier did not—that there were only two other planes left in the entire formation (Peaslee remembers seeing only two planes: Normand's and one other)—wisely elected to fly with the group directly ahead, since the fighter attacks were still continuing. The bombs from these three airplanes, reported the bombardier, fell to the left of the aiming point, toward the center of Schweinfurt. No sooner had the bomb-bay doors closed than Major Normand watched another of his bombers plunge away from the formation, wrapped in flames.

The course change near the Initial Point, final evaluation reveals, assisted a major percentage of the bombing Fortresses in gaining temporary relief from the attacking fighters.

Bomb release

The German pilots hammered without respite at Peaslee's formation, as he and Normand recalled grimly.

Captain James C. McClanahan, bombardier in the lead Fortress of the 384th Group, reported at the debriefing after the mission: "The visibility was good over the target. I saw our bombs hit and I can say we knocked hell out of it. The bombs burst and the smoke rolled up, then there was a big explosion and all of a sudden there was a great splash of fire right in the center of everything."

During the bomb run of several groups, starting at about the time the Fortresses approached the Initial Point, there occurred one of the most baffling incidents of World War II, and an enigma that to this day defies all explanation.

As the bombers of the 384th Group swung into the final bomb run after passing the Initial Point, the fighter attacks fell off. This point is vital, and pilots were queried extensively, as were other crew members, as to the position at that time of the German fighter planes. Every man interrogated was firm in his statement that "at the time there were no enemy aircraft above."[1]

At this moment the pilots and top turret gunners, as well as several crewmen in the plexiglas noses of the bombers, reported a cluster of discs in the path of the 384th's formation and closing with the bombers. The startled exclamations focused attention on the phenomenon, and the crews talked back and forth, discussing and confirming the astonishing sight before them.

The discs in the cluster were agreed upon as being silver colored, about one inch thick and three inches in diameter. They were easily seen by the B-17 crewmen, gliding down slowly in a very uniform cluster.

And then the "impossible" happened. B-17 Number 026 closed rapidly with a cluster of discs; the pilot attempted to evade an imminent collision with the objects, but was unsuccessful in his maneuver. He reported at the intelligence debriefing that his "right wing went directly through a cluster with absolutely no effect on engines or plane surface."

The intelligence officers pressed their questioning, and the pilot stated further that one of the discs was heard to strike

[1] Memorandum of October 24, 1943, from Major E. R. T. Holmes, F.L.O., 1st Bombardment Division. Reference FLO/1BW/REP/126, to M.I. 15. War Office, Whitehall, London, S.W. (copy to Colonel E. W. Thomson, A-2, Pinetree).

the tail assembly of his B-17, but that neither he nor any member of the crew heard or witnessed an explosion.

He further explained that about twenty feet from the discs the pilots sighted a mass of black debris of varying sizes in clusters of three by four feet.

The SECRET report added: "Also observed two other A/C flying through silver discs with no apparent damage. Observed discs and debris two other times but could not determine where it came from."

No further information on this baffling incident has been uncovered, with the exception that such discs were observed by pilots and crew members on missions prior to, and after Mission 115 of October 14, 1943.

The 1st Air Division's Circular Error Report[2] for its groups read as follows:

92d Group	1,800 feet for 61 bombs
305th Group	2,000 feet for 8 bombs
306th Group	1,920 feet for 16 bombs
91st Group	1,100 feet for 39 bombs
381st/351st Groups	5,930 feet for 60 bombs
379th Group	1,010 feet for 34 bombs
384th Group	1,660 feet for 18 bombs
303d Group	2,369 feet for 19 bombs

The 388th Group, which formed as the low group of the lead combat wing of the 2d Air Task Force (entire 3d Air Division), reported the target area as heavily obscured by smoke from the previous attack of the preceding division. The lead bombardier was unable to identify either the target itself or the marshaling yards that were located to the south. He set up his horizontal cross hairs on the bridge over the Main River which was southeast of the target. Unfortunately, the prearranged check point for the course, which was to have passed over the marshaling yards, was also obscured by smoke and the bombardier had no positive check on his course.

The bombs of this division, strike photographs revealed,

---

[2]Circular error: a bombing error measured by the radial distance of a point of bomb impact, or mean point of impact, from the center of the target, excluding gross errors.

fell slightly to the right of the target, enveloping the southern half of the target and the eastern end of the marshaling yards.

Colonel Van DeVander, leader of the 385th Group, which led the 4th Combat Wing, 3d Air Division, reported: "We had perfect visibility and could see the target from forty to fifty miles away. The lead wing never did make a definite turn, and did not drop any flares. I was going to go inside of the wing ahead; however, after firing two flares, they started swinging back in front of us. I had to swing over, and that may have bothered the 94th Group. I set up the Automatic Flight Control Equipment and gave it to the bombardier. The pilot turned it off accidentally, but I immediately switched it back on again, and we had a perfect run. Flak was not bad in some areas, but intense over the target. Then I could see many bursts. We made a fairly sharp turn off the target, but we pulled into fairly good defensive formation. I could not catch up on any distance on the lead wing without increasing speed. The 94th Group said that they could increase their speed, and we then made up distance and fell into formation. There were some fighter attacks, not heavy."

Of all the Fortresses dispatched, it will be recalled, a final number of 228 bombers reached the target area. One additional B-17 was forced to get rid of its bomb load, which it dropped on the first "target of opportunity," and did not contribute to the attack.

The B-17 force struck the targets—the primary of the ball-bearing works and the secondary of the city of Schweinfurt—in two waves that extended from 21,000 to 24,000 feet altitude. The first wave—1st Air Division—started its bomb runs at 1439 hours, and the last plane passed over the industrial center of Schweinfurt six minutes later, at 1445 hours.

Six minutes later the first wave of the 3d Air Division (2d Air Task Force) moved into its bombing run; this continued for exactly six more minutes. From the beginning to the end of all bomb runs eighteen minutes were consumed.

The 1st and 3d Air Divisions, as noted in an earlier chapter, dispatched an effective total of 291 Fortresses on Mission 115. Of this force, 26 bombers turned back to England because of mechanical and equipment failures. Five aborted the mission from personnel failures, two became lost in the overcast during attempt to assemble, and excessive fuel consumption forced another abort.

The loss of these 34 bombers, plus that of the 60 B-24's of the 2d Air Division, and other aborts, depleted Mission 115's strength to 257 bombers. The fierce Luftwaffe fighter attacks on the approach and penetration into Germany cut another 28 bombers out of formation before the target was reached, leaving 229 Fortresses. Battle damage forced one of these to dump its bombs on the first available target.

There was no question—either then or after careful study of the results of the attack—that in respect to effective bombing, Mission 115 was an unqualified success.

Nearly four hundred tons of high-explosive bombs and 88 tons of incendiaries fell on or about all three of the major ball-bearings works. The plants were struck heavily, much more effectively, in fact, than in the initial raid of August 17, which had caused a severe drop in the production of one plant.

The success of Mission 115 left no question but that it was the most important of the sixteen raids carried out during the war against the Schweinfurt complex. Beyond any doubt it was the most effective in bombing, and it caused the most damage to plants in the city. It also caused, directly, the greatest interference with production. The repercussions of the raid that swept the industrial hierarchy and the government itself led directly to a reorganization of the entire German bearings industry.

"The raids of 14 October," states the army air forces in its official history, "coming upon the still fresh damage of 17 August, alarmed the German industrial planners to a degree that almost justified the optimistic estimates made by Allied observers in the fall of that year."

All this, however, still lay in the future. For the moment there was the task for the bombers of surviving to reach England.

The prospects of survival were not good. Just after the lead group of the 3d Air Division came off the target a force of 160 single-engine fighters rushed in for "a very intense attack." The worst losses of Mission 115 were yet to come.

15

HOW THE GERMANS FOUGHT

Mission 115 earned its niche in the history of war as the most savage aerial battle ever fought. Not the least of the factors contributing to this distinction were the unprecedented fury and efficiency of the defending Luftwaffe fighter force. The presence of Thunderbolt escort fighters for approximately two hundred and forty miles out from England served substantially to reduce the initial effect of the enemy attack. Thirteen fighters definitely destroyed, as well as several damaged, resulted in an immediate if minor depletion of the enemy strength. More important, however, the aggressive Thunderbolt maneuvers broke up attacking German formations. This reduced the total time of enemy attack on the B-17's, and prevented the terrible casualties from becoming even greater.

As we have seen, the German pilots hit the bombers shortly after they penetrated the airspace over the continent. The harassment all the way to Schweinfurt was constant and brutal, and to a lessened degree the enemy struck again and again at the battered force as it struggled to reach the safety of England. In some instances single-engine fighters harried bomber groups more than midway across the Channel. It is unfortunate that weather kept the Thunderbolts and Spitfires which were to have provided withdrawal escort on the ground. An effective withdrawal screen would have saved several more Fortresses.

Most of the tactics that the Germans employed against Mission 115—formation attacks, use of rockets and heavy nose-mounted cannon, air-to-air bombing, concentration on one bomber group at a time, and hitting swiftly at all stragglers—had been used before, especially in the terrible three days of October 8, 9, and 10. But not until October 14 did the Luftwaffe reach such efficiency in the maximum coordination of all their weapons and tactics.

The blows hurled against the B-17 formations varied from wing to wing, but consistent general patterns emerged. The most dominant of these was the large screen of single-engine

Bomber destroyer—cannon, machine guns, rockets. The Junkers
Ju-88 modified for the killer missions

fighters, usually Messerschmitt Me-109's or Focke-Wulf FW-190's. These raced into the bombers with an attack from dead ahead, firing their 20-mm. cannon and machine guns until very close to the formation. On the heels of the single-engine fighters, thus protected from B-17 defensive fire until the last moment, were large formations of twin-engine fighters. These roared in to attack in waves, the fighter mass launching deadly rockets in heavy salvos (with four rockets released from under-wing positions by each fighter).

The majority of single-engine attacks came from the nose, between ten o'clock and two o'clock, and were pressed home with three to five fighters. While these nose attacks closed to point-blank range, other single-engine fighters attacked simultaneously from high and low positions "in such rapid succession that gunners could not even make observations. At the same time the twin-engine fighters stood out from our tail positions and lobbed rockets into the formation."

Another pilot reports: "Flights of the two-engine aircraft stood off at 1,500 yards at both sides and on the tails of the formations to lob rockets or heavy cannon shells into formations. They hit with devastating effect. Simultaneously the single-engine fighters attacked from the nose, from high and low, spraying us with 20-mm. cannon. During the interval between waves of the twin-engine aircraft, the single-engine fighters dived through the formations from all angles.

"Those single-engine boys resorted to every tactic of aerial combat known, and from all angles. They even dreamed up a couple of new ideas. They barrel-rolled wildly through the formations, hurling out streams of cannon shells and tracers."

The moment the single-engine fighters exhausted their ammunition, they dived at high speed for the nearest fields to refuel and to replenish ammunition, and returned at once to the battle as it marched across Germany. Since re-forming into tight groups was impossible for most of these fighters, they swarmed individually into the Fortresses like hornets, striking targets of opportunity, and racing into and through the formations from all directions. During the intervals when the twin-engine fighters dropped away to refuel and rearm, the single-engine planes especially harassed the bombers. And soon afterward the heavier fighters returned. They reassembled in tight formations, sweeping in with their advantage of massed waves in precision attacks.

Messerschmitt Me-110, twin-engine fighter mainstay

As the stream of Flying Fortresses neared the target, a definite change in the pattern of attacks emerged. The Germans began to concentrate on a single formation, closing in to point-blank firing runs. This was the most feared of all the tactics the Germans might adopt, and its effectiveness was appalling. The masses of twin-engine strikes sent rockets into the midst of the formations, scattering the planes and diluting the effectiveness of their defensive fire screen. Pressing their advantage to the utmost, both single- and twin-engine fighters rushed in close, pressing their runs with heavy cannon and machine guns. The moment a cripple showed, a swarm of single-engine fighters immediately pounced to deliver the *coup de grâce*.

The Germans changed completely one previous pattern in their air-defense maneuvers. On earlier raids, a cripple that straggled from the formation was left to the attentions of fighters such as the Messerschmitt Me-110. Heavily armed with four cannon and two machine guns firing forward in a massed stream from the nose, the Me-110 was handicapped by a much slower speed than the single-engine airplanes. Against a crippled Fortress, however, its speed was excellent, and its ability to deliver tremendous bursts of firepower usually assured that the B-17 went down. On this mission, however, the Germans' single-engine fighters swooped away from the mass formation to hit cripples and stragglers, while the heavier and larger fighters stayed with the bomber stream.

As best they could, the planners of Mission 115 routed the two bombardment divisions around German ground defenses. The bombers reported "en route meager inaccurate flak" at Domburg, West Schouwen, Woensdrecht, and Antwerp, and "en route meager accurate flak" at Limburg, Friedberg, and Würzburg. Flak over the target was "intense and accurate."

Bomber crews reported anti-aircraft bursts as red, white, and black, and also caught the interest of intelligence officers with descriptions of flak that burst with a rich "purple flash, and produced a purple smoke cloud." For the first time in any numbers the Germans employed flak rockets. These were seen near Worms as intense bursts of flame near the ground and thin smoke trails racing into the sky after the bombers. They proved ineffective, and were more interesting than dangerous.

The array of aircraft thrown into the battle was unprecedented, not merely in number but in types. The single-engine fighters included the familiar Messerschmitt Me-109's and Focke-Wulf FW-190's. For the first time in daylight intercepts the crews also sighted the small Heinkel He-113. "They were unmistakable as the He-113's," a pilot reported. "They were flown by green kids, were sloppy in their maneuvers, and they left themselves wide open for our gunners. They got the hell shot out of them."

German twin-engine fighters included the twin-tailed Messerschmitt Me-110's and swarms of Messerschmitt Me-210's, much faster than the earlier fighters. Also among the twin-engine attackers were the Junkers Ju-88 bombers modified to carry rockets and heavy armament batteries. Focke-Wulf FW-189's, normally seen close to the ground in support operations, also swept in against the Fortress stream.

B-17 pilots identified the vintage Heinkel He-111 bomber with its broad, unmistakable elliptical wings, which the Germans used primarily as rocket launching platforms. At 22,000 feet several bomber crews were startled to see single-engine Junkers Ju-87 Stukas, broad fixed landing gear unmistakable, as they struggled in the thin air. Dornier Do-217 twin-engine bombers, bristling with rockets and cannon, also attacked in waves.

Into the savage air struggle the Germans threw even their two main four-engine bombers. Heinkel He-177's made rocket and cannon attacks against the Fortresses, while the giant Focke-Wulf FW-200K Kuriers, raiders of Atlantic merchant convoys, cruised behind the Fortresses to radio to fighter vector stations and flak headquarters sites the exact altitude, speed, and position of the American bombers.

The enemy fighters were marked with a dazzling variety of colors and stripes. Me-109's were distinctive with gleaming paint surfaces that featured an orange-colored nose and underside of the cowling, with the rest of the airplane black. Several FW-190's were completely yellow, and polished to a high gloss. Me-110's had a large yellow patch on the center underside of the airplanes, and many Ju-99's were seen with all-white bellies and multicolored striped tops.

The 3d Air Division reported still further variations in fighter identifications. They saw Ju-88's with all-black bellies and upper surfaces painted white or cream. Me-109's appeared with green bellies and the rest of the aircraft all silver. The four-engine FW-200K Kuriers were all painted silver. Several FW-190's were seen with yellow noses and green cowlings, and the He-177 four-engine bombers appeared in mixed black-and-white color schemes.

The 1st Air Division reported that between 250 and 300 enemy fighters were airborne and in positions to attack their formations in a continuous running air battle. Groups of from 50 to 60 fighters pressed home their attacks to "ramming distance," and broke off their repeated passes only when fresh groups arrived as reinforcements to institute new sweeps into the formations. Other attacks were made from various positions of the clock in groups of three to seven fighters, with every firing run "pressed home most vigorously." These served to distract much of the firepower from the heavy massed fighter runs from dead on.

The first attacks of the day against the lead air division began at 1333 hours, after the Thunderbolts turned back near Aachen. They continued until the French border was reached near Ludwigshafen. At 1647 hours—after three hours and fourteen minutes of continuous air battle—the Germans left.

"The air was literally filled with single-engine and twin-engine fighters," states the official report of Mission 115 by the 1st Bombardment Division, "with FW-190's acting as diversion screens for the twin-engine ships. The single-engine aircraft attacked to attract the gunners, and at the same time twin-engine fighters in formations of three, four, and five slipped in behind the diversionary groups. When the Germans attacked in this fashion, twin-engine fighters released their rockets as close as two hundred yards and then slipped away. Most of these attacks were made against tail positions."

The 1st Division encountered most of its intense opposition en route to the target; attacks by German fighters dropped off considerably after the bombs were released, with only a few attacks made on two of the withdrawing task forces in this division.

The 3d Air Division in its withdrawal suffered a particularly severe and determined attack. "A very intense attack was made against the lead group by approximately 160 single-engine fighters just after the target," reported a 3d Air Division wing commander. "They attacked in waves of ten to twenty." The 3d Air Division commander reported that "the enemy aircraft approached our formation in compact groups and in overpowering strength."

Certain groups were virtually slaughtered by the Germans, and others miraculously found the gaps in the air battle and met only mild defense by the German pilots. "The whole German Air Force was there," reported a weary Major George W. Harris, Jr., who led the 384th Group. "They dived in sixes and in fours and everything else, and they stayed with us until we had reached France on the way back."

"We had no trouble until the P-47's left," said the leader of the 306th Group, "then all hell broke loose. Between the Rhine and the target our formations were attacked by at least three hundred enemy aircraft. Rocket guns mounted under the wings of enemy aircraft fired into our tight defensive formation caused the highest rate of casualties. The crews described the scene as similar to a parachute invasion, there were so many crews bailing out." This group lost ten bombers and 100 men.

The 388th Group, as part of the second attacking wave of bombers, was one of the few units to enjoy a miraculous reprieve from the slaughter in the air. Eighteen bombers took off, two aborted, and the remaining 16 bombers went on. "Enemy fighter opposition was moderate," reported the group leader at debriefing. "Fighters attacked from the vicinity of Eupen in eastern Belgium, in to the target, and all the way back to the French coast. There were never more than ten fighters in the air around the group at any one time, generally five to six. Most attacks were from the tail." All 16 bombers came home, and only one man out of the 160 aboard was wounded.

The 92d Bomber Group (first wave) reported that ten minutes after the first German planes appeared in sight, a large flight of twin-engine Me-210's came in fast from astern and a little high. "At 2,000 yards they split four ways to attack the groups in the rear of the formations. From then on both twin-engine and single-engine fighters attacked viciously."

Usually the heavy fighter planes released their rockets from beyond the range of the bombers' .50-caliber guns, though many also came in as close as 200 yards. Single-engine fighters carried these projectiles beneath the belly, and the twin-engine planes held two rockets beneath each wing, making a total of four. When fired, the rockets trailed a brilliant and long red streak.

Several crews reported Me-210's closing in to about five hundred yards, when "suddenly the aircraft seemed to disappear in a brilliant glare. There were four very bright flashes.

Me-210 diving away from three oclock...

The rockets were on the way. Then they came in close to use the 20-mm. cannon."

All reports were consistent that the rocket bursts were at least as large, or larger, than a heavy flak burst. Many of the rockets obviously were of a larger size, for the crews stated emphatically that these were "at least four times as large and as powerful in their effect as an 88-mm. gun burst."

In the Ruhr area the fighters released rockets that "burst in a continuous stream of flashes. A red flare exploded first, followed by dense black smoke. Out of each burst came clusters of smaller shells that exploded a few seconds later. Some rockets were extremely large, bursting with four times the size of flak."

A pilot of the 92d Group reported: "Whenever a Fort was hit by such a projectile, it immediately exploded or fell apart." One such victim was the one reported by Colonel Peaslee, hit directly ahead of his own airplane. A careful check of observations from all crews surviving in this group revealed two bombers lost within seconds. The first dropped from the formation in a steady dive, the number three and four engines burning, and the propeller of another engine feathered. Nine parachutes blossomed: "a slightly cheering prospect in the middle of hell."

Then, exactly at 1357 hours, a rocket sailed into the wing root of B-17 Number 321, piloted by Lieutenant Clough. "The wing blew off, a tremendous sheet of flame ripped out of the airplane, and it whipped into a very tight spin. One chute was seen to come out before the airplane exploded at 21,000 feet."

Another report described a new type of cannon never experienced before Mission 115: "Several large twin-engine aircraft closed to 850 yards to fire their rockets, or to blaze away with cannon shells of a large size and type never before experienced. Large flashes were seen from the leading edges of the wings close to the wing roots. Continuous fire for a short time was observed, until the aircraft turned away. Gun flashes and projectile bursts were larger than 20-mm. fire, and the bursts exploded in the formation with black smoke on top and white smoke on the bottom. The bursts were equivalent in explosive force to flak.

"B-17's hit by these projectiles invariably started to burn fiercely, and immediately. One projectile, not otherwise identified, was observed to hit the number-four engine nacelle of the lead aircraft of the second element of the 92d Group, and after one-half minute the engine caught fire. The shell seemed to sit on the wing of the nacelle and burn brilliantly."

Both air divisions reported attempts by German fighters to bomb the formations from higher altitudes. In one instance five Focke-Wulf FW-190's drifted in above the 92d Group, approximately fifteen hundred feet over the bombers and flying parallel. When almost directly overhead several objects, "which looked like small standard bombs," fell away toward the B-17's. White smoke streamers trailed the bombs, which fell in a tight spiral. None of these bombs struck the Fortresses, and they all dropped out of sight without exploding.

Several times single-engine fighters made individual bombing attacks, which varied in approach. An Me-109 flew 1,000 feet above and parallel with one group formation. Directly above the bombers it dropped "several objects which appeared to be small and round. The crews stated that they believed these objects were dropped over the side of the enemy aircraft by hand, in rapid succession. No strikes were made. . . ."

A bomber group in the 3d Air Division was attacked by an Me-109 which flew along the same course as the Fortresses. This fighter stayed high; at 32,000 feet it was at least 5,000 feet above the B-17's. The bomb dropped ahead of the formation, "about a thousand yards out, and exploded well below the group. Strings of smoke were observed when the bomb was dropped."

Still another group reported a number of incendiaries which showered down. "These were spider-like in appearance; they burst with a heavy black smoke that looked like oil smoke. They exploded with a dull flash."

And to add a final note to these attacks, several Me-110 twin-engine fighters were observed to fly above and ahead of the formations, releasing aerial mines slung beneath parachutes. These drifted wide of the formations—their closest approach was reported to be at least 5,000 feet. Several exploded with a "blinding light" in the air, the others drifted out of sight without any detonation.

In no instances were the attempts to destroy the Fortresses by these aerial bombing attacks reported as successful.

One sighting—made up by the crews of several bombers— has to this day remained unexplained. The sighting is included in the mission report of the 92d Group, and is reproduced verbatim:

> Four P-47's, thought to be friendly American aircraft flown by the enemy, were observed on the approach to the Initial Point at 22,000 feet, heading 120° Magnetic. These aircraft flew out to the side and parallel with the combat wing formation in the manner of fighter escort. They suddenly executed a 90° turn in toward the head of the combat wing formation. These aircraft were originally at 800 yards on the port beam. They approached to 300 yards when they nosed up and away, showing a full-plan view of themselves. *Positive identification is claimed.* The aircraft had brown fuselages and the wings were a very dark color, almost black. No white cowling and no white tail markings were observed. No insignia was observed and the aircraft did not open fire. Several B-17's fired on them. The last P-47 escort had long since departed and the enemy aircraft had been attacking for some time at this point.

Heavy anti-aircraft shells and rockets from the ground, and in the air machine guns, cannon, rockets, bombs, aerial mines, incendiary bombs, and even hand-thrown weapons, made up the arsenal the Luftwaffe hurled against Mission 115. There was still another; this report is typical of many:

> On three different occasions FW-190's swooped down and just over the parachutes of our men who had bailed out. They raced in close, propellers just clearing the chutes. The slip stream either scooped air out of the chutes or collapsed them, and on each occasion the chute and wearer plummeted to the ground.

16

TIME HACK

To tell in full detail the stories of the hundreds of gunners engaged in Mission 115 who returned to their British bases for debriefing would obviously fill a large volume in itself. In addition to those men, moreover, there were some 480 gunners in the 60 heavy bombers lost on the mission. They can contribute nothing to this chapter, in which the typical work of a few gunners in only three groups, during a period of less than sixty seconds, will be selected as representative of the whole titanic struggle.

In the debriefing records of these three groups alone it was possible to find the details of eleven attacks on the bombers of those groups that took place within the single minute from 1515 to 1516 hours. I must emphasize, however, that unfortunately the gunner debriefing reports do not include the attacks of those fighters that stood off out of range of the Fortress guns and lobbed rockets into the bomber formations. Out of this time period of one minute in which we shall describe eleven attacks, it is estimated—on the basis of report times of rocket launchings into the Fortresses—that no less than forty to fifty German fighter attacks were taking place *simultaneously*.

An explanation is necessary here of the basis on which gunnery claims are made and evaluated. Beyond any doubt the accurate tabulation of German fighters destroyed in air battle was plagued by an overlapping of claims which tended to increase in almost geometrical progression with the number of bombers engaged. With dozens of gunners sometimes firing simultaneously at the same target, such duplication was inevitable. And then, how to establish accurately whether or not a fighter had *definitely* been destroyed? The German pilots had the trick, after firing a burst at a bomber, of flipping over on their backs and plunging straight down, black smoke pouring from their exhausts. Inexperienced gunners, in the heat of battle, could well mistake the flame and smoke from a fighter's four or six cannon as battle damage inflicted by their own guns.

For a gunner to receive credit for an enemy plane as *Destroyed*, it must be witnessed descending completely enveloped in flames, and not merely with flames coming out of the cowling or a wing. A claim for *Destroyed* was granted when the airplane was seen to disintegrate in midair, or if the complete wing or tail assembly was shot away from it, but not if only parts were shot away; experience with our own planes made it all too obvious that an airplane could be shot almost to pieces, and still return safely.

If the fighter were single-engine, and the pilot bailed out, credit would be given for a *Destroyed*. *Probably Destroyed* or *Probable* included those fighters of whose destruction there was no certainty, but which seemed so badly damaged, or so completely on fire, that it was unlikely they would survive. If any of the fighter's parts were shot away, it would be listed as a *Damaged*. Bullets striking an enemy fighter with no sign of the foregoing would mean no claim.

In addition, an elaborate checking and cross-checking system to prevent duplication of claims was worked out. The time of the encounter, the type of enemy aircraft claimed destroyed, the method of destruction, the geographical location of the engagement, the altitude at which the combat took place—all these factors were entered on diagrams in such a way that a virtual three-dimensional reconstruction of the action was achieved.

For Mission 115 against Schweinfurt, the total claims came to 186 fighters *Destroyed*, 27 *Probables*, and 89 *Damaged*. We know today that these claims include duplications, and that the Germans more accurately lost somewhere about one hundred fighters—the exact number will never be known. Enemy records show total combat losses for the day, exclusive of those not attributable to army air forces' action, of 43 fighters destroyed in combat and 31 damaged. The problem is that the Germans did not employ a system similar to ours in evaluating their own losses. Their records would not support a gunner's claim for a *Destroyed*, *if the pilot survived* the destruction of a fighter. Germans who worked in command headquarters have related that often, when (for example) 26 fighters were destroyed and 19 pilots escaped with their lives, only seven planes would be listed as destroyed.

Time Hack—1515 hours to 1516 hours:

B-17 Number 250 flying low position of 548th Squadron, at 21,000 feet, part of 385th Group: Sergeant T. E. Cavanaugh in the right waist watched a Junkers Ju-88 closing from three o'clock level. Cavanaugh fired 40 rounds; at 400 yards the Ju-88 smoked heavily, and whirled crazily out of control. Two chutes came out.

As Cavanaugh fired at the Ju-88, another fighter came in dead astern, level. Sergeant W. N. Sweeney in tail-gunner position opened fire at 1,200 yards. Fighter wavered in midair, flipped over on its back and dropped qucikly, trailing flames from the right engine. Cavanaugh was given a *Destroyed*, Sweeney a claim for *Damaged*.

B-17 Number 547 in number-three position of lead squadron, 549th, of the 385th Group at 22,500 feet: One Me-110 attacked from eleven o'clock low. Sergeant A. R. Millican in second gun position behind top turret opened fire at 800 yards. Tracers struck the nose and the left wing. Left engine burst into flames, and the fighter whirled out of control. Man in left waist position watched the airplane hit the ground and explode, Millican was credited with a *Destroyed*.

B-17 Number 717 of 548th Squadron, 385th Group, flying position number six of high squadron at 23,000 feet: One Me-110 dived from ten-thirty o'clock. Lieutenant R. C. Howard, navigator, fired 65 rounds. Tracers seen to strike fuselage and wing. Fighter peeled off into a long glide. *No claim*.

B-17 Number 439 of 410th Squadron, 94th Group, flying twenty-five miles south of Schweinfurt: Me-109 came in fast from ten o'clock, swinging to seven o'clock, and passing out at two o'clock. Sergeant C. T. Troott tracked fighter, squeezed out 50 rounds, struck cockpit area heavily. Fighter exploded, disintegrated in midair. Troott received a *Destroyed*.

B-17 Number 3446, same squadron, same group: Sergeant F. F. Riordan tracked an Me-109 coming in at six o'clock high. Opened fire at range of 700 yards. At distance of 100 yards watched tracers hitting Me-109, saw pieces flying off. Bullets hit behind cockpit. Fighter slow-rolled and dived, trailing smoke. Airplane dived for 15,000 feet, then pulled out. *Damaged.*

B-17 Number 301 of 332d Squadron, same group: Ju-88 came in at six o'clock level. Sergeant E. E. Hunt fired at 150 yards with long burst into fighter. Cockpit canopy flew off suddenly and Ju-88 went into a steep dive, trailing flame and smoke. Plane did not pull out and crashed, exploding on impact. *Destroyed.*

B-17 Number 30444, same squadron, same group: Me-210 dived in from two o'clock high at lead group of formation, penetrated directly through mass of bombers, firing steadily. Sergeant G. A. Elkin in top turret tracked and fired, then held fire because of B-17's behind Me-210. Fighter banked steeply at four-thirty o'clock, and Elkin opened fire again. A long burst sprayed the length of the Messerschmitt, which plunged into a steep dive. *No claim.*

B-17 Number 264 of 348th Squadron, 303d Group, last plane in formation at 23,000 feet: An FW-190 passed to the rear of the high squadron about six hundred yards out. Sergeant H. H. Zeitner in ball turret fired when fighter reached six-thirty o'clock. At five-thirty o'clock the FW-190 whipped into a spin, then exploded. It tore to pieces in the air, the tail and rear of fuselage breaking off. *Destroyed.*

B-17 Number 930 of 360th Squadron, same group: Bomber was at 24,000 feet when Me-110 came in slightly low at six o'clock. Sergeant J. P. Deffinger in ball turret fired series of bursts at range of 800 yards. At 200 yards, boring in, the Me-110 burst into flames. Slid off on one wing, seemingly out of control and burning. *Damaged.*

B-17 Number 341 of 427th Squadron, same group, at 25,000 feet: Me-110 closed from dead astern, and at 300 yards fired a salvo of rockets. These exploded with violent force directly beneath the Fortress. At same time Sergeant R. R. Humphreys in tail turret was firing steadily, and scored bursts in both engines. Me-110 went down out of sight with left engine and wing on fire. *Damaged.*

Sixty seconds, eleven attacks noted by these gunners, an estimated forty to fifty attacks unlisted. In this same period crew reports show several B-17's badly hit, of which at least two went down immediately afterward.

Strange things occur sometimes in battle, and even in the air war over Germany the American funny bone is apt to reveal itself under odd circumstances. The following incident *did* happen—literally—on Mission 115.

The opening series of attacks had passed, and there was a lull as fresh German fighters moved into position behind one group. They were still several thousand yards behind the Fortresses when a waist gunner, on his first mission and still in a state of nervous tension after the initial attacks, sighted the enemy planes. In a high-pitched voice that was barely controllable he shouted over the interphone of a "big bunch of many enemy fighters closing in!"

His pilot, thinking in terms of the clock system of identification, snapped back: "What time is it?"

To which the excited and vexed gunner screeched: "Jesus Christ, sir, *NOW!*"

It is exceedingly regrettable that many of the gunner reports of the wild fighting over Germany were committed to the historical records in only the briefest of terms; and that it is virtually impossible today to recapture those grim but often stirring moments in the lofty amphitheater of German skies. While the action of the crew aboard B-17 Number 782, of the 306th Group's 369th Squadron, may not be typical of all the gunners on this mission, it reflects accurately the caliber of the men who stood firm aboard their bombers and slugged it out with the best the Germans had to offer.

Fortress Number 782 was near the Initial Point at 23,000 feet when a yellow-nosed FW-190 raced in from seven-thirty low. Five minutes before this attack, Technical Sergeant Robert J. Conley at the left waist was thrown from his gun. An exploding 20-mm. cannon shell blew Conley's left hand completely from his arm. Staff Sergeant B. H. Perlmutter at the right waist position immediately applied a tourniquet to Conley's forearm. As he finished tying the bandage the FW-190 swept in and opened fire. Conley shoved Perlmutter aside and struggled to his feet, grasping his machine gun with his right hand.

The German fighter was at the point-blank range of 150 yards, hurling a stream of cannon shells into the Fortress, when Conley braced himself and squeezed the trigger, holding it down. His accuracy was perfect: a long river of tracers blazed into the Focke-Wulf and seconds later the German airplane disappeared in a blinding explosion, hurling pieces of wreckage in all directions.

Conley fainted, and fell heavily to the deck of the bomber. When he regained consciousness—during a bitter fight—the crew was astonished to see him crawl to his feet and fight his way back to his gun position. He grasped the weapon with his one hand, cursing with pain and at his inability to maneuver the heavy gun in the slipstream, and fainted again.

In this chapter I have portrayed a single slice of one minute out of the total of 194 minutes of almost continuous air fighting. Now it is appropriate to select from these 194 minutes the case histories of five individual bombers, four from the 92d Group and one from the 94th, to illustrate better another page in this bloody saga of Mission 115.

This is a different sort of *time hack*. In the case of each bomber I have selected only the major firing engagements reported in detail by that Fortress's gunners. Again it is necessary to emphasize that with each airplane, the gunners' reports are but a segment of the encounters of that airplane from 1333 to 1647 hours, and do not include many of those times when mass formations of German fighters swarmed through the B-17's with a single attack involving as many as 60 to 70 fighter airplanes. At such times, obviously, it was "every man for himself and to hell with reports."

Top turret, B-17 bomber

Neither is it possible to record the fighters which stood off out of range to launch their rocket salvos. And also absent are the gunner reports of snap shots flung out as fighters whipped by; when there were seemingly no results, these were stricken from the record.

Missing, too, must be the thunder of the battle itself, the hammering noises of guns and cannon and rockets, the explosions, the roar of motors, the singsong whine of shell cases, the thin metallic scream of the fighters. . . .

The first airplane is B-17 Number 383, of the 332d Squadron, 94th Group (which lost six bombers on the raid):

1405 Hours: The B-17 was in the vicinity of Luxembourg at 22,000 feet, when Sergeant R. E. King in the tail turret called out an Me-109 while it was still high above and behind the bomber. The Messerschmitt dived well below the B-17, gaining great speed in the dive, and then hauled up into a swift, soaring climb to begin its attack. Tracking the fighter through the whole of the maneuver, King opened fire at 700 yards, leading the Me-109. He fired in short, continuous bursts, scoring hits repeatedly. At 400 yards range, riddled with bullets, the Me-109 rolled slowly over on its back, and then flipped suddenly out of control. It whirled down out of sight in a spiral. King received a *Damaged.*

1415 Hours: An Me-109 bored in from six o'clock high, firing steadily with its three heavy cannon and two guns. Sergeant W. P. Wetzel in the radio operator's position (second dorsal) fired steadily at the steeply diving fighter. At a distance of 300 yards he watched his tracers meeting the entire frontal area of the Me-109, and hosed them into the engine and wing root areas. The airplane exploded in a brilliant flash. It was a complete disintegration, and the pieces showered out in all directions, several striking the B-17. *Destroyed.*

1417 Hours: The attacks of the two previous fighters had seriously crippled this bomber, and the B-17 was in critical danger. On a heading of 83° Magnetic, riddled with holes and with the number-four engine dead and the propeller feathered, the Fortress began to drop back from formation. One could almost feel the staring eyes of the German fighters as they clawed around to finish the kill. Sergeant N. P. Loupe in the ball turret called out an FW-190 far out and level with the bomber. The fighter dropped down suddenly, leveled off, and trailing smoke from its exhausts, raced at full speed under the ball turret. Loupe opened fire at 600 yards, tracking the FW-190 with high accuracy as it swept in and by. Suddenly the airplane emitted heavy smoke; the next instant a searing ball of flame enveloped the cockpit, and then swept the entire machine. It spiraled down, visible only as a fireball. Loupe was given a *Destroyed*.

Three minutes later the crippled B-17 was ten miles east of Luxembourg. The call was out, and four FW-190's screamed in to finish what the other fighter had failed to do. Sergeant S. H. Rodeschin in the right waist opened fire at long range, and had barely squeezed the trigger when the lead Focke-Wulf exploded violently. Rodeschin was amazed; he had fired only four rounds from his gun. The bullets struck, apparently, a rocket beneath the FW-190's wing, for the explosion ripped the entire wing free. The sudden stress of the tumble broke the fighter into pieces and it fell as wreckage. Rodeschin received a *Destroyed*. The B-17, in the meantime, was descending rapidly and down to 20,000 feet. The fighter attacks were to continue until below 8,000 feet.

1421 Hours: By now the Fortress was in a steep spiral, and nearly torn to pieces in the steady attacks. Several Me-109's had joined the Focke-Wulfs in their firing runs, all queueing up as though they were on practice gunnery missions. An Me-109 came in fast from eight-thirty o'clock low, sticking girmly with the spiraling B-17. As it came within range of the left waist gun, Sergeant D. A. Nowlin fired at a range of 400 yards. It appeared that his tracers went into the Me-109's gas tank. Suddenly the airplane exploded, was flung into a whirling spiral, completely out of control, and enveloped from nose to tail in flames. *Destroyed*.

That made, from 1405 to 1421 hours, four confirmed kills and one damaged. B-17 Number 383 was named *Brennan's Circus;* we shall return in Chapter 18 to this particular Fortress.

The second airplane is B-17 Number 301 of the 332d Squadron (same squadron as B-17 Number 383), 94th Group:

1431 Hours: The Fortress was twenty-five miles southwest of Würzburg at 22,500 feet, when an Me-109 came in fast at six o'clock level. Sergeant E. E. Hunt in the tail fired at a range of 500 yards. Then he noticed two other Me-109's behind the lead fighter, peeling off. The lead Me-109 closed in to point-blank range, then flashed directly beneath the tail, only several yards away. Without any serious damage showing, the pilot bailed out. Seconds later, reported the ball-turret gunner, the fighter exploded. *Destroyed.*

1440 Hours: Nine minutes later, just before the bomber reached its turn at the Initial Point, a swarm of fighters struck the B-17. Hunt in the tail again opened up, firing at an Me-109 diving from five o'clock high. Hunt's aim was accurate, and a shower of incendiaries bracketed the Me-109. The fighter at once burst into flames and the canopy flew off, but the expected body of the pilot failed to show. Hunt lost sight of the blazing Me-109 as he tracked and fired at another fighter; eight planes in all were attacking. Later, two fighters were seen to strike the ground and explode, but it was impossible to confirm Hunt's target. He received a *Damaged.*

1451 Hours: This time the fighters were twin-engine, and a Ju-88 came in from four-forty-five o'clock, very high, and diving steeply. Sergeant F. C. Mancuso in the top turret fired steadily, scoring hits in both engines. He and the other crewmen believed the pilot was also hit. The Ju-88 steepened the dive and never pulled out. Hunt in the tail watched the explosion as it crashed. *Destroyed.*

1515 Hours: At 20,500 feet, in the Bad Mergentheim area, Hunt got into the fray again. A Ju-88 slipped in close at six o'clock level, surprising the tail gunner, who was occupied firing at another fighter on a side attack. Hunt spotted the Ju-88 when it was barely 150 yards away, but closing slowly —a perfect target. The entire nose of the Ju-88 was blazing from its firing cannon when Hunt opened up. He scored direct hits into the cockpit. The canopy flew off, and the fighter plunged away in a dive, sheets of flame pouring from the cockpit. He never pulled out. *Destroyed.*

1525 Hours: Between the target and the Rally Point, at 22,500 feet, a Ju-88 came in firing rockets and cannon from eight o'clock level. Sergeant S. J. Maciolek in the left waist kept shooting steadily as the Ju-88 closed in, and suddenly whirled over on its back before flipping into a dive. As it dived, flames came back from both engines and completely enveloped the fighter. It crashed and exploded. *Destroyed.*

Score: Four destroyed and one damaged.

The third airplane is B-17 Number 439, 410th Squadron of the 94th Group:

1400 Hours: At 21,000 feet, thirty miles east of Eupen, an

Me-109 came in from four-thirty o'clock, low, attacking the low squadron. Sergeant McCabe in the right waist fired a short burst. For a moment the Me-109 rolled out of the attack, and presented an excellent target. McCabe now squeezed out a long burst, covering the fighter from nose to tail. The Me-109 rolled rapidly onto its back and dived vertically. The ball-turret gunner, Sergeant C. L. Burkhardt, watched the fighter hit the ground and explode. *Destroyed*.

1445 Hours: Sergeant L. Rand in the left waist position called out an Me-109 coming in slightly low at seven o'clock; the bomber was then at 22,000 feet, twenty miles west of Würzburg. At 1,000 yards Rand opened fire, with three bursts of 25 rounds each, and watched his tracers striking the engine. The pilot went over the side and his parachute opened at once. Brown in the tail confirmed the appearance of the chute. *Destroyed*.

1510 Hours: Fifteen miles southeast of Schweinfurt, at 21,000 feet, a twin-engine fighter approached from five o'clock high, closing slowly, and firing 20-mm. cannon in short, repeated bursts. Sergeant W. P. Brown in the tail fired several bursts, and then squeezed off a steady 60 rounds. Pieces of the large fighter came off, and he fell away, tumbling slowly. Smoke streamed back, and suddenly sheets of flame erupted from the tanks. The crew failed to get out, and the airplane tumbled all the way to the ground, where it exploded. *Destroyed*.

1515 Hours: An Me-109 closed in from a steep dive, pulling out, and firing steadily at the Fortress. As he swung into the ten o'clock position, Sergeant C. T. Troott in the top turret tracked but held his fire. The Me-109 raced in to come over from seven o'clock and banked steeply; at that moment Troott poured 50 rounds into the cockpit. The fighter spurted flames and, seconds later, reported the bombardier, exploded violently. *Destroyed*.

Score: Four destroyed.

The fourth airplane is B-17 Number 248, same squadron:

1425 Hours: The first attack came as the bomber approached the Initial Point at 22,000 feet. Two FW-190's peeled off at two o'clock high, and Sergeant A. A. Ulrich in the top turret poured 100 rounds into the lead fighter. He opened fire at 800 yards and kept firing as the FW-190 rushed in to less than 50 yards' distance. The FW-190 spurted flame, and then careened wildly over the bomber, scant feet away. By now the flames engulfed the Focke-Wulf from nose to tail. It raced by the Fortress, fell below, and exploded, sending pieces in all directions. No parachute was seen; the fighter passed so close that Ulrich said that the pilot seemed to be dead before his ship exploded. *Destroyed.*

1435 Hours: Near the Initial Point an Me-210 came in from six o'clock low, and 1,000 yards out he salvoed his four

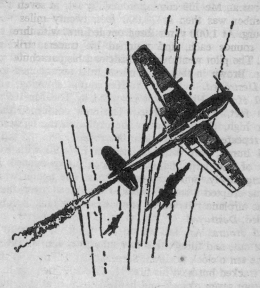

"Me-109G, last seen burning, diving away. *Damaged.*"

rockets. Sergeant C. T. Noulles in the ball turret started firing with short bursts, maintaining this fire as the Me-210 closed to 400 yards. The twin-engine fighter peeled off, came around again, firing its 20-mm. cannon. Noulles kept tracking and firing his steady bursts. After a long burst into the Me-210 the fighter blazed suddenly and, low at about four o'clock, erupted into a fireball, scattering pieces in all directions. Noulles had fired 300 rounds of armor-piercing bullets to score. *Destroyed.*

1526 Hours: Ulrich made his second kill just after the

B-17 turned for home. Starting its run about fourteen hundred yards out, an Me-109 dived from seven o'clock high. At 700 yards Ulrich opened up with the twin guns of his top turret, squeezing out a long, continuous burst of 200 rounds. At a distance of 300 yards he stopped firing—more than satisfied with the results. The Me-109 had attempted to pull up suddenly while Ulrich's tracers wreathed the airplane. He burst into flames; the nose came up, then fell again as the Me-109 whipped into a spin. Moments later it began to disintegrate, and literally shredded apart in midair. *Destroyed*.

1533 Hours: Now it was Sergeant B. Lewis's time to score. Near Werback at 22,000 feet an Me-109 came in level at six o'clock. Lewis opened fire with his two tail guns at 600 yards, gunning the fighter with short bursts as it approached to 200 yards. After 75 rounds the Me-109 started smoking, and as it swept by the B-17, flames engulfed it. The Me-109 went into a steep dive and exploded. The crew confirmed that no chute appeared, and that after the explosion the fighter spun wildly, shedding pieces as it fell. *Destroyed*.

1538 Hours: Five minutes later an FW-190 with a belly tank came in slightly high at six o'clock. Lewis opened fire at 600 yards and maintained steady bursts. The fighter whipped in close and less than 20 yards away raced over the tail. Lewis saw flames streaming from the belly tank before the FW-190 passed out of his view. The top turret gunner watched the airplane fall off on one wing, burst completely into flame, and explode. He saw no chute. Lewis received a second *Destroyed*.

Score: Five destroyed.

The fifth airplane is B-17 Number 351Z, 407th Squadron, of the 92d Group. There are no specific times or locations of the attacks. The harried crew—which earned the awe of even their fellows—stated to the debriefing officers that "we were too goddamned busy to be worried about what time and where they hit us. There were fiighters *everywhere,* and they never let go." B-17 Number 351Z flew the lead squadron position on the right flank of the bomber box; Colonel Peaslee remembers this unit as being subject to "constant and fierce enemy air attacks."

It is agreed by many veterans of the raid that 351Z was the outstanding performer in defending itself against the German fighters and exacting the heaviest toll of the enemy. This airplane's saga during Mission 115 is one of the most remarkable of all World War II. Some of the engagements are presented in the words of various crew members.

"A big gaggle of Ju-88's had rushed through the formation, going like hell and firing steadily at all the B-17's in front of them. I don't know how many fighters, at least 30 of them. Then a single Ju-88 closed in from five o'clock level. Sergeant D. M. Radney in the tail tracked him, and fired in short, steady bursts. The Junkers poured in his shells; his nose was lit up like a Christmas tree. At 500 yards Radney called out that the fighter's port engine was aflame. The fighter closed to 200 yards, Radney still firing, when it broke away sharply. Fire licked back from the engine along the entire fuselage. Nobody saw it crash or the crew go out." A disgruntled Radney received a *Damaged* claim for this one.

In another mass attack, this time by single-engine fighters, Sergeant J. W. Disher in the ball turret called out an FW-190 rushing upward from seven o'clock, and firing everything he had. Cannon shells exploded all over the belly of the Fortress as Disher fired several long bursts. Suddenly Disher was hit by fragments from a shell; he kept firing, and was rewarded with smoke trailing from the Focke-Wulf. It nosed over into a dive, and the smoke thickened to obscure the fighter. The pilot leaped clear. Disher received a *Destroyed*.

Another heavy attack was made by Ju-88's blasting away with their grouped cannon. One fighter closed in at two o'clock to 300 yards, firing steadily. Sergeant B. L. Boutwell in the top turret fired a steady series of bursts as he tracked the Ju-88 in. The fighter dropped suddenly, and as it raced closely beneath the B-17, the ball-turret gunner reported that both engines were burning. The dive steepened, and the copilot shouted back to Boutwell that the Junkers was a complete ball of flame. Two parachutes blossomed out, and Boutwell got a *Destroyed*.

Almost at the same moment as this attack, a Ju-88 came in slightly low at five o'clock. Radney in the tail fired at 500 yards, hosing a stream of tracers into the fighter as the range closed to 350 yards. Even as the B-17 shook badly from the exploding shells the tracers set the Ju-88's entire right wing aflame. Then the left engine blossomed out in fire as the plane fell into a dive. No one saw the airplane crash, and there was no time to follow it in the dive to look for parachutes. Cannon shells burst with a series of roars around Radney, and he swung his guns immediately to meet another attack from a line of Ju-88's. He received a *Probable*.

A newcomer to the attacks was a large Dornier Do-217 bomber which climbed at a shallow angle from four o'clock low, pumping very large cannon shells into the B-17. Disher in the ball turret fired three long bursts, scoring steadily. The big German airplane staggered in the air, and Radney in the tail called in as both engines flamed, and the Do-217 fell out of control. Nearly two miles below it exploded, and Disher had his second *Destroyed*.

The Dornier disappeared from sight, and then a swarm of Ju-88's enveloped the Fortress in a cascade of exploding cannon shells. From his tail position Radney snapped out burst after burst at the Junkers, and frantically swung his guns to track an FW-190 which raced in from dead astern. Radney had the horrifying view of staring into the FW-190 from only 25 yards away, the wings and nose blazing with firing guns and cannon. Radney's well-directed fire set the Focke-Wulf smoking heavily, but the German plane rushed in. A collision seemed imminent; at the last second the fighter swerved sharply to the left. There was no mistake about this one. Slightly below and 150 yards out a blinding explosion racked the FW-190, and then pieces fell in all directions. Radney received a *Destroyed*.

Lieutenant K. A. Pfleger, bombardier: "Two FW-190's came in at one-thirty o'clock and I opened fire at 400 yards. I continued firing at the first ship to the limit of movement of the gun. The first FW-190 was seen by Hultquist in the right waist, going by out of control. It tumbled and crashed into another FW-190 which was coming in at five o'clock from above. Both ships exploded in flames when they crashed into each other." At the debriefing they gave Pfleger credit for *Two Destroyed*.

Sergeant C. T. Hultquist in the right waist: "Me-109's from above at seven o'clock. He divided on us, firing, and I caught him in my sights at 600 yards, and opened fire. His right engine suddenly flamed. He went out of sight at three o'clock; Hultquist saw him going down in flames in a steep dive. He struck the ground and exploded." *Destroyed*.

Sergeant C. T. Hultquist in the right waist: "Me-109's came in a bunch just below the right wing at two o'clock. I

"One FW-190. Confirmed destroyed."

fired at the second ship. Right away a stream of smoke poured from underneath the engine. Radney in the tail saw him come out, smoking heavily. Then the airplane exploded into small pieces." *Destroyed.*

The final attack came from the nose. Lieutenant P. L. Stebbins, the navigator, tracked a Ju-88 coming in level at one-thirty o'clock, firing steadily. Stebbins opened fire at 400 yards, squeezing out long bursts through the limit of arc of his gun. As the Ju-88 raced by the Fortress Boutwell in the top turret reported the fighter trailing heavy smoke from both engines. The Junkers dropped in a steepening dive and never recovered; Disher in the ball reported the crash and explosion. *Destroyed.*

B-17 Number 351Z was a busy airplane. Score: Nine destroyed, one probable, one damaged.

17

THE TRAIN TRAVELER

Six heavy bombers of the 384th Group went down before the attacks of German fighters on Mission 115. Sixty men that night were missing from the mess halls and the barracks at Grafton Underwood. One of those men was Staff Sergeant Peter Seniawsky.

Early in December, six weeks after the mission, a "ghost" with a grin splitting his face from ear to ear walked into the operations room of the 384th. It was Pete Seniawsky, who had been shot down on the raid—and then crossed part of Germany, all of France, and into Spain on an extraordinary journey on foot, by truck and by train.

Seniawsky, a waist gunner, related that his Fortress was virtually riddled with cannon shells and bullets. "We were hit everywhere and she started to burn," he said. "The pilot told us to get out, and as fast as we could, we jumped. I delayed my jump intentionally from 20,000 feet down to 5,000 feet, and while falling I watched the ground carefully, waiting until the layout of farm lands was clearly visible. Then I pulled the ring. After my chute opened I saw the B17, burning heavily, disappear in level flight. I counted only three chutes. . . ."

That was the beginning of Sergeant Seniawsky's amazing tale of working his way from Germany back to Grafton Underwood. For several hours after he hit the ground he concealed himself in thick bushes, as German farmers armed with shotguns scoured the countryside where they had seen his parachute descending.

Until sundown Seniawsky remained frozen where he was, aware that any movement would earn him either a shotgun blast or immediate capture. Under cover of dark he crept from his hideout, but all Germany, it seemed, was searching for the hundreds of airmen who had gone down during the day. No sooner had he walked into nearby woods when he stumbled into the midst of a military search party—which didn't ask any questions in the dark but opened up with a withering barrage of fire from rifles and machine guns.

Flat on his belly and hugging the ground as the bullets ripped through branches over his head, Seniawsky crawled on his knees and elbows until away from the immediate fire. Safe for the moment, he ran as fast and hard as he could through the dense underbrush. Gasping for air, he threw himself down beneath thick bushes and waited, his lungs heaving, as the cursing Germans fanned out for the kill. Staying on his belly now, Seniawsky crawled away from the search party, and managed to cover several hundred yards. His escape was successful. The German troops moved off in one direction, and the sergeant happily took off in the other.

He walked all night, making sure to remain under concealment of the trees and heavy brush. After midnight he swallowed anti-fatigue pills from his escape kit to stay fully alert and awake. Once again—by now he thought the Germans were living in the woods—he ran into the enemy. Almost facing a German officer, Seniawsky slipped noiselessly to the ground and rolled under some bushes as the man passed only several feet away.

Luck fell when the sergeant neared a large town. A thick ground fog rolled in, to the grateful relief of Seniawsky, weary of half-crouching and crawling at every sudden sound. He walked rapidly to the south, making excellent time as the fog blanketed his movements. When the first streaks of dawn brushed the sky, Seniawsky searched for a hiding place where he would be concealed from the Germans and where he could also sleep. A large haystack seemed as good a place as any, and the tired sergeant crawled in. "It was a lousy spot. The hay was wet and cold, and it was impossible to sleep. At sunup I sneaked a look through the hay—and almost fainted."

Barely 200 yards away were nearly fifty German soldiers and a large gun emplacement. The horrified Seniawsky did not dare to move, and he passed the day shivering from the dampness and the cold—to say nothing of his reactions to the German troops at the gun site and a constant stream of heavy military traffic on a nearby road.

Late that night he crawled out of the hay and made his way on his belly to the edge of the field. He moved rapidly through the woods, anxious to get away from the unnerving company of the German soldiers. That night, still moving steadily to the south, he sneaked up to a farmhouse and quickly filled his canteen from a pump in the yard.

Suddenly a large dog barked loudly, and came skidding around the house, making "enough noise to wake the dead." The dog howled lustily as Seniawsky ran as fast as possible into the outskirts of a nearby town and dashed down a side street. The dog lost interest and trotted off, and the exhausted gunner barely had time to fling himself behind a fence as a car moved down the street. The game of hide-and-seek was getting rough.

At dawn Seniawsky climbed into the largest and thickest tree in sight and clambered high into the thick foliage. He wrapped himself around a tree branch, wedged in tightly, and spent the day sleeping. That night he moved out again, this time to the west, navigating with his hand compass. Occasionally dogs barked and howled as he passed isolated houses, but none joined in the chase. Before dawn he climbed gratefully into a hayloft, pausing only to snatch some apple peelings he found on the ground. His rations were exhausted, and to the weary gunner the prospects of continued flight were anything but cheery.

Late in the afternoon he slipped from the hayloft and moved into a nearby woods, anxious to keep moving. It was a mistake; travel in daylight in Germany was simply too dangerous. As a farmer spotted him moving beneath the trees, Seniawsky froze into position. It was a wasted effort. Less than thirty minutes later four men moved purposefully across the field adjoining the woods—directly for him.,

Fate smiled benevolently on the Fortress gunner; the men were French! After Seniawsky identified himself—not too difficult a task because of his clothing—the Frenchmen used sign language to indicate they would help him as best they could. One man in broken English told Seniawsky that he was then 65 kilometers (about forty miles) east of Metz. Nearby railroad tracks, the Frenchmen indicated, led directly to the city, but the way between was thick with Germans. The Frenchmen—conscripted farm workers with no love for the enemy—gave Seniawsky food and whiskey. Then he was on his way again.

For the next several days he dodged both soldiers and civilians alike, moving furtively, hiding like a rat in a corner at the slightest sound. Whenever it was possible, he stole food and refilled his canteen with water. Near the French border, at the edge of a field, he stumbled into a man and a girl. The three stared at one another, and cautiously Seniawsky identified himself as an American airman. The girl was French, the man a Serb—again a conscripted worker. They warned the gunner to hide carefully until dark, saying they would return to sneak him across the border into France.

At sundown Seniawsky spotted the man running frantically across the field to his hiding place; the Germans were scouring the area, he warned. The Serb shoved a package of bread, butter, and sardines into his hands, and bade him leave at once. Seniawsky shook the Serb's hand gratefully, and took off at a run. For the rest of the night he followed the railroad to the south, taking every step with precaution.

Before dawn he sneaked into a barn to hide. This time he was convinced the jig was up, for it was obvious the Germans were looking for him. Several minutes after he sneaked into the barn, a heavily-armed German patrol moved purposefully toward the same building, bayonets fixed and ready. Desperately, Seniawsky dropped into a hole in the floor, and pulled hay after him to cover his head and shoulders. For what seemed like an eternity two soldiers stood within inches of his head, slowly turning as they scanned the barn. Seniawsky was weak with tension as they moved away. Again he was safe!

For several days Seniawsky worked his way closer to France. He lived like an animal, drinking from streams, sleeping in the open fields, in abandoned shacks, and whenever possible in barns. German troops were everywhere, and the gunner was fast becoming a nervous wreck, starting fitfully at every sudden sound. Then luck befriended him again. A conscripted Polish worker spotted him at the edge of a field, kept silent, and joined him under cover of the brush. Seniawsky spoke Polish fairly well. That night the friendly Pole hid him in a barn, brought him food, and set him off in the proper direction to cross the border.

The prospects of reaching France were grim. Between Seniawsky and the occupied land lay several consecutive high fences of barbed wire, armed sentries, and many vicious dogs which were trained to kill any man or woman they encountered. Seniawsky slipped through the first fence on his back, eased over to his stomach, and noiselessly crawled a hundred yards in the dark on his hands and knees. At the second fence he rolled over again, and on his back eased beneath the barbed-wire strands. He could hear the German soldiers walking patrol nearby.

The next 200 yards Seniawsky covered on his stomach, freezing instantly to the spot whenever he heard any sounds. He had just cleared the last fence when thick clouds slid in front of the moon to bring almost total darkness. Gratefully Seniawsky clambered to his feet and ran.

The next morning he abandoned his furtive movements and decided to brazen it out. He walked openly through the streets of several towns, looking for all the world like a man weary from hard work. The French were wonderful; the moment his identification was positive, all suspicions vanished. They fed him as best they could, burned his flying suit, and gave him working clothes. For the first time since he had bailed out of the flaming Fortress, Seniawsky was able to bathe and to shave the thick stubble from his face. In most towns the people never even looked twice at him as he walked through the streets; if anyone noticed anything unusual about the gunner, they did not give him away by staring.

A Frenchman moving south joined him in his travel, and the two men walked along a country road. Waving their hands, they stopped a truck, and persuaded the driver to give them a lift to Nancy. They walked again for a while, and were joined by a Polish worker traveling to a nearby small town. The Pole studied Seniawsky carefully, learned his name, and grinned. That afternoon he took the two men to a restaurant where the Pole excitedly introduced them to a group made up of Poles, Russians, and Serbs—all conscripted laborers. The restaurant owner piled food in front of them, and Seniawsky ate with gusto.

In the midst of the meal a French detective walked in and eyed the group suspiciously. Immediately the American gunner, his mouth full of food, started talking boisterously in Polish to the rest of the men. The detective looked hard at him, then turned and left. Seniawsky slumped in his seat with relief; the policeman had not asked for identification papers. It was a narrow escape.

That night a young French boy hid Seniawsky in his room. He spent the following day walking the side streets, brushing by German soldiers constantly, standing shoulder to shoulder with them at street corners Early in the afternoon he bought cake in a bakery, stuffed it into his pockets, and joined a line waiting for a movie to open. He slept for several hours in the theater.

That evening capture again loomed close. In a bar Seniawsky pointed to a glass of beer and dug in his pockets for money. A German soldier stared curiously as the gunner fumbled with the French currency. Seniawsky waved his glass in a toast to the German, downed the beer, and walked out.

He walked slowly into the railroad station and studied the timetables on the wall. Carefully, trying not to arouse any interest, he watched the people buying tickets, especially what kind of people went to certain windows. Then he walked casually to a third-class seat window, mumbled incoherently in his meager French, but said "Dijon" clearly. The agent pushed the ticket at him and took his money.

He bought coffee in the station bar, then walked in the streets until darkness fell. In the gloomy station he stretched out on a bench and slept. Boarding the train presented no problems, and Seniawsky counted his blessings as the miles flashed by beneath his feet.

At Dijon, however, when the train pulled in at noon, he faced the bleak prospect of the French police checking the papers of all passengers leaving the station. He slipped into the restaurant and slowly sipped coffee. One hour later his patience was rewarded: the police left.

Seniawsky then bought a ticket to Lyons, boarded the train as it arrived, and stood the entire journey in the vestibule, happily out of sight of most of the passengers. At Lyons he ran to a ticket window, purchased a ticket to Marseilles, and sank wearily into a third-class seat. Despite his determination to stay awake, in minutes he was fast asleep.

Again at Marseilles a large force of police met all debarking passengers, and Seniawsky took pains to avoid these inquisitive gendarmes. The moment he stepped off the train he walked in the direction opposite from the police check, unobtrusively joined a group of workmen walking through the yards, and slipped away when he reached a side street.

In minutes he was back at the railroad station and marched nonchalantly right past the police. To get out of Marseilles he bought a ticket back northward to Avignon, but the earliest train would not leave until the following morning. Seniawsky didn't dare be seen loitering at the station; this alone would be enough to arouse the suspicions of the police in an occupied country. He sneaked beneath a train platform and there slept soundly until sunup. Brushing off his clothes, he walked through the yards again, left by the same side street, and bought grapes from a street vendor for his breakfast. At 7:30 A.M. he was safely aboard the train bound for Avignon.

He was incredibly lucky. So far, by dodging the police and managing to look like any tired, dirty worker, he had avoided being asked for his papers. Once that happened, he knew the game was up. But so long as things moved so smoothly, he intended to pull off every trick he knew to work his way south. At Avignon the streets seemed to crawl with German soldiers, and in their midst Seniawsky put to its severest test his ability to melt into the crowds. Trying not to watch for anyone who might be noticing him—acting the part of any worker—he moved from bakery stall to stall, spending 200 francs to buy twelve small cakes, which he stuffed into his pockets.

By now he felt like an experienced train traveler, and with his new experiences behind him, felt no qualms about returning to the ticket windows. He bought a ticket to Sète. This time he broke precedent and started a conversation with an elderly woman, who spoke French fluently—Seniawsky didn't —and some Polish. Between the two languages and a timetable he learned that he must change trains en route in order to reach Sète.

As the trains bore him to the southwest, he lost his direction in trying to reach Perpignan, and ran the risk of drawing attention to himself by dashing madly through the station to catch the right train at Narbonne. Here his luck began to thin. A conductor was openly curious as to his mad dash and not a little hostile. Before the man could press him for his identification papers, Seniawsky grasped his hand and shook it enthusiastically, as though meeting an old friend. The conductor glanced down at the 100-franc note which had appeared in his palm, and immediately lost all interest in the scruffy workman before him.

One narrow escape followed another. Seniawsky sat at one end of the railroad car, as two German soldiers entered the car at the opposite end, demanding papers from all passengers. As they studied the passengers' credentials, Seniawsky scurried from the car, ready to jump from the speeding train. But his luck held. He swung to the side of the train, clutched a handhold, and held grimly to the side of the swaying train for thirty minutes. By some miracle no one who watched this performance from the side of the tracks reported the unusual sight. When Seniawsky clambered back into the car, the Germans were gone. The French passengers favored him by not so much as a glance.

At Perpignan he slept from midnight until dawn in the wating room, and then slipped out a side door as the police took up their positions at the main exits. Within another hour he was outside the town; using his compass and reading the road signs, he began to walk toward Céret. Outside this town, hungry and weary, he stopped at a small café to buy soup. The woman who owned the shop seemed friendly; Seniawsky took a chance and when the woman spoke to him in French, he replied that he was an American.

To his astonishment, the woman showed no surprise, as though it was the most ordinary thing in the world for escaping Americans to drink soup in her café. As Seniawsky finished his meal, she sat down at the table beside him and warned him to avoid Céret; under no circumstances must he enter the town. The dreaded word *Gestapo* was more than reason enough. The woman bade him wait at the table while she stood at the door, looking around for Germans. She signaled him to follow quickly, and led him to an isolated mountain road that led due south. Seniawsky thanked her and left.

Long hours later, exhausted and suffering from the bitter cold, he reached the ridge of the mountains. Ahead of him was a small shack, and he stumbled through the door, desperate for rest. Panic welled up in him: the shack was occupied! In the dim light Seniawsky saw an old man, and with relief sat down beside him. Once the Frenchman accepted Seniawsky as an escaping airman, he thrust a bottle of wine and a bag of chestnuts—all the food he had—into his hands. Gratefully, the gunner ate and drank.

As dusk fell, he renewed his journey, his hopes raised higher and higher. For in the distance, nestled in a deep valley, was a town showing its lights without caution. Spain!

All night long Seniawsky crawled down the mountainside. This stretch—the final leg of his amazing trip—was the most dangerous. German patrols clumped through the woods, many of them with dogs. At the slightest sound Seniawsky froze to the spot, and then resumed his journey.

Just before dawn, with several miles behind him, he walked directly into the hands of two soldiers. *Spanish!*

The soldiers hustled the jubilant Seniawsky off to prison where they questioned him closely for several hours. Later that day they transferred him to another prison, in Figueras. A week later Seniawsky joyfully greeted the American consul, who obtained his release and took him to Gerona. Two weeks later, after traveling through Barcelona, Saragossa, Ahlama, and Madrid, he stepped onto British soil at Gibraltar.

On December 1—six weeks after he had bailed out four miles above Germany—Peter Seniawsky walked back into the operations room of the 384th Group.

It had been quite a trip.

18

THE FORTS COME HOME

In Chapter 16, I listed a series of five gunnery engagements of B-17 Number 383—*Brennan's Circus*—of the 332d Squadron, 94th Group. The battle between this rugged Fortress and attacking German fighters as reported covered a time period of only sixteen minutes, but these seemed an eternity to the ten men aboard the bomber. B-17 Number 383 was one of those rare Forts that struggled for some distance homeward on *one* engine and the rest of the airplane shot to pieces. The *Circus* failed to bring her men home to England, but she brought the crew close enough, and not a man had anything but kind words to say about their valiant bomber.

Ten minutes before the target run the fighters shot out the first engine, which burst into flames. For another five minutes the pilot, First Lieutenant Joseph Brennan, twenty-one years old, struggled to keep up with the group formation. The Fortress was sluggish and unresponsive, and both Brennan and his copilot, Second Lieutenant Gordon E. White, twenty-two years old, were forced to work at the controls together But even with the throttles jammed all the way forward, the crippled bomber couldn't make it.

Their only chance of remaining with the other bombers, of continuing to fly under the protection of the massed fire screen, was to jettison the heavy bomb load. Brennan ordered Second Lieutenant Joseph E. Genone, twenty-four years old, to salvo the bombs. Unhappily, the Fortress was in far worse condition than they realized, and the bomb-release mechanism was a shambles of twisted metal. "I decided right then that we had to peel off," Brennan said. "We were far behind the rest of the formation by then, and the fighters were making terrific passes at us. We were at 25,000 feet when I swung her over and let her go."

Shaking badly, shivering from nose to tail in a series of eerie vibrations, the *Circus* swooped down in a dive, and quickly reached a speed of more than three hundred and fifty miles per hour—still with her lethal bombs in the bays. Seeing the burning engine and the sudden plunge, the fighters closed in, blasting away with guns and cannon. Then four more FW-190's swept in while the gunners were engaged. Four rockets whipped past the B-17, blazing fiercely. They missed.

Technical Sergeant Willard R. Wetzel, twenty-three years old, the radio operator-gunner, was on his twenty-fifth (and final) mission. As the *Circus* dropped away, the target of the furious German attacks, Wetzel had one of the worst moments of his battle-studded combat career. "The pilot kept circling as he went down," Wetzel related back in England, "because if we had gone down in a straight dive, all a fighter had to do was get on our tail and stay there while he was letting us have it. As it was, the Jerries managed to hit another engine. The prop began to run away at such a speed it made the most horrifying noise I have ever heard. I didn't know then it was the prop. I thought the wings were falling off. I was all alone in the radio compartment and didn't have my headset on. I thought, with the wings falling off, the pilot had ordered us to bail out and I hadn't heard him. I opened the radio compartment door and looked to see if the bomb-bay doors were open. They were. I thought then that I was left all alone in the ship, with no one at the controls.

"That really hit me. I turned to ice.

"I fumbled around, finally managed to plug in my headset, and called the pilot. There was a minute—one hell of a long minute, too—before he answered, and I think I kept holding my breath. Then he said, 'Stick with us,' Boy, was I relieved!"

As the *Circus* swirled around steeply in her spiral, the bombardier finally managed to jettison the several tons of high explosives. Almost as if she was glad to be rid of the bombs, the *Circus* responded faster and more effectively to the wrestling motions of Brennan and White in the cockpit. Still the bomber fell, while the navigator, Lieutenant Verne D. Viterbo, shouted to Wetzel to get him a radio "fix" to home on.

"Things were rapidly going straight to hell"—so the pilot later described the moments of the spiral from 25,000 feet down to the ground—a spinning blur of flames, exploding shells, singing bullets, the roar of the engines, the shouts of the crew, and the blasting noise of the runaway prop. The *Circus* had only one chance, and Brennan took it by diving the battered Fortress right to the deck—scarcely fifteen feet over German soil.

From then on this B-17 certainly had what must be described as one of the "hairiest" flights in bomber history. With one engine out and its prop spinning crazily, another worthless and streaming flames, the B-17 lit out for the Channel with the fighters on her tail like a wolf pack in full cry. The shells and bullets crashed into the wings like hail, but the fighters could not make steep diving attacks and had to slow down as they came in, for fear of striking the ground. All the gunners blazed away and finally the fighter pilots, either discouraged or else convinced that the Fortress didn't stand any chance of making it home, turned tail and went after fresher game.

With only his two good engines and the *Circus* resembling something that had gone through a meat grinder, Brennan coaxed the staggering bomber directly among the trees and buildings. Frequently he had to lift a wing to clear a tower or a church steeple, missing the ground obstacles by scant inches.

By the time the *Circus* was floundering its way across Holland and Belgium, ground fire replaced the attacks of the Luftwaffe. The area was so strewn with small fighter airfields that it proved impossible to avoid all nests of flak and, occasionally, a half-hearted pass by a single fighter plane whose pilot must have stared in some disbelief at the wreck hedgehopping over the land, leaving behind it a long pall of smoke.

Low as it flew, the thunder of the *Circus's* two remaining motors was heard for miles ahead. People rushed out of their homes and shops, jumping up and down in excitement, waving happily, and raising their arms in "V for Victory" salutes to the bomber. Everywhere the people appeared— men, women, and children—and their reaction was spontaneous. The sight of an American bomber so close to the ground—with the crew members leaning out of turrets and hatches and waving back!—was cause for cheer. But there were enemy troops on the ground, too.

"They fired everything they had at us," said Staff Sergeant Denver A. Nowlin, the right waist gunner. "We were so close to them that the noise was terrific. They were firing machine guns and everything else. Troops were lined up on rooftops and in the streets and fields, blazing away with rifles. Their officers also were outside, firing pistols. If they'd had more time, they probably would have thrown rocks at us also."

The *Circus* took a terrific beating from the withering ground barrage. If she was cut up before, now she began to fall apart. Pieces of metal curled up on the wings, gaping holes appeared magically in the wings and fuselage, and bullets twanged through the ship like a swarm of bees.

Then a final barrage struck home. A waterfall of tracers soared up from the earth and smashed into one of the two remaining good engines. The *Circus* faltered visibly as the third engine cut out, then struggled on—carried by only one engine.

It is impossible for a B-17 to fly on one engine, but maybe Brennan in the cockpit hadn't read the book that said so. Revved up to maximum power, that engine dragged the Fortress away from the land, while the tail turret gunner cheerfully described the hail of bullets splashing in the water behind them, unable to reach the staggering bomber. Wetzel had already flashed out the plane's identifying radio signal to British shore stations, saying they would be coming in right on the deck. But the *Circus* just didn't have it any more; she began to lose the precious few feet beneath the wings. Brennan told Wetzel to flash the *Mayday* distress call; they would have to ditch in the Channel.

Only five miles from the British coast line the crippled bomber gave up the ghost. Brennan and White held the nose high as the crew gathered in the radio room, and then they settled her gently to the water. She drifted down like a feather, trailed a high plume of spray, and slowly came to a stop. As the Fortress began to settle, the crew cut the dinghies loose and climbed aboard. Not a man got his feet wet. Within an hour a British rescue boat picked them up.

Lieutenant Miles McFann was a navigator aboard the B-17 named *Paper Doll* on Mission 115; it was his seventh—and his most memorable—attack of the war. Before training as a navigator in the army air forces, McFann had flown airplanes—little light planes with 65 horsepower that might do 80 miles per hour if you flew them straight down with the engine shaking itself loose. But he came back from Mission 115 as a pilot, simply because there wasn't much choice.

The pilot was dead, the copilot was badly wounded and bleeding profusely, and the *Paper Doll* had 132 big holes in her. McFann brought the battered Fort down on a strange field to write another epic chapter of Mission 115.

Paper Doll flew the trailing position in the lead element of the attack. Through the worst of the German fighter attacks and flak barrages over Schweinfurt she sailed along with what seemed like a sorcerer's ability to dodge bullets, shells, and flak bursts. Seven minutes from the French coast on the return leg her luck gave out.

"Everybody was happy," related the weary McFann at the end of the flight. "We'd been through a tough time in the target area, but things were going nice and we hadn't even been hit once. The bombardier asked me how long it would be before we got out of the danger zone. I calculated that we'd be over the French coast and out of the mess in seven minutes. Then flak started popping up and our right wing was hit."

That's when everything went to hell. *Paper Doll's* pilot threw the big Fortress into wild, evasive maneuvers; the flak batteries had the bomber pinned neatly, and unless it evacuated that block of airspace, it was only a matter of seconds before the shells must score directly. So violent were the flak and the pilot's reaction that when the crew looked around again they were alone. The formation was far off in the distance, and at that moment everyone began to feel distinctly uncomfortable. They had good reason to be.

Without warning two fighters flashed in to attack directly out of the sun—their shells crashing into the B-17 even before anyone called out their positions. As the crew hastily swung their guns around another fighter raced up from beneath and stitched a deadly wreath of holes in the Fortress's belly.

The fighters making the attack from out of the sun had rockets, and one of these flashed brightly before it exploded with a thundering roar against the right side of the cockpit canopy. The bomber reeled wildly, out of control as steel fragments screamed through the cockpit. A moment later a 20-mm. cannon shell slashed in between the copilot and the back of his seat, exploded, and almost tore the pilot—

Lieutenant Robert H. Bolick—to pieces. Shell fragments ripped his face all over, struck his neck, and opened deep wounds in his leg. There was no respite; cannon shells exploded in the bomb bay, blew holes all through the rudder, and turned the number-one engine into spinning junk.

The stricken Fortress skidded to the left, dropped her wing, and began to slide earthward. McFann called desperately to the cockpit, but the exploding shells had knocked out the interphone system. The navigator clambered up to the cockpit and stared at the bloody mess in front of him. Bolick was slumped over the control wheel, but even with all his wounds and the terrible loss of blood he straightened up, grasped the controls, and righted the B-17 from her fall. Weakly he motioned to the copilot, Lieutenant Edward F. Downs, to take over the controls; then he slumped over again, unable even to hold up his head.

"See—see what you can do for Bolick," gasped the copilot as he grabbed the wheel. McFann stopped short as Bolick raised his hand once more in an effort to take over the controls. It was his last effort. He slumped once again over the wheel, and fainted.

All this time Downs had only asked that Bolick be given assistance. Then, quietly, he informed McFann that he would also need some help. The navigator looked in wonder at his copilot; Downs had been hit in the right arm, the right side, in his right leg, and in both knees. Blood trickled down from multiple wounds in his head.

The engineer and bombadier came to McFann's assistance, and the three men, as gently as they could, moved Bolick from his seat and carried him into the nose. The pilot did not regain consciousness again; several minutes later he died.

McFann climbed back into the cockpit and moved into Bolick's seat. On several previous occasions the pilot had let him fly the Fortress, but only in straight and level flight, many thousands of feet above the ground. But if Downs didn't get any better, McFann was going to have to fly this airplane right onto the runway—or else everybody was going to hit the silk. One of the crew attended Downs' wounds as McFann held the airplane in a steep glide, dropping below the thick overcast.

McFann lit a cigarette and handed it to Downs; when the copilot made no move to take the cigarette he had just requested, McFann knew he had real trouble on his hands,

Bolick was dead, and Downs, unconscious and bleeding badly, close to death.

"Fred [Downs] would go in and out; he'd be conscious a while and then pass out again," McFann related. "Whenever he came to he tried to give me advice on flying the Fortress. I couldn't see a thing and wasn't certain exactly where I was, because in the thick of the fighting I didn't have time to keep my navigation up to date.

"So I got the radio operator to send out an SOS. We finally got an escort of two Spitfires, who guided us to a Royal Canadian Air Force field with long runways which would handle the big Fort. Fred was conscious at this time and told me to put down the landing gear. Then, through sheer guts—for his right arm was ripped from the elbow to the shoulder—Fred put both hands on the controls to help me.

"He couldn't do much talking, so he'd shake his head as a signal to retard the throttle, and nod it to signal me to give it more gas. As we neared the ground, he tried to pull back on the wheel; I helped him, but two thirds of the way down the runway we still hadn't settled.

"I could see Fred was trying to pull the wheel all the way back, so I yanked hard on it and pulled it all the way back into my stomach. The plane settled okay, but Fred was so weak he couldn't handle it well. It veered slightly, but I kicked right rudder and got it straightened out and safely stopped.

"When we had all this trouble, we could have bailed out, of course, instead of risking a possible crash landing. I suppose a lot of fellows wouldn't want to take a chance on having a navigator act as pilot, but they weren't sticking because of their confidence in me.

"They all knew that Bolick was dead inside that ship, and none of us was going to bail out and leave him in there. We just wouldn't do it, that's all."

Brennan's Circus failed to reach England on her return from Mission 115, but she brought her crew right to the doorstep. *Paper Doll* made it home, by little more than the insane courage of her wounded copilot and the amazing pinch-hit flying of Lieutenant McFann.

There was a third B-17 that, by all the odds of combat, should have made the losses in combat for Mission 115 a total of 61 bombers. Again the crew provided the difference when everything was held together by little more than the sinews of courage. This B-17, nameless but affectionately called just *741* by her crew, did *Brennan's Circus* one better in the mad dash over occupied Europe. Where the *Circus* barely cleared obstacles on the ground, *741* dropped a little lower and literally clipped treetops across Germany and France. She did so with her metal skin torn to fragments and with several of her crew badly shot up.

For an hour and a half *741* with the rest of her formation bore the brunt of furious attacks by waves of German fighters. On the bombing run their luck ran out; a fighter hosed a stream of cannon shells into one engine, and the pilot, First Lieutenant Harold R. Christensen, shouted to the copilot, Second Lieutenant Stuart B. Mendelsohn, to feather the battered engine. Mendelsohn hit the feathering button, the fuel cut-off switch, and chopped the throttle.

What should have happened didn't. Instead of the propeller blades turning slowly to knife into the wind—useless but presenting little drag—the blades stayed at the same angle, windmilling and imposing severe drag on the Fortress. One of the gunners stared out at the windmilling blades and muttered to no one in particular on the interphone: "Something tells me we have bought the farm. We ain't going nowhere with that goddamn fan doing that out there. . . ."

For twenty minutes, adding power to the other three engines, Christensen managed to keep *741* within the protecting firepower of the rest of the formation. Then the other Fortresses began to climb, and the ghost was up. The bomber simply didn't have the power, and an unhappy crew watched the rest of the B-17's pulling away. Suddenly the sky seemed very big and *741* very small and naked.

The German pilots called out the news of the cripple, and at once the Messerschmitts and Focke-Wulfs closed in like sharks for the kill. They were good, and so was their aim.

In the midst of the running fight the ball-turret gunner, Staff Sergeant Walter J. Molzon, gasped suddenly with pain. A moment later he called on the interphone to the bombardier, First Lieutenant Homer E. Chatfield. "I've been hit," he grated. "I'm coming up to have you dress the wound." Molzon extricated himself from the turret, staggered forward through the lurching bomber to the bombardier's station. Chatfield attended his wound, bound it tightly, and Molzon went back to his turret and climbed in. Moments later his guns added to the ear-blasting din.

The Fortress could not survive these attacks for long, and Christensen dived wildly for clouds beneath the bomber. He didn't make it in time. Three Me-109's dived almost vertically after *741*, pulled out on her tail in a wide fan, and blazed away. Within seconds the rear compartment of the Fortress was a sieve, with more and more daylight showing through the airplane's ribs as bullets tore through the skin and the cannon shells exploded. By some miracle the tail gunner, Staff Sergeant James J. Sweely, suffered no more than minor wounds. Almost every inch of metal around him was dented or cut up by the exploding shells.

The Fortress slewed around crazily like a cork in a storm as Christensen evaded constantly to throw off the fighters' aim. Then the wonderful oblivion of grayness within the clouds surrounded the bomber. The crew nearly cheered with relief. In the nose the navigator studied his maps of Switzerland, for there was now serious doubt that the Fortress could make it back to England. Christensen called the crew on the interphone, and told them they could have their option— bailing out over Germany, heading for Switzerland for internment, or trying the unlikely task of making the English coast.

"Home, James, home!" shouted a gunner, and a chorus of assent decided the issue. The best chance was a hedgehopping flight to avoid being spotted by fighters. Despite very poor visibility, Christensen pushed forward on the wheel and dived *741* for the deck. Brushing the treetops, he eased the crippled Fortress from her dive and raced for the Channel.

"In France we swept over one small hill and almost ran into a city in the valley," Chatfield later explained. "A nest of machine guns and light flak opened up on us with everything they had as we passed over—and they had plenty. A shell tore a big hole in the side of the cockpit and hit Chris in the upper arm. He stayed at the controls until the ship was over the next knoll and out of range of the German guns, which actually were firing right through French homes at us as we left them."

The copilot, Mendelsohn, took over the controls as Christensen crawled down from the cockpit, collapsing in the entrance to the nose. He was wounded more seriously than anyone had imagined. The bombardier and navigator made him as comfortable as possible, applied a tourniquet to his arm, which was severely lacerated and spurting blood. Then they injected a shot of morphine to deaden the pain.

The outside visibility grew steadily worse with each passing minute, and Mendelsohn was in trouble attempting to stay near the ground. He swept over a hill, frantically hauling back on the wheel, but not in time to avoid smashing into the top of a tall tree. The Fortress shook with a terrible roar; the entire plexiglas nose was smashed in.

Then the coastline was in sight, but not the end of the fight. Machine guns and light flak opened up with a terrible barrage, and again the airplane shuddered from the impact of bullets and shells. Mendelsohn banked the plane to give the radio operator—the only gunner with any ammunition left—a chance to fire back. He picked off several German gunners along the edge of the sea wall and the others scattered. Then they were out of range.

Their ability to reach England was doubtful. Empty fuel gauges stared at the worried Mendelsohn, who lost interest quickly in that problem when a gunner called in that one of the engines was burning. Somehow, 741 made the coast, and her copilot headed straight for the nearest British airfield. The visibility was lousy, the wind howled in through the smashed nose, a tire was flat, and the engines were coughing drily as Mendelsohn brought her around. It wasn't the best landing, but 741 stopped right side up. They were home.

Lieutenant Christensen died the next morning.

At the fields in England, still lying hidden from the broad sweep of the sky by the thick haze and fog, everything goes on as normal—if the feeling of suspended animation can be accepted as normal. For this is the time—waiting for the Fortresses to come home—when the long hours become unbearable, and men are afraid to think, because thinking means they may imagine all sorts of things that have happened "out there." The waiting is hateful, because the man who waits is helpless. There are friends out there above the haze, and brothers, and men who are closer to each other than brothers.

Along the flight line, in front of the hangars, on and near the vehicles, at the hardstands, are small bunches of men.

Ground crews, mostly. But you can see the rest of them as well, all waiting, all hating every minute, all frightened for their friends—even those they do not call by name and do not recognize by face. The administrative personnel are out. Armorers, drivers, the cooks, and the KP's. The control-tower balcony again holds its knot of men, the operational staffs. In the tower the Flying Control Officer waits, standing by a special short-range radio so that he can "talk down" someone who may be in serious trouble.

The meat wagons are ready, the big red crosses on their sides ominous with meaning. The crash trucks wait, motors running, drivers at the wheel, ready to roll with no more effort than a foot slammed down on the accelerator. The firemen, who may have to push into the center of a raging holocaust fed by gasoline, are attired in their asbestos suits, only the headpieces waiting to be donned.

Everyone studies the sky, and waits, and feels the knot of fear twisting harder and harder....

In the sky over Germany ... let us return to the B-17 with Colonel Peaslee and Captain McLaughlin in the cockpit. Colonel Peaslee: "Suddenly we feel as though we are having a vacation with pay—no fighters. There is an outburst of chatter and wisecracks. We are all exhilarated again. Once across the French border, our chances of survival increase many fold. We realize for the first time that it is a glorious day. We do not even think of what is behind us, that the mission has· been successful, that there will be awards and decorations out of this. We don't even worry abut the fighters that will intercept us over France. It's just good to be here now. We live only in the present moment.

"Our progress across France turns out to be uneventful. A few fighters heckle us, but their attacks have lost their zing. They do not press home, but fire and zoom away at extreme range. For the most part they are busy preying on the wounded. We begin to look for friendly fighters, and when we see none we assume they are busy elsewhere. It never enters our heads that they are earthbound by weather in England. The cloud deck has risen to nearly our level, for there is now a 20,000-foot overcast over our bases. We see it ahead and start our descent over the Channel.

"I call the leaders to take command of their groups for the letdown. This is routine for such an occasion. We will return to our splashers and descend as we climbed, each bomber coming down singly along the predetermined course. It's as simple as climbing out, but there is a mental hazard involved —the thought of hard ground, of clouds with rocks in them. We discover a hole in the cloud deck and see England. It looks good, and the hole is of good size, so there is a last-minute change of plan. We decide to hold our formation together and descend visually, circling down through the hole.

"We come out of our last turn and head north toward our base. Scraping through the low hills above London, we enter the plains of the Midlands and suddenly we are over home at 300 feet. We can see now. As we break into the landing pattern, we spot the men at the hardstands, the ambulances and the fire trucks along the runway, standing with their engines running and their crews watching us. Everyone down there is watching—counting the bombers, trying to read the symbols painted on them. All they see is one squadron.

" 'Where are the other two?' I can almost hear them saying. 'Must have headed south of here because of the weather.'

"The bombers string out behind us as we turn over the runway and head for the landing. From one of the rear aircraft a red flare blossoms, and the men in the ambulance spring to life—there are wounded aboard.

"Captain McLaughlin sets her down on glass—it's hard to tell when flight ceases and the landing roll begins. As we start to slow and the weight of the bomber relaxes, we feel the roughness of the runway.

"We roll to the end of the runway, past the waiting jeep and the ambulance, and turn smoothly onto the taxi strip. Jockeying the plane is easy now in the daylight, and as we move through the woods we pass the hardstands with their waiting crews. Invariably they wave and make victory signs in our direction. In a few moments many of them will return silently and sadly to their squadron headquarters to receive the condolences of more fortunate comrades and to wait for a new bomber and a new combat crew assignment. Some may get a forty-eight-hour pass and head for London to find distraction with the girls of Piccadilly or oblivion in a sodden drunk.

"We approach our own hardstand and turn in. My boss Slim Turner, the wing commander, and Bill Reid, the group commander, stand by the staff cars and smile and wave as my pilot wheels the bomber onto the hardstand to be made ready for tomorrow's mission. As the engines roar out, then die into silence, I stand up.

"It's wonderful to stand up after so many hours in one position. It is an indescribable feeling—I stagger a little at first, and with the vibration of the engines missing, I feel a little numb all over. I ignore the slow exit route around the gun turrets, through the bomb bay, through the radio compartment, past the waist guns, to the door in the rear of the fuselage. I simply step down to the catwalk into the bombardier's and navigator's compartment and drop out of the forward escape hatch in the nose. I stagger noticeably as Slim and Bill both reach for my hand. Their faces are bright with smiles that are about to fade. The questions start.

" 'How did it go? Where is the rest of the group—southern England or still on top? Have any trouble letting down? Hear it was a milk run. How was the bombing? Did you get the target?'

"I hold up my hand. I suppose I'm guilty of making a try at the dramatic.

" 'You have just watched the group land—all that's left of it,' I say. 'We had a hell of a fight.'

"The bright faces sag, there are seconds of silence, then come expressions of disbelief, punctuated by curses. They want to think I am lying or joking, but they know I am doing neither. The crew has debarked, and each member becomes the nucleus of a questioning group.

"They fire questions at me, many questions, but they all lead up to two words. *What happened?*

"I look at the silently waiting crews on the empty hardstands. I tell them—the highlights only—what took place in that terrible sky over Germany. They remain silent until I have finished. There are a few more scattered questions, then Bill says, his shoulders slumped, 'Let's go to my quarters.'

"I know what that means—a drink, and I need a drink. Bill needs one, too, for he has lost two thirds of his boys, the boys he has trained, criticized, disciplined—made members of the official family. Tomorrow he will be signing letters to their folks. Inside he will be crying, just as all the parents will weep with visible tears.

"I don't envy him. How many times can a man's heart break?"

And so the crews at all the fields wait, hoping, praying, and suffering the deep pangs of fear. Everyone studies the sky. Then, quietly, a man says in a dead, flat voice: "There's one."

It is only a single bomber, and she comes in low and fast, away from the rest of the formation. The B-17 rushes across the field, winging into a bank, and then is hidden from sight by the line of trees at the edge of the field. As she comes back, the engines cough and backfire in the glide—and suddenly all eyes are riveted to the sight of a red flare racing out from an open hatch of the bomber, arcing up and over. Inside the B-17 a man is white-faced. He is bleeding to death.

The ambulance races down the runway. The Fortress comes in, one wing dragging low. She hits on the low wheel, rocks to the other, wobbles dangerously, and then settles down, trailing dust. She is 3,000 feet down the runway when the squeal of brakes hits the ears. The bomber is a sieve; she turns slowly and swings onto the turf. The medics are running to the door before the crew has a chance to step out.

They come in steadily. Tiny spots in the sky, growing bigger and bigger. They wheel, and turn. Battered airplanes. Holes and gashes and smashed plexiglas, stripped metal, long scars, the deep and angry marks of fire. But there are too few, too few!

The *Windy City Avenger* came in on her final approach to the landing field more a junk heap than an airplane. One elevator was shot to ribbons, but remained in a locked position. As the Fortress settled down in her glide toward the runway the elevator "went completely berserk," and at the impossible height of only 150 feet the terrified crew prepared to abandon their wild-flying bomber. But in the cockpit the pilot and copilot, white-faced and scared nearly to death, brought the ship out of her gyrations, and managed to climb to 1,000 feet. When the pilot shouted to everyone, "Let's get the hell outa here," the airplane was empty in seconds. Everyone got out, and the airplane crashed in the mist.

At Grafton Underwood the haze was so thick that only the lead Fortress, with Major George W. Harris, Jr., at the controls, returned to the field. The other survivors landed at emergency fields. That night the crews on the ground received the news. Six bombers down over Germany. Sixty empty bunks tonight.

"It is little wonder that airmen of Grafton Underwood have by this time developed the idea that it is impossible to complete a full tour of duty," wrote a man in despair that night. "It has come to be an accepted fact that you will be shot down eventually. The 384th entered combat four months ago with a combat flying strength of 363 officers and men. In these four months we lost more than we started with. We are just as strong, due to replacements that are continually coming in, but there are few originals left. . . ."

At the Thurleigh airdrome the feeling of a crushing disaster overwhelms the men on the ground. This day the 306th Group has lost ten bombers—100 men are never coming back. Fifteen four-engine B-17 bombers had gone on the raid—only five returned.

"You never forget those sights, and I know I never will," one of the ground crewmen at Thurleigh that day recalls. "The day was wet and cold, and in that biting wind the field was ringed with little bunches of men peering anxiously at the low gray clouds. Our planes are five minutes overdue . . . and there they come now, but only five of them.

"Red flares pop up, and the meat wagons dash past us. The watchers turn to pick out the other planes that are expected. The roar of engines approaches, a welcome and warm sound; these *must* be ours. No, they pass on, and the cluster of watching figures grows tense.

"From the first plane to land word trickles back. 'Those goddamn rockets! They hit a plane and it just disappears. Seventeens blowing up all around. Never saw so many goddamned fighters in my life, the sky was saturated with 'em.'

"As the crews come in their faces are drawn and wan, not just from weariness, but because too many friends have gone down in flames in front of their eyes. Too many. Jerry had thrown so many planes at them they were bewildered. And for another reason. There was still tomorrow, and the tomorrow after that. What answer could they find to this kind of stuff on the next raid, perhaps even tomorrow morning?"

And then there is the airdrome at Chelveston, home of the 305th Group. Sixteen bombers took off. One aborted, returning early with mechanical troubles. Fifteen Fortresses went on.

Two bombers returned on schedule to land at Chelveston. Where are the others? Have they landed elsewhere? Where are they?

There are no others. Of the 15 heavy bombers that left Chelveston this morning of October 14, 1943, 12 fell in flames before the crews ever saw Schweinfurt. Another made its bombing run and then plunged earthward, torn to pieces by a salvo of rockets.

The 305th Group is virtually wiped out. One hundred and thirty men! The men in 13 ground crews stare at each other in stunned disbelief. It cannot be; *it just cannot be.*

But it is. Thirteen crews, 130 men. Men they have worked for and worked with, waved good-bye to, shouted greetings to on their landings.

The concrete, stained with oil and grease where the big bombers have stood, is empty, a terrible aching void. The ground crewmen scruff their feet aimlessly, walk off. Every man looks as if he has just lost his brother.

Fifty-nine Flying Fortresses went down over German-occupied Europe, or over the Third Reich itself. One crippled and battered B-17, *Brennan's Circus,* made it back to the Channel, and ditched, saving the life of its crew in its amazing struggle to remain airborne.

Three bombers have been abandoned over England, low on fuel, lost, their pilots not daring to hazard a landing in the murk covering their fields. The empty airplanes crashed and exploded, with a sudden glare of light in the fog.

Two others make it down, and their pilots lose all control. The bombers careen wildly, and crash. They are destroyed.

Sixty-five Flying Fortresses gone forever. Seventeen more that come home are so badly shot to pieces, so ruined and slashed and battered and cut and burned, that they will never fly again.

Five hundred and ninety-four men of the VIII Bomber Command are "missing" over Europe, an unknown number of them prisoners. In the bombers that return there are five dead men. There are also ten men so badly wounded that their survival is questionable. There are 33 more suffering to a lesser extent from wounds.

Three Thunderbolts are gone. One fighter pilot is missing, one is dead from his crash in England.

Two hundred and fifty-seven Fortresses made up the combat force that reached into the enemy's airspace. One hundred and ninety-seven returned, and five of these were abandoned, or crashed. That leaves 192 bombers of the combat force. Of these, 142 are damaged. Only 50 bombers—in the wings that miraculously escaped with only negligible opposition—were not punctured by the enemy's defenses.

There is one last episode to which the surviving crews must contribute. This is the debriefing. Intelligence must get its information at once, before the crews are relieved.

In the debriefing rooms each crew collects at a large table. The questions are asked quietly, with more than a little consideration. But the answers must be obtained now. It is vital. The war still goes on.

"What was your bombing altitude? Your magnetic heading? Your position in the formation?

"How many fighters? What types? What kind of attacks? What kind of weapons? Any special markings?

"What about flak? Where? What kind? Accurate? How much?"

Hot news is flashed to Air Division. The flak reports are shuffled together by Intelligence; a new pattern emerges. Tomorrow's briefings will be altered. In the darkrooms nearby sergeants and corporals swirl paper in developing baths. The pictures begin to emerge; outside the doors a "hot messenger" waits, ready to rush them to Air Division.

"Any comments?"

"Yeah. Jesus Christ, give us fighters for escort!"

Usually the debriefings are less solemn. The men are relieved to be home, to be alive. On this afternoon the relief is buried deep, swamped by the shock of the mission. Few of the men can find it in themselves to laugh, even with a touch of hysteria, at the mad thrill of just being *alive*. Many of these men still don't believe they are here, safe, on the ground.

They are tired and bone-weary and they are sick. Their faces reflect death. It has missed them but it has struck down their friends, their brothers. They stare at the floor, suck on cigarettes, tastelessly drink coffee. They answer the questions numbly, hands moving in fitful jerks, eyes glazed.

In one room a pilot abruptly moves back his chair and leaves his debriefing table. He shuffles awkwardly to a corner of the room, where he hides his face. Wordlessly his crewmen stare at him, then turn away. The lieutenant is weeping.

He cries for all of them. . . .

PART IV
THE SUMMING UP

19

THE BOMBING: EVALUATION

A flash report of Mission 115 to Headquarters, VIII Bomber Command, with copies to Generals D. D. Eisenhower and George C. Marshall, stated that the attack had produced "... good bombing results and *possible total destruction of target."*

Soon after this cheering news was disseminated through official channels, the public received from Brigadier General Frederick L. Anderson its first detailed official statement on the raid.

"The entire works are now inactive," announced the general. "It may be possible for the Germans eventually to restore 25 per cent of normal productive capacity, but even that will require some time. A tremendous amount of clearance, repair work, and rebuilding will be necessary before plants can again be operative. Fires raged throughout three of the plant areas, burning out not only factories, but stores and dispatch buildings as well."

Both in official documents and in public statements the army air forces hailed its tremendous accomplishment at Schweinfurt. On October 18, four days after the mission, a jubilant General Henry H. Arnold, commanding general of the army air forces, announced dramatically to a press conference, *"Now we have got Schweinfurt!"*

Headquarters VIII Bomber Command passed on to Eighth Air Force headquarters its *Interpretation Report S. A. 628,* which said:

"The brunt of the attack fell solidly on the target area, with at least 100 separate distinguishable hits within factory confines. In addition there are four areas of heavy concentrations of bursts which partially blanket factories. A total of nine large fires are seen and one explosion is noted."

The report showed photographs of bomb concentrations and bursts, including "a concentration of at least 40 bursts in a wooded area on the east side of Aschenhof, 3.5 miles southwest of Schweinfurt." The Bomber Command realized from its photos that many of its bombs had missed and scattered wildly; despite these normal far spreads, however, Intelligence was convinced of the overwhelming success of the mission. In a subsequent report, *No. K. 1785,* it stated:

"Very heavy and concentrated damage is visible within the target area, due probably as much to fire as to H.E. [high explosive]. All three main factories of the Schweinfurt ball-bearing industry and the two closely allied therewith have been affected, those of VKF Works I and II and Fichtel & Sachs suffering very severe damage. In many cases, buildings damaged in the previous raid have now been destroyed or have received further damage."

During the first week of November, 1943, a telegram from the United States diplomatic service, transmitted from Göteborg, Sweden, and classified *Secret,* arrived at headquarters of the VIII Bomber Command. Dated "2 November, 11 A.M.," it carried cheering verification of the strike photo interpretations, and stated:

"The principal stockholders of the Swedish Ball Bearing Company have been advised by officials of that company that the recent American bombing at Schweinfurt irreparably destroyed the entire ball-bearing industry there. According to the Swedish officials, the precision of the bombing deeply impressed the German military and industrialists because the property was utterly devastated whereas the adjoining properties were untouched."

In the Volume I, Number 8, issue of *Impact* magazine, an official army air forces publication with the classification of *Confidential,* the editors reported of the Schweinfurt attack of October 14 that: "All five plants—representing about 65 per cent of the ball- and roller-bearing capacity of Germany— were so heavily damaged that *our bombers may never have to go back.*"

After receiving photographic reconnaisance and intelligence interpretation of the attacks, and with possibly too much concern for public reaction to the success of his command, General Arnold stated in a report to the Secretary of War:

All five of the works at Schweinfurt were either completely or almost completely wiped out. Our attack was the most perfect example in history of accurate distribution of bombs over a target. It was an attack that will not have to be repeated for a very long time, if at all.

> H. H. ARNOLD, General, USAAF, Commanding

The statements by Generals Anderson and Arnold, the telegram from Sweden, the report carried in *Impact* magazine —*not one of these was true*—they were extraordinarily optimistic.

Despite the conviction that we had wrecked the German bearings industry, Mission 115 did no more than to affect a minimum of Schweinfurt's capacity to produce the vitally needed bearings. The wording of the telegram from Sweden leads one to believe that the informant, whoever he might be, could well have passed on this information quite deliberately, to the delight of the Germans. That the Germans regarded the raid as a major crisis was true enough, but only because of what the future held in the possibility of a series of continued attacks, rather than as a result of the bombing that had allegedly "irreparably destroyed the entire ball-bearing industry there."

After the war the United States Strategic Bombing Survey, from the incomparable vantage point of the victor, prepared a detailed analysis of the results of Mission 115. "Best results were obtained from the 24 HE and seven INC bombs which hit VKF Works II. As though designed to complement the effects of the August bombing on FAG, here again it was the ball-producing plant which suffered most heavily. The loss of ball output affected operations not only here, but in other plants as well, since Works II made all the balls used by the entire VKF firm, including the Erkner and Cannstatt complexes, and sold balls to outside firms. In other parts of Works II, 23 machines were destroyed and 54 damaged, mostly in the cage-making department and tool shop.

"Thirty-eight HE bombs hit various parts of CKG's Works I, but the six-story building housing the bulk of its productive operations was scarcely damaged. Sixteen machines were destroyed and 15 damaged, mostly in the department producing small bearings. Apart from this single instance, the plant resumed operations as soon as power had been restored and a little plaster had been dusted off the machines.

"In this same attack, FAG lost 374 machines—84 totally destroyed and 290 damaged. Chiefly affected was the production of large bearings and of rollers and cages; as a result this section was subsequently dispersed to a large extent or moved into basements. Bombs fell also on the departments housing assembly and grinding of medium bearings, on the tool shop, and on the forge. The damage was substantial, but it was considerably less than in the raid of 17 August.

"Despite the crippling of some departments and sections, production on the whole received no more than a temporary setback. Over-all machine damage for the two VKF plants and the FAG plant amounted to only 10 per cent—3.5 per cent destroyed and 6.5 per cent damaged."

If this figure—10 per cent of the capacity of the three main Schweinfurt plants—is correct, it is disappointingly low. Some observers consider it too low, pointing out that it was usually necessary for the Strategic Bombing Survey to try to determine damages after repairs had been made, and that it had to base its findings in considerable part on German statements as to the extent of such damage. Such statements by Germans, these students of air warfare believe, tended unduly to minimize the effectiveness of our bombing. These statements often reflected, they feel, a psychology similar to that of a fighter who when lifted out of the ring with a bloody nose and black eye, insists, "He didn't lay a glove on me."

Notwithstanding the low percentages, in any case, Mission 115, on the whole, cost the Germans twice the destruction and damage inflicted by any other single attack of the war on the bearings industry, including a heavy blow the next year with more than three thousand tons of bombs.

In spite of all their hopes and the substantial successes they achieved, the planners of the aerial assault against Germany failed in their dedicated campaign to inflict crippling blows against the enemy's war machine by destruction of the ball-bearings industry. There are several major reasons for this failure, and they involve a crippling weakness on the part of the VIII Bomber Command to resume and sustain immediately its attacks on the bearing industry, which *would* have achieved the results desired.

Even the relatively limited damage inflicted in Schweinfurt

raised the danger signal throughout Germany. Reichsminister for Armaments and War Production Speer, as we have seen, regarded the situation with utmost gravity. Not only were he and his associates aware of the acute vulnerability of the bearings industry, but they realized fully that the target analysts of the American and British air forces shared this knowledge. Subsequent attacks were inevitable, and the Germans responded accordingly.

"The raids on the ball-bearings industry at Schweinfurt in August, 1943," stated Speer, "evoked a . . . crisis, the full import of which was made known to the Führer in all its gravity. Here again the delay in development of repetitions of the attack gave us the necessary time to take defensive precautions. . . .

"After the attack on the ball-bearings plants at Schweinfurt the first steps were taken to transfer this industry to Lower Silesia and to disperse in various groups in Franconia. The dispersal of important plants following attacks upon vital points was undertaken."

The dispersal of the German bearings industry was more than successful. No matter how strong and genuine the original conviction of the army air forces that they had "got Schweinfurt," the Germans were able to boast, right to the very last day of the war:

"Es ist kein Gerät zurück geblieben weil Wälzläger fehlten."

"No equipment has been held up because of a shortage of bearings."

20

IN THIS WE FAILED

On October 18, four days after Mission 115 had become history, the commanding general of the army air forces, Henry H. Arnold, made this statement to the press: "Regardless of our losses, I'm ready to send replacements of planes and crews and continue building up our strength. The opposition isn't nearly what it was, and we are wearing them down. The loss of 60 American bombers in the Schweinfurt raid was incidental."

It is impossible to explain General Arnold's words, for they conflicted in the highest degree with the situation which then existed. Rather than showing a downward trend ("the opposition isn't nearly what it was"), the German aerial defense of Schweinfurt on October 14 was unquestionably the most masterful, most viciously pressed home, and most effective onslaught of fighter planes in the entire war. It is even more difficult to reconcile with fact the incredible remark that the "loss of 60 American bombers in the Schweinfurt raid was incidental"; this same loss, coming so swiftly on three consecutive raids that had cost the VIII Bomber Command another 88 bombers lost in combat, *was the direct cause of the failure of the strategic bombing campaign to destroy the German bearings industry*.

In the simplest terms, the inability of the VIII Bomber Command to continue its attacks on the bearings industry— an inability caused by losses so disastrous that they were beyond capacity of the United States to replace at the time—prevented the Fortresses from returning to Schweinfurt for another four months. And by that time the opportunity to deliver the *coup de grâce* had vanished; the Germans had not failed to take advantage of the losses they had inflicted upon the American bomber forces.

"The Allied air attacks remained without decisive success until early 1944," declared Albert Speer. "This failure, which is reflected in the armaments output figures for 1943 and 1944, is to be attributed principally to the tenacious efforts of the German workers and factory managers and also to the haphazard and too scattered form of attack of the enemy, who, until the attacks on the synthetic oil plants, based his raids on no clearly recognizable economic planning."

Speer asserted further: "Armaments production would have been materially weakened over a period of two months and would have been brought to a complete standstill at the end of four months if:

"1. All ball-bearing plants had been attacked at one and the same time.

"2. The attacks had been repeated three or four times at intervals of fourteen days each, without regard to the bomb plots.

"3. Each attempt at reconstruction had been attacked every eight weeks by two consecutive heavy raids, and if the execution of this total bombing policy had been continued for six months."

Had all this transpired, Speer stated, the German war machine could not possibly have survived. "The destruction of the ball-bearings industry, at the cost of a small expenditure of effort, would have caused a complete standstill of armaments and war production within a period of four months, and in certain important spheres even within fourteen days to eight weeks."

During the course of the strategic bombing campaign in Europe, this hope was not to be fulfilled, despite a very major effort through the Combined Bomber Offensive. From August 17, 1943, until the end of the war in Europe in the spring of 1945, both the American and British bomber commands participated in a series of 40 separate air raids aimed at the bearings plants in Germany, Austria, France, and Italy, plus 11 other raids in which bearings plants suffered by proximity to targets undergoing attack.

In all, the Eighth and Fifteenth Air Forces, and the Royal Air Force Bomber Command, unleashed 12,000 tons of bombs on the bearings industry. Of this total, two thirds—8,000 tons—fell on Schweinfurt. The vast weight of bombs did not do the task expected of it.

Destruction of buildings in the raids was more than substantial, since it amounted to almost half of the entire pre-raid floor space of the bearings industry, while eventually the equivalent of another half was heavily damaged. *It was not because of bombing failures that the bearings industry survived.* The failure rested in the serious underestimation by Allied planners of the recuperative powers of German industry.

Also, we did not know during the war—such things are not revealed by the best of reconnaissance photographs—that damage to machine tools in German industry was not at all proportionate to damage to buildings. The machine tools destroyed equaled but 12 per cent of the original inventory, and those that were damaged came to another 30 per cent. These were small dividends for the bomb tonnage involved and especially in view of the disastrous toll exacted by the enemy defense system.

It proved impossible to establish a specific pattern of effectiveness for the attacks on the bearings industry, for both the intensity and the accuracy of the raids varied too greatly. The Fortresses were able to strike with stunning effectiveness at the small plants at Annecy and Ebelsbach, literally pounding them into junk and bringing all production to a complete standstill. At Setyr and at VKF Berlin the Fortresses struck with such precision that the plants were unable to function as producing units for months at a time. Even the large plants—at Schweinfurt—were partially disrupted.

Successive raids proved to the satisfaction of the Germans, however, that their factories enjoyed a resiliency not even they could have anticipated. The suceptibility of machine tools to damage was not so great as had been believed. High-explosive bombs were used in preponderant quantities, but fire proved far more effective than blast. Machine tools, which contained a great deal of oil, were prime targets for flames. Although appearing to be in good condition after the raids, the machines that had fed the fires with their own oil, or that had been heated by incendiary bombs or by the fires in the buildings, were found to be twisted, or broken in the frames and parts by the water used in fire fighting.

Stocks of raw materials and semi-finished bearings suffered some damage, but they could not be hit so badly as to cause the industry to falter seriously. And even hits on buildings housing vital processes proved insufficient to wreck a plant or put it out of commission. This was in direct contradiction of the beliefs of the Allied planners.

A careful study of German records reveals that high-explosive bombs, except in the case of direct hits, failed to destroy the heaviest and most important machine tools. On these machines the more sensitive electrical gear proved to be the most vulnerable area.

The most elaborate studies by the United States Strategic Bombing Survey failed to provide a yardstick of bomb effectiveness. "The variation in destructiveness of bombs was very great, so that it is impossible to state any coefficient of the number of machines destroyed or damaged per bomb hit." In a strike on April 13, 1944, for example, a single bomb that exploded directly in the production shop destroyed the majority of the machines in Kugelfischer's ring-grinding department for medium bearings. Other bombs that struck the factory building "did virtually no damage to machines." On one raid in February, 1944, a single bomb appears to have caused more damage than all the rest of the bombs dropped in the attack. One hundred and sixty-one machines in VKF's machine storeroom in Works II were destroyed as a result of a fire set by this bomb that subsequently swept the storeroom.

Ingenious organization of the German factories also paid off handsomely. Through the establishment in the bearings plants of many departments, each of which carried through the complete manufacture of one component, a plant that was heavily damaged was able to continue its production even though the production of one or more components was halted: the other manufacturing processes continued unabated, or with only minor lessening of production, and the plant accomplished its vital final assembly by drawing on stocks. In addition to this resilient compartmentation, much machinery in one department could be quickly adapted for use in another, so that even when a vital process was destroyed in an attack, the Germans were able readily to provide substitute machine tools.

Nevertheless, by April, 1944, the heavy bomber raids had inflicted a significant blow. The best efforts of the Germans in the face of these attacks failed to prevent a drop in bearings production to less than 50 per cent of the pre-raid levels. Had continued attacks taken place at this critical moment, the objectives of the strategic bombing campaign might have been achieved. The bombers failed to return, however, for reasons we shall soon see.

By September, 1944, the German production had recovered to its full pre-raid level. Indeed, their total loss of production amounted to barely three months' output, calculated at the rate obtaining before the first raid of August 17, 1943. Nor did all this loss result directly from the bombing attacks, but rather from the combined factors of direct-bomb damage and the German policy of dispersal with the immobilization of machinery and equipment that it demanded.

There can be no other view than that the Germans accepted the problem of bearings shortages, and met that problem, in superb fashion. Engineers worked day and night in an aggressive program to ramrod the redesign of armaments so as to eliminate anti-friction bearings wherever they were not absolutely necessary. This materially reduced requirements, and again contradicted the supposition of the Allied target analysts that this procedure would produce no vital beneficial results. Hardly had the dust cleared from the exploding bombs of the first Schweinfurt raids, moreover, than an exceedingly rigid system of bearings control went into effect throughout Germany in both the bearings plants and the user plants. In this manner the essential weapons manufacturers were further protected from lack of essential bearings.

Thus many factors contributed to the German effort to prevent crippling of industrial production as a result of the attacks against the bearings industry. Vigorous production measures, the dispersal of production lines from the large centers of manufacturing to numerous small plants, the bombproofing and erection of blast walls around vital machinery, and the amazingly rapid repair or replacement of damaged or destroyed machinery and equipment—all these measures enabled production to return to adequate levels before the cushion provided by reserve stocks and the shortening of the pipeline between producer and user plants ceased to exist.

This is the German side of the story that enabled them to boast in all truth: *"Es ist kein Gerät zurück geblieben weil Wälzläger fehlten. . . ."*

The consequences of our heavy loss of bombers in the Schweinfurt raid were ominous. *"In one raid,"* states the Strategic Bombing Survey, *"the Eighth Air Force had temporarily lost its air superiority over German targets."*

This was the concrete fact that the Eighth Air Force had to live with, and in the last analysis it was for this reason, and no other, that the German bearings industry survived the weight of all the attacks made upon it.

"The incalculable advantage of a breathing spell from further attacks for another four months," states the official history of the army air forces, "was granted the Germans, who regarded the 'omission' on the part of the army air forces as nothing less than miraculous."

Four months passed before the Fortresses of the Eighth Air Force returned to Schweinfurt, and that was all the miraculous "breathing spell" the Germans needed. By December, 1943, two months after Black Thursday, the long-range fighters to escort the bombers all the way to Schweinfurt were ready. By then, however, continuing storms and heavy cloud masses over England and the continent interfered with projected raids, and the acceleration of other bombing commitments lowered Schweinfurt on the priority target list. Not until late in February, 1944, was the army air forces able to resume its attacks against the German bearings industry in general and Schweinfurt in particular. The Luftwaffe had battered us so badly that we lacked the strength—and the recuperative powers—to repair sooner the losses experienced on October 14.

On the evening of February 24, 1944, the Royal Air Force struck at Schweinfurt. The next morning heavy bombers of the army air forces took off from England to smash the plants in a follow-up daylight raid. And that night, completing the long-needed consecutive raid against the target, another Royal Air Force armada attacked. A tremendous weight of 3,000 tons of high explosives and incendiaries cascaded into the city and the bearings plants.

It was a case of locking the barn door after the horse was galloping down the road. The VKF works alone had transferred 549 vital machines to their new locations in dispersal plants, and this was 27 per cent of the VKF total in Schweinfurt. Even more machines had vanished from the Kugelfischer works.

More than 40 per cent of the target was no longer in Schweinfurt. Despite the overwhelming weight of the bomb tonnage involved, the February attacks produced *less* results than had the October 14 mission.

On March 24, 1944, 60 United States Army Air Forces

bombers struck in a "precision" attack against the bearings works in the city. This proved to be one of the classic bombing failures of the war; not a single bomb of the hundreds dropped struck any bearings factory.

Less than one week later heavy bombers of the Royal Air Force struck with 104 tons of bombs in a night attack. The explosions and fires damaged some buildings but left the machines and productive facilities unscathed.

On April 13, two weeks after the Royal Air Force attack, the Eighth Air Force returned to score its most effective mission since the October 14 assault. The attacks that followed for the remainder of the war, despite some damage, proved to be largely ineffectual. The heaviest of these came on October 9, 1944, when in a daylight strike the Eighth dumped 820 tons into the target. By now, however, more than 70 per cent of Schweinfurt's former facilities for producing ball bearings had been effectively dispersed throughout Germany, and the damage wrought by the 820 tons of bombs, mostly high-explosive, came to perhaps 18 per cent that of Mission 115. This attack, states the Strategic Bombing Survey, "virtually marked the end of the strategic bombing attacks on Schweinfurt."

The final tally at the war's end revealed disappointing figures. For the Schweinfurt raids, the percentage of machines destroyed per raid averaged well under 5 per cent and the percentage damaged under 10 per cent. The Germans had restored the bulk of the machines damaged in the raids to productive condition within sixty days, and almost all of them within four months.

The great Fortresses and their crews of the VIII Bomber Command had done their best to cripple German bearings production. It was not enough.

At the war's end, however, with Germany prostrate and defeated, it became possible to review in its full perspective the role of our air power and to assess objectively its impact upon the enemy's capacity to fight.

"Allied air power," states the Strategic Bombing Survey, "was decisive in the war in western Europe. Hindsight inevitably suggests that it might have been employed differently or better in some respects. Nevertheless, it was decisive. In the air, its victory was complete; at sea, its contribution, combined with naval power, brought an end to the enemy's greatest naval threat—the U-boat; on land, it helped turn the tide overwhelmingly in favor of the Allied ground forces. . . .

"By the beginning of 1945, before the invasion of the homeland itself, Germany was reaching a state of helplessness."

In that European air war the separate missions by the Fortresses and the Liberators merged into a great and extended struggle of machines and men. In the course of that air conflict the United States lost some 160,000 airmen and many thousands of planes.

We fought many battles; some were so vast as to be individual campaigns. We emerged the victor from most, and our strength in the air prevailed to bring about the ultimate victory.

To all those men who fought the Schweinfurt battles, who watched their crew mates die, nothing would be more satisfying than to know that the campaign against Schweinfurt, against its industry whose destruction would have brought the enemy's war machines grinding to a halt, was successful.

But it was not to be so; we did not win all our battles, and this was one that we lost.

EPILOGUE

Thus Mission 115 passes into history. Black Thursday saw the most violent, savagely fought, and bloodiest of all the battles in the titanic aerial conflict waged in the high arena over Germany.

The curtain of time has rung down on the vast stage on which the grim drama was enacted. Never again will there be a Mission 115, never again will a bullet-riddled wreck struggle across the Channel to ease the weary metal and the bloody men to their black runway. The Fortresses now belong to history. The need for the air crews of ten men, the pilots and copilots, bombardiers, navigators, radio operators, and all the gunners, no longer exists.

The roar of thousands of powerful motors in unison will never be heard again; the echo may persist long after we have gone, but the cry is a historical thunder, as extinct as that of the dinosaur. There are no more flashing propellers on our bombers, no more ball turrets in which a man curls himself up for the punishment of long hours in such an unnatural position. There are no more open hatches or gleaming belts of .50-caliber bullets. They are all anachronisms.

The book of their blazing pages of history is closed. Perhaps it is fitting that Mission 115, that long, bloody, and savage battle of seventeen years ago, cannot be hailed in retrospect as a victorious venture. It is so easy to write of conquests and of an enemy routed; Black Thursday was not one of those battles.

There is a far better reason for committing Mission 115 to its documented niche in the history of our air war. On October 14, 1943, the American bomber force that struggled to reach Schweinfurt was mauled, shot to pieces, and raked viciously by the superb pilots of the enemy Luftwaffe.

Those German pilots, many of them still with us today, knew only too well their unprecedented effectiveness against our bombers. They saw the burning planes, the Fortresses with their torn wings, the mutilated and burning bodies, the crews tumbling through space.

And they wondered how those crews could take such punishment, could accept the losses, could fly onward without wavering, in the face of the hundreds of miles of further unremitting struggle that would continue to reap its macabre toll.

Mission 115, you see, contributed to a tradition. Despite the most intense aerial opposition in the history of man's combat in the air, our bombers did not turn back. The men in the great Fortresses did not falter. Despite their fear—and terror was a companion aboard those bombers—they did not consider forfeiting the mission. No matter how cruel the test, no matter how many giant bombers writhed in flame, no matter how many formations split apart and plunged earthward, there was no question but that the survivors would continue.

That is their contribution to a tradition—that no American bomber force, once committed to battle, has ever turned back.

APPENDIX

MISSION 115

Air Task Forces dispatched to Schweinfurt by the 1st and the 3rd Bombardment Divisions
1st Air Division

Group	Base	Type of Aircraft	Number Dispatched
91st	Bassingbourne	B-17	11
92d	Alconbury (Podington)	B-17	19
303d	Molesworth	B-17	19
305th	Chelveston	B-17	16
306th	Thurleigh	B-17	18
351st	Polebrook	B-17	16
379th	Kimbolton	B-17	17
381st	Ridgewell	B-17	17
384th	Grafton Underwood	B-17	16
			149

Group	Failed to Bomb a	b	Attacked	Lost	KIA	Wounded	MIA
91st	4	0	7	1	0	2	10
92d	1	5	13	6 + 1*	1	4	60
303d	0	1	18	1 + 1*	0	5	11
305th	1	12	3	13	0	3	130
306th	2	11	5	10	0	2	100
351st	3	3	10	1	0	5	10
379th	0	0	17	6	0	3	60
381st	2	0	15	1	0	3	10
384th	3	0	13	6 + 3*	0	2	60
	16	32	101	45*	1	29	451

ᵃFor mechanical or equipment reasons
ᵇFor all other reasons
*Total losses were 50 B-17's. In addition to 45 lost in battle:
One B-17 of 92d Group crash-landed at Alden Maston.

231

Of the returning bombers in the 1st Bombardment Division, 63 were damaged.

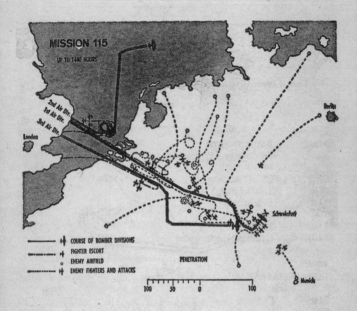

MISSION 115

UP TO 1440 HOURS

Berlin

2nd Air Div.
1st Air Div.
3rd Air Div.

London

Schweinfurt

Munich

——— ⊬ COURSE OF BOMBER DIVISIONS

—·—·— ⊬ FIGHTER ESCORT

·········· o ENEMY AIRFIELD

········— ⊬ ENEMY FIGHTERS AND ATTACKS

PENETRATION

100   50   0   100

One B-17 of 303d Group crashed near Riseley; crew bailed out.
One B-17 of 384th Group crashed near Blatherwycke; crew bailed out.
Two B-17's of 384th Group abandoned over England; crews bailed out.

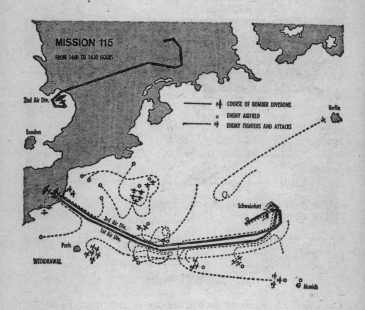

3d Air Division

Group	Base	Type of Aircraft	Number Dispatched
94th	Bury Saint Edmunds	B-17	21
95th	Horsham Saint Faith	B-17	18
96th	Grafton Underwood	B-17	41
100th	Thorpe Abbotts	B-17	8
385th	Great Ashfield	B-17	21
388th	Knettisham	B-17	18
390th	Framlingham	B-17	15
			142

Group	Failed to Bomb a	b	Attacked	Lost	KIA	Wounded	MIA
94th	0	0	21	6	1	2	50
95th	2	0	16	1	0	0	13
96th	6	3	32	7	2	5	70
100th	0	0	8	0	0	0	0
385th	1	0	20	0	1	2	0
388th	1	1	16	0	0	1	0
390th	0	0	15	1	0	1	10
	10	4	128	15	4	11	143

aFor mechanical or equipment reasons
bFor all other reasons

Of the returning bombers in the 3d Air Division, 79 were damaged.

2d Air Division

One Air Task Force of B-24 Liberator aircraft from the 2d Air Division . . .

93rd Group at Hardwick   15 aircraft dispatched
392d Group at Wendling   14 aircraft dispatched

. . . was assigned to attack targets in Schweinfurt, but all elements were unable to make formations because of adverse weather conditions over bases. Eight B-24's returned to bases, 21 B-24's carried out a diversionary sweep to Frisian Islands in the North Sea. No incidents.

Fighters

103 P-47 Thunderbolts of the 353d and 56th Fighter Groups were assigned for escort. The 353d escorted the 1st Air Division to

Düren, first engaged enemy fighters over Walcheren Island. The 56th Fighter Group, escorting the 2d Air Task Force to Dison, had less opposition.

One P-47 was lost in combat. The Thunderbolts shot down 13, probably destroyed one, and damaged five German fighters.

A total of 56 P-47 Thunderbolts of 352d Fighter Group was assigned as escort to B-24 Liberator bombers of 2d Air Division. Fighters and bombers rendezvoused; fighters returned to home bases as 21 B-24's departed for diversionary sweep to Frisian Islands.

Some Totals

1. First wave of B-17's struck Schweinfurt on bomb run from 1439 to 1445 hours.

2. Second wave of B-17's struck Schweinfurt on bomb run from 1451 to 1457 hours.

3. Casualties:

>   5 crew members killed in action
>   10 crew members seriously wounded
>   33 crew members slightly wounded
>   594 crew members missing in action

4. 40 B-17's lost from various causes; exact reasons unidentified.
    2 B-17's lost from flak; positive identification.
   18 B-17's lost from fighters; positive identification.
    5 B-17's lost in England on return.

5. 228 B-17's attacking Schweinfurt dropped a total of:

>   450 1,000-lb. high-explosive bombs
>   663   500-lb. high-explosive bombs
>   1,751   100-lb. incendiary bombs

6. 1st Air Division expended 321,126 rounds .50-caliber ammunition.
   3d Air Division expended 376,702 rounds .50-caliber ammunition.
   Total for mission: 697,828 rounds

7. The two waves of B-17's that attacked Schweinfurt extended in formations from 21,000 to 24,000 feet.

INDEX

ABOUT THE AUTHOR

MARTIN CAIDIN, a versatile writer with more than 100 books to his credit, is also a commercial and military pilot, a stunt flyer, a parachutist, the owner and pilot of a huge three-engine German WWII bomber, and a recognized world authority in the fields of aviation and astronautics. After military service in the U.S. Merchant Marines and U.S. Air Force in many parts of the world, he served as nuclear warfare specialist for the State of New York and as international consultant on mass-destruction weaponry systems from 1950 to 1954. He analyzed in great detail the effects of nuclear, biological, chemical and other weapons on potential targets in the United States. As a commercial multi-engine pilot, Mr. Caidin has owned and flown a wide variety of civil and military aircraft and he flies often throughout the U.S. He has flown fighters and multi-engine bombers to and within Europe, has earned the permanent title of "Thunderbird Fight" from flying with the USAF team, is a member of the Army's Golden Knights jump team, and has flown as a stunt pilot in movies and air-shows.

Martin Caidin's first novel, *Marooned,* a thrilling account of a space rescue, became a major motion picture, and many other novels were bought for films. *Cyborg,* published in 1972, became the world-acclaimed TV series, *The Six-Million-Dollar Man* and *The Bionic Woman.* Mr. Caidin is the author of an impressive list of authoritative books on military air history. Many of them, including *Samurai!* and *The Ragged, Rugged Warriors,* are considered classics in the field. Martin Caidin is a Charter Member of the Congressional Hall of Fame, a Fellow of the British Interplanetary Society, the founder of the American Astronautical Society, the Rebel Flying Corps and other world-known organizations. He and his wife, Dee Dee, who is also a pilot and balloonist and former parachutist, live in Gainesville, Florida where they teach a wide variety of subjects. Mr. Caidin continues to devote much of his time, in addition to flying and writing, to advanced scientific projects and the problems we have fashioned for ourselves with sophisticated weapons. Among his most recent books are *Aquarius, Starbright,* and *The Final Countdown.*